GW01606374

Whitaker's Almanack

WORLD HEADS OF STATE 1998

Whitaker's Almanack

World Heads of State 1998

Roger East
Assistant editor: Catherine Ashment

London:
THE STATIONERY OFFICE

ISBN 0 11 702204 7

Typeset by Spire Origination, Norwich
Printed in Great Britain by The Stationery Office

A CIP catalogue record for this book is available from the British Library.

Published by The Stationery Office and available from:

The Publications Centre
(mail, telephone and fax orders only)
PO Box 276, London SW8 5DT
General enquiries 0171 873 0011
Telephone orders 0171 873 9090
Fax orders 0171 873 8200

The Stationery Office Bookshops
59–60 Holborn Viaduct, London EC1A 2FD
temporary until mid 1998
(counter service and fax orders only)
Fax 0171 831 1326
68–69 Bull Street, Birmingham B4 6AD
0121 236 9696 Fax 0121 236 9699
33 Wine Street, Bristol BS1 2BQ
0117 9264306 Fax 0117 9294515
9–21 Princess Street, Manchester M60 8AS
0161 834 7201 Fax 0161 833 0634
16 Arthur Street, Belfast BT1 4GD
01232 238451 Fax 01232 235401
The Stationery Office Oriel Bookshop
The Friary, Cardiff CF1 4AA
01222 395548 Fax 01222 384347
71 Lothian Road, Edinburgh EH3 9AZ
(counter service only)

Customers in Scotland may
mail, telephone or fax their orders to:
Scottish Publications Sales
South Gyle Crescent, Edinburgh EH12 9EB
0131 228 4181 Fax 0131 622 7017

The Stationery Office's Accredited Agents
(see Yellow Pages)

and through good booksellers

Preface

This is the first edition of *Whitaker's Almanack World Heads of State*. It brings together in one volume a succinct portrait of every current head of state in the world. A companion volume covers world heads of government.

The entries cover the current situation as at 1 January 1998. In only one case has this rule been varied: Lithuania, where the presidential election was held in two rounds on 21 December and 4 January, and where the eventual winner is included. For several countries the portraits included here are, strictly speaking, those of presidents-elect (as in Guyana, Honduras and South Korea) rather than their "lame duck" predecessors, but all were scheduled to take office well before the publication date of this book.

The portraits combine factual biographical information with a description of each individual's political significance, in the context of his or her current office and previous career. Each begins with a single paragraph summary, set in italic script, which highlights how and when the incumbent came to office, and the role they play as head of state.

The book is arranged alphabetically by country. Country names are those in most common usage – thus for example North Korea and South Korea (under K), rather than the Democratic People's Republic and the Republic of Korea. There are entries for all sovereign states, as well as for entities which make a claim to statehood, even where this is generally not recognised internationally. In a similarly deliberate spirit of inclusivity, where there are competing regimes claiming legitimacy, such as in Afghanistan, the book gives a profile of the leader of each, without any implication that the claim of either is preferred.

This book could not have been written without the invaluable assistance of embassies, high commissions and government departments around the world, whose official biographies and information sheets have provided essential details not available from any other source. At the same time, an enormous range of other material has been collected, quarried and sifted. The resulting portraits are designed to inform their readers, rather than to praise, condone or criticise their subjects. At the same time they do not pretend that the careers of leading political figures are without controversy, and they could not have been written without the exercise of political judgement. Responsibility for this, for the selection of what is deemed significant, and for any errors which have crept in despite our best efforts to be meticulous, rests with the author.

Roger East, Cambridge, January 1998

Acknowledgements

Thanks are due to the many people who have assisted in a range of different ways in the preparation of this book. Charlotte Honebon, Iain McDaniel, Ken Skates and many other people helped greatly in the considerable task of gathering information, and in putting together draft entries. Among those who have much improved the final portraits by commencing on and revising them in various stages, Frances Nicholson and Philippa Youngman are especially to be thanked for contributions far exceeding the normal duties of copy editing.

Grateful acknowledgement is due to the staff of embassies and governments throughout the world, for providing information which has been invaluable as source material for the portraits contained in this book. Photographs, except those specifically mentioned below, have also been provided by the relevant embassies and governments, and are again gratefully acknowledged.

The photographs on pp. 57, 85, 143, 174, 263, 271 were supplied by Rex Features; those on pp. 30, 51, 59, 66, 86, 118, 128, 131, 133, 142, 187, 199, 202, 236, 240, 260, 275, 277 by Frank Spooner Pictures; the photograph on p. 25 by S.F.I. (copyright SOFAM); that on p. 74 by the Danish Embassy with thanks to Rigmor Mydtskov; that on p. 99 by the German Embassy with thanks to Inter Nationes Bonn Press; that on p. 166 by Dr Iain Stevenson; that on p. 175 by the Embassy of the Netherlands with thanks to photo Thuring; that on p. 177 by the New Zealand High Commission with thanks to Woolf; that on p. 183 by the Norwegian Embassy with thanks to ScanFoto; that on p. 234 by the Swedish Embassy with thanks to Kungl. Husgeraadskammaren, Stockholm; that on p. 242 by the Embassy of Thailand with thanks to the Royal Household Bureau; that on p. 243 by Tibet Images with thanks to Brian Beresford; and that on p. 258 by the Central Office of Information. In all cases copyright is acknowledged, with thanks for permission for reproduction in this book.

Burhannuddin **Rabbani**

Burhannuddin Rabbani was chosen in June 1992 as president of the Leadership Council, part of an attempt to create a government structure from among rival mujaheddin groups, after the ousting of the former Soviet-backed Najibullah regime. The leader of the Jamiat-i-Islami, *whose supporters were mostly of Tajik origin and fundamentalist Sunni Muslims, Rabbani was himself from an Islamic university background before he became a mujaheddin guerrilla organiser. His presidency effectively ended when he and his supporters were ousted from the capital, Kabul, as the ultra-fundamentalist taliban militia forces extended their control over most of the country in 1996. Despite the establishment of a* de facto *taliban government, however, Rabbani continued to be recognised as president of Afghanistan by most foreign countries.*

Born in 1940 in Faizabad in Badakhshan province, Rabbani went to Darul-uloom-e-Sharia (a religious school) in Kabul and then studied Islamic law and theology at Kabul University, graduating in 1963, when he became a professor there. In 1966 he went to Egypt, and in 1968 received his master's degree in Islamic philosophy from the University of Al-Azhar in Cairo.

On his return to Afghanistan he became an organiser for the *Jamiat-i-Islami* movement within the university system, where he worked as a member of the research department at Kabul University. After a spell of further research in Ankara, Turkey, he returned to Kabul, where his increasing prominence within the *Jamiat-i-Islami* led to his being targeted in an anti-Islamist clampdown by the regime of the then President Daoud. He evaded capture when police came to arrest him at Kabul University in early 1974, escaping from the city and subsequently going into exile in Pakistan. It was from Peshawar that he became a prominent member of the mujaheddin struggle to oust Soviet forces following their 1979 invasion of Afghanistan. In 1991, after the Soviet withdrawal but before the final defeat of the Najibullah regime, Rabbani as leader of the *Jamiat-i-Islami* became a co-founder of the National Liberation Front.

Only two months separated the eventual fall of Najibullah, and Rabbani's election in June 1992 as head of the Leadership Council. This was intended originally to provide for rotation of the state presidency among mujaheddin faction leaders, but Rabbani went on to be endorsed formally as president by a Constituent Assembly in December 1992. In the event, with the Leadership Council a dead letter and inter-faction conflicts continuing, he had still not passed on the presidency when in September 1996 the taliban forces captured Kabul and declared their own government.

Mohammad **Omar**

Mullah Mohammad Omar was chosen on 3 April 1996 as Amir-ul-Momineen *(Commander of the Faithful) of the taliban, the radical religious student militia which at that time was rapidly establishing itself as the most effective military force amid the complex factional conflicts in Afghanistan. Little is known about his rise to power within the taliban, and when he first emerged as leader he was sometimes represented as a figurehead, trained and controlled by Pakistani military intelligence. He became* de facto *head of state, although without widespread international recognition, when the taliban took Kabul, the Afghan capital, in September 1996.*

Born in 1963 or 1964 in the central province of Uruzgan, Omar studied in several Islamic madrassahs (schools) before joining the jihad (Islamic holy war) against the Soviet occupation in the 1980s. During that conflict, in which he reportedly lost an eye and a leg, he rose to be a deputy chief commander in the *Harakat-i-Inqilab-i-Islami* guerrilla movement or mujaheddin led by Mohammad Nabi Mohammadi.

When the Soviet army withdrew from Afghanistan in 1989 and the war became a power struggle between different mujaheddin groups, he withdrew from the fighting and taught in an Islamic school. Later, however, the behaviour of marauding mujaheddin troops in the Kandahar region in 1994 prompted Omar to support the creation of the so-called taliban or student movement, which soon became a full-blown militia. The taliban regarded the then President Rabbani, a former mujaheddin leader who had also fought against Soviet occupation, as a criminal. Taliban offensives brought their forces rapidly through eastern areas of Afghanistan and culminated in the capture of Kabul on 27 September 1996. With Omar as *de facto* head of state, a strict Islamic regime was immediately imposed and on 2 October forced prayer, five times a day, was introduced. On the same day Amnesty International accused the taliban of carrying out a reign of terror in the Afghan capital, to which Omar responded on 3 December, instructing taliban members to relax their treatment of people in Kabul.

Rexhep **Mejdani**

Rexhep Mejdani has been president of Albania since July 1997, having been elected for a five-year term by the People's Assembly following the resignation of his beleaguered predecessor Sali Berisha. Mejdani entered politics late in life, after a distinguished academic career in Albania, and was never a member of the communist party, although he was briefly secretary-general of its reformist successor, from September 1996 until his election as head of state.

Mejdani was born on 17 August 1944 in Tirana, the son of an army officer and a teacher. Having graduated in physics from Tirana University in 1966, he went on to research solid-state physics in Cannes and Paris. He returned to Tirana to lecture in theoretical physics in 1976. From 1986 he held a variety of chairs in physics at Tirana and edited several scientific journals. Then, when the country began to move towards multiparty democracy in 1990, he became chairman of the state electoral commission, while also remaining physics professor at the university. Mejdani has participated in many commissions and organisations seeking to promote the democratisation of the education system. He also chaired the board of the Centre of Human Rights Documentation from November 1994, campaigning for the strengthening of non-governmental organisations such as "For a Democratic Albania".

Mejdani was never a member of the former ruling communist Party of Labour of Albania and only joined its successor, the Socialist Party of Albania (PSS) in July 1996, but was elected secretary-general that September. As such he was responsible for directing the party away from its former Stalinist stance towards more pragmatic social democratic policies.

The PSS at this stage formed the main parliamentary opposition to the free-market-oriented Democratic Party regime under President Sali Berisha. A disastrous economic collapse at the end of 1996 unleashed a popular rebellion, particularly in the south, with widespread lawlessness, violence and political instability. This was only brought under control following the formation of a government of national reconciliation and the deployment of an international protection force. Berisha eventually resigned his post as head of state on 23 July 1997.

The PSS won an overall majority in the People's Assembly in the July 1997 general election, and PSS chairman Fatos Nano formed a new coalition government. Mejdani was elected president on 24 July 1997, winning 110 out of the 122 votes cast by members of the Assembly. He immediately resigned all his duties and functions within the PSS. Mejdani has vowed to lower crime, to ensure the economic and social emancipation of his citizens and to integrate Albania into the global economy.

Mejdani is married to a mathematician. They have two children.

Liamine **Zeroual**

Brig.-Gen. Liamine Zeroual has been head of state since January 1994, when the military-dominated High Security Council chose him to end a political impasse over who should replace the five-member collective presidency. Presidential elections held in November 1995 gave him a five-year mandate, in conditions of effective civil war as the confrontation with Islamist terrorists deepened. Zeroual, a career soldier, had fought as a young man in the war to end French rule, and had risen to be army chief of staff by 1989. Sent off in the last years of President Chadli's regime to be ambassador to Romania, he was brought back to the centre of power in 1993 by the military regime, initially as minister of defence.

Liamine Zeroual was born on 3 July 1941 in Batna, and joined the National Liberation Army at the age of 16, becoming a junior officer in the war of independence against the French. After Algeria achieved independence (in 1962), he received more formal military education in Cairo, in Moscow and in Paris. Rising to the rank of brigade commander, he was head of the Cherchell officer training school in the late 1970s and held a succession of regional military commands in the 1980s until his appointment in 1988 as the army's deputy chief of staff. Promoted at this point to the rank of brigadier-general, he became army chief of staff the following year.

A disagreement with the then President Chadli in 1990 provoked Zeroual's resignation over plans to reorganise the armed forces, as Chadli pressed ahead with the transition from the single-party rule of the National Liberation Front (FLN) to a multiparty political system. Zeroual was posted as ambassador to Romania, and a year later retired from public life. However, Chadli was replaced by a military-based regime in Algeria, imposed when elections in late 1991 threatened to produce a parliament dominated by the radical Islamist party FIS (the Islamic Salvation Front). The military leadership appointed Zeroual as minister of defence in July 1993.

Zeroual's appointment as president, on 27 January 1994, followed the failure of a national conference, which the regime had called in an attempt to win consensus on who should take over as head of state for a proposed three-year transitional period. The conference was boycotted by all the main parties save for *Hamas*, and broke down when it became clear that the most credible civilian candidate would not accept nomination, because of the extensive powers which the military intended to retain. Abandoning the attempt at consensus, the military leadership nominated Zeroual, who was sworn in on 31 January. He also retained charge of the national defence portfolio.

Zeroual had been in contact with FIS leaders the previous December about a possible national reconciliation process, but various proposals from both sides in 1994 and 1995 produced no agreement. The regime accordingly went ahead with a nationwide presidential election on 16 November 1995, from which the FIS was excluded, and which other main parties (except *Hamas*) consequently boycotted. Zeroual's victory over three other candidates, with 61 per cent of the vote on the first round, was of less significance in conferring legitimacy on his position than the fact of a respectably high voter turnout. Further stages in the re-establishment of political institutions included parliamentary elections in June 1997, held without the FIS and won by a newly created pro-Zeroual party, the National Democratic Rally (RND), in alliance with the former ruling FLN. The so-called transition process, however, was taking place in the context of an escalating campaign of increasingly indiscriminate terrorism by Islamist extremists. Zeroual's government showed no sign of being able to contain or control this violence, still less to resolve it, and accusations persisted that soldiers were implicated in, or stood aside and allowed, some of the mass killings.

Liamine Zeroual is married with three children.

Joan Martí **Alanis** and Jacques **Chirac**

The principality of Andorra has as its two co-princes (joint titular heads of state) the Spanish bishop of Urgell, currently Bishop Joan Martí Alanis (illustrated above), and the president of France, currently Jacques Chirac. This so-called paréage *dates from an agreement in 1278 between the bishop of Urgell and the French count of Foix. The representatives of the co-princes in Andorra are the* Veguer Episcopal *and the* Veguer de França, *who are Francesc Badia Batalla and Jean-Pierre Courtois, respectively.*

Mgr Joan Martí Alanis has been co-prince since his induction on 31 January 1971 as bishop of Seo de Urgell. Since 1989 he has also been a member of the pontifical council on social communication. Born on 29 November 1928 in El Milà in the archdiocese of Tarragona, he graduated from the University of Salamanca with a degree in classical humanities, and was ordained as a priest on 17 June 1951. He remained in his native archdiocese for 19 years as an episcopal vicar of doctrine of the faith and teaching; he was also director of the Colegio Episcopal de la Mare de Déu de la Mercé in Montblanc and founding director of the Colegio Menor de Sant Pablo in Tarragona. Two years after he became bishop of Urgell in 1971, he and the then French president, Georges Pompidou, held in 1973 the first ever personal meeting between two co-princes to discuss matters affecting the future of Andorra.

For **Jacques Chirac**, see under France.

José Eduardo **dos Santos**

José Eduardo dos Santos succeeded to the presidency in 1979 on the death of Antonio Agostinho Neto, Angola's leader since independence in 1975. Involved since his youth in the struggle to end Portuguese colonial rule, as a member of the Marxist–Leninist guerrilla Popular Movement for the Liberation of Angola (MPLA), he rose to hold a place on the party politburo and was also a government minister before becoming president. His regime has had to contend with a protracted civil war against Jonas Savimbi's UNITA, backed for much of this time by South Africa and the USA. Dos Santos was most recently confirmed in office in 1992, when under a peace formula he contested the first round of a presidential election against Savimbi in disputed circumstances. The president, whose normal term of office is five years, is head of state and government, appointing the prime minister (a post restored only in 1992) and presiding over the council of ministers.

Born in Luanda on 28 August 1942, the son of a bricklayer, dos Santos joined the MPLA in 1961 while still a student in Luanda, and set up a youth organisation within it. In November of that year he fled north across the border, initially to Leopoldville (now Kinshasa) to escape the Portuguese colonial authorities. Enlisting in the MPLA guerrilla army the following year, he soon became the organisation's chief representative in Brazzaville.

In 1963 he went to study in the Soviet Union at the Baku Petroleum and Gas Institute, receiving degrees in petroleum engineering and in radar communications. After completing his studies in 1969 he did a one-year military communications course before returning to Angola in 1970 to resume his role in the anti-colonial struggle. He was head of the MPLA's principal communications centre on the northern front, where he became in 1974 a member of the Readjustment Commission and also head of finances. In September 1974 he was elected to the MPLA central committee.

In June 1975 he was named as the MPLA's foreign affairs secretary, and after the proclamation of independence on 11 November he was appointed minister of external relations, later transferring to become minister of planning. He also held the office of first deputy premier until it was abolished in 1978, and was put in charge of national reconstruction on the party central committee.

After Neto's death in 1979 dos Santos moved up to take over the MPLA leadership, carrying with it the roles of state president and commander in chief of the armed forces (FAPLA), to which he was sworn in on 21 September 1979. The dos Santos succession marked a setback for hardline pro-Soviet elements within the embattled party leadership, and the ascendancy of those who favoured a sustained attempt to negotiate an end to the civil war with UNITA. For most of the next decade this proved unattainable, however, with the Reagan administration in the USA, and the South African apartheid government (itself also embroiled in Namibia) both increasingly committed to backing and arming UNITA. The MPLA regime for its part remained militarily reliant on the Cuban forces which had helped avert its defeat in the months after independence.

Prospects for peace apparently improved with two sets of agreements in which dos Santos played a major part, those signed in New York in 1988 to end South African and Cuban involvement, and the 1991 Bicesse accord with UNITA which provided for a peace process, a UN presence, and a transition to multiparty democracy. Elections held in September 1992 were dominated by the presidential contest between dos Santos (who won 49.6 per cent of the vote) and Savimbi (who won 40 per cent). UNITA responded by launching an intensified civil war, however, which prevented the holding of a second-round run-off. Peace process negotiations were eventually resumed in 1994, but fighting continued and as of the end of 1997 the power-sharing provisions of a Lusaka Protocol signed in November 1994 had yet to be implemented in full.

Dos Santos is generally credited with supporting the peace process, and with having overseen the reorientation of the MPLA away from its Marxist–Leninist ideological foundation in the wake of the collapse of communism in eastern Europe and the Soviet Union. At successive party congresses in December 1990 and May 1992, reforms were adopted and he was re-elected as party chairman. A more hardline element in the party, however, backed the election of Lopo do Nascimento as secretary-general in 1993, and reflected concern that the party's forces had weakened themselves dangerously *vis-à-vis* UNITA by observing the terms of the peace process. Moreover, the war has left the economy crippled, with rampant inflation and growing signs of discontent in the capital, Luanda, in spite of the deployment of special forces to forestall public protest. The president, his family and his immediate circle of advisers have been accused by critics of lacking answers to the country's pressing problems, and of corruption and preoccupation with their own business interests, while dos Santos himself has suffered serious illness, believed to be prostate cancer.

Sir James **Carlisle**

Sir James Carlisle has been governor-general of Antigua and Barbuda since 1993. He represents the monarch, Queen Elizabeth II, as titular head of state. His appointment came after a long career in dentistry.

Born on 5 August 1937, James Carlisle attended Bolans Public School, Antigua, between 1946 and 1954, and afterwards worked as a primary school teacher. In 1960 he went to Britain, joining the Royal Air Force while also pursuing courses at North West London Polytechnic and (in 1963/64) at Singapore University. Returning to Britain he did an A-level course at Northampton College of Technology and then went to the University of Dundee in 1967, qualifying as a dentist in 1972.

From 1972 to 1992 he worked in general practice in Scotland, Wales, England and Antigua, and was also a part-time school dental officer in Scotland and Antigua. Between 1981 and 1983 he was a volunteer dentist at the Baptist Dental Clinic, and from 1983 to 1986 was manager of the fluoride programme with the Catholic Dental Centre. In 1990/91 he studied laser dentistry at Orlando, Florida. In 1993 he instituted a free dental care programme for children and the elderly. He was also chairman of the National Parks Authority (1986–90) and chairman of the Tabitha Senior Citizens' Home (1987–90). He was created a Knight Grand Cross of the Most Distinguished Order of St Michael and St George in November 1993.

Sir James Carlisle is married with five children.

Carlos **Menem**

Carlos Menem has been president of Argentina since July 1989, having won the election the previous May. He was re-elected for a further term in 1995, after successfully pushing through a constitutional amendment to allow an incumbent to seek re-election; the normal length of a presidential term was reduced by this amendment, however, to four years. The executive presidency combines the functions of head of state and head of government. Menem was an active Peronist from his youth, but has followed free market liberal economic policies as president rather than maintaining the Peronist tradition of corporatism and welfare spending. Imprisoned under the military regime from 1976 to 1981, he subsequently built up his power base as governor of La Rioja province and makes a feature of his flamboyant "macho" style.

Carlos Saúl Menem was born on 2 July 1930 in Anillaco in La Rioja province. The son of Sunni Muslim immigrants from Syria, he converted to Catholicism, and was active in student politics at university in Córdoba, where he completed a doctorate in law and founded a Peronist youth group. In 1955, the year in which Juan Perón's dictatorship was overthrown, Menem began a 15-year link with the Peronist trade union confederation as a legal adviser. He was also involved from 1955 in defending political prisoners, and became implicated in the abortive attempt to restore Perón to power in 1956, which cost him a brief period in detention.

Menem first stood for election as a provincial deputy in La Rioja in 1958, and was a candidate for deputy governor in 1972, but the intervention of another military coup prevented that election from taking place. Provincial leader of the Peronists (formally known as FREJUPO or the Justicialist Party, PJ) in La Rioja from 1963, he was three times provincial governor between 1973 (when Perón made his triumphant return from Spain) and 1989. However, he spent five of these years in prison or under house arrest, from 1976 to 1981, after Perón's widow had been forced out of power by a military coup. The 1983 elections marked the restoration of democratic rule, but with the Radical Civic Union (UCR) winning power at national level the Peronists became increasingly faction-ridden in opposition.

Menem's nomination as the Justicialist Party presidential candidate for the 1989 election was based on his support among the Peronist trade unions and the "federalism and liberation" faction, against the hostility of a left-wing "renewalist" faction. He won over 47 per cent in the popular vote on 14 May and thus the support of 310 of the 600-member electoral college, responsible for his formal election as president. Although not due to take over power until the end of the year, he was sworn in early, on 8 July, at the instigation of the outgoing president, who thereby avoided making a decision on an amnesty for human rights violations under military rule. Menem subsequently pardoned many of the former military leaders, attempting to placate the armed forces on this issue in the wake of a military revolt in late 1990.

Once in office, and facing a sharp deterioration in the economy, Menem also made a pronounced shift to the right on economic policy. The third strand in the Justicialist Party, the traditionalist Peronists or so-called *"oficialistas"*, criticised this and disagreed with his prescription of liberal free market policies. In response, however, Menem tended to point to his government's record of economic achievement from 1991 onwards. This success boosted the party's performance in the October 1993 partial legislative elections, encouraging Menem to go ahead with his project for a constituent assembly to reform the constitution. The assembly, elected on April 1994, duly adopted in October of that year a new constitution allowing a president to serve two consecutive four-year terms, enabling Menem to seek re-election at the end of his term in 1995.

Menem won re-election convincingly in 1995, receiving 49.8 per cent of the vote in the nationwide poll on 14 May, although without a corresponding success in the concurrent legislative election. The formal procedure of the electoral college had been abolished under the 1994 constitution. Menem was sworn in for his second term on 8 July 1995.

Carlos Menem was married in 1966 to the equally flamboyant Zulema Fátima Yoma; it was a turbulent relationship which ended in divorce.

Levon **Ter-Petrossian**

Levon Ter-Petrossian, who led Armenia through the process of establishing independence from the Soviet Union in 1990/91, was confirmed by the electorate as the country's first president in October 1991 and was re-elected for a second five-year term in a controversial poll in September 1996, but his position subsequently came under serious challenge. As president he is head of state and has executive powers which were strengthened under the 1995 constitution, although formally the head of government is the prime minister (whom the president appoints). A philologist and scholar of ancient Armenian history, Ter-Petrossian came to prominence in the pro-independence movement in the late 1980s and is the leader of the Pan Armenian National Movement (PANM).

Ter-Petrossian was born on 9 January 1945 in Aleppo, Syria, and emigrated with his family in 1946 to Soviet Armenia. On 28 April 1965, the anniversary of the start of the Turkish genocide in Armenia which lasted from 1915 to 1917, he participated in unprecedented protests by hundreds of thousands of demonstrators against the Soviet regime and was as a result imprisoned for several months.

After graduating in 1968 from the oriental studies department of the state university in Yerevan, he went to Leningrad (now St Petersburg) to do postgraduate study in that city's prestigious institute of oriental studies, working on Armenian and Assyrian philology. He then worked on a variety of academic projects in research institutes within Armenia and Russia, including at the institute of literature of the Academy of Sciences of Armenia (1972–78) and the Matenadaran Library of Ancient Manuscripts (1978–88); his doctorate was eventually awarded in 1987.

In 1988, Ter-Petrossian became more widely known through the agitation of the Karabakh Committee, of which he was one of the co-founders, for the transfer to Armenia of the mainly Armenian-populated Nagorny Karabakh enclave within Azerbaijan. In December 1988 he was arrested, along with other members of the committee, and imprisoned in Moscow for his role in organising nationalist and pro-democracy demonstrations. Following his release in 1989 he was elected chair of the newly formed PANM, making him a key figure in the nationalist campaign for Armenia's independence from the Soviet Union. In elections in May 1990, the PANM became the dominant element in the Supreme Council of the Armenian Soviet Socialist Republic. Five months later Ter-Petrossian was elected chair of the Council (*de facto* head of state), shortly before the Supreme Soviet's declaration of independent statehood on 23 August 1990.

When a decision to declare full independence had been confirmed overwhelmingly in a September

1991 referendum, Armenia's first direct presidential elections were held on 16 October 1991. Seeking a popular mandate to continue in office, Ter-Petrossian won a sweeping victory with 83 per cent of the vote. Over the ensuing five years his administration maintained its hold on power, seeking to achieve a transition to a market economy in clearly adverse conditions while retaining the support of communist-era managers. Ter-Petrossian's position was reinforced by the success of a PANM-led republican bloc at legislative elections in July 1995 and the approval at the same time of a new constitution strengthening the powers of the presidency. This was overshadowed, however, by a protracted and unresolved conflict with Azerbaijan over Nagorny Karabakh, and by deterioration in the economic situation, to which Ter-Petrossian responded by replacing one cabinet with a more pro-reform team, launching an accelerated privatisation drive in 1995, and taking a firm line with protest demonstrations. Ter-Petrossian was re-elected for a second five-year term in presidential elections held on 22 September 1996, although this poll was marred by serious breaches of the electoral law. Ter-Petrossian was credited with winning 52 per cent of the vote against 41 per cent for his main rival, former prime minister Vazgen Manukian. Public demonstrations over the results, which led to the storming of the parliamentary building, were put down by a show of military force, and Ter-Petrossian was inaugurated for his second term on 11 November 1996. By late 1997, however, he was under severe pressure to resign, having been outflanked by critics with more intransigent views on Nagorny Karabakh when he delayed recognition of a "declaration of independence" in the enclave and instead sought an accommodation with Azerbaijan to end the conflict.

Olindo **Koolman**

Olindo Koolman has been governor of Aruba since 1992. Since the island was accorded status aparte *from the Netherlands Antilles in 1986, Aruba has been a self-governing territory responsible for its own internal affairs, and thus one of the three fully autonomous elements of the Kingdom of the Netherlands. As governor, Koolman represents the monarch, Queen Beatrix, as titular head of state and is appointed by the queen on the advice of the government.*

Koolman, who served as a member of the commissions dealing with the island's *status aparte,* had worked as an inspector of customs and excise in Aruba since 1986. His appointment as governor, in succession to Felipe B. Tromp, was announced on 29 January 1992 and he was sworn in by Queen Beatrix on 5 February.

In a speech following his investiture Koolman stressed the importance of respect for human rights, while also indicating that the protection of the environment and the prosecution of the war against drug trafficking would be among his principal priority concerns.

Sir William **Deane**

Sir William Deane, a retired high court justice, was sworn in for a five-year term as the 22nd governor-general of Australia, and Chancellor of the Order of Australia, on 16 February 1996. In this post he is the representative of the monarch, Queen Elizabeth II, as titular head of state, with powers limited mainly by unwritten convention. Since the passage of the Australia Act in 1986 the appointment of the governor-general is made by the federal government and does not require formal confirmation by the monarch. The residual link with the monarchy is currently under review, with ideas under discussion which would provide for Australia instead becoming a republic within the Commonwealth.

Deane was born on 4 January 1931 in Melbourne. He was educated at St Christopher's Convent in Canberra and St Joseph's College in Sydney, before graduating from Sydney University in the arts and law. After a brief period working for the attorney-general's department in Canberra, he studied international law in Europe and was awarded the diploma of The Hague Academy of International Law. In 1956/57 Deane was an acting lecturer in international law in Sydney and worked with a law firm before he was called to the Bar in 1957. He remained a teaching fellow in equity at Sydney University until 1961.

In 1966 Deane was appointed Queen's Counsel. In 1977 he became judge of the Equity Division of the Supreme Court of New South Wales; in the same year he was appointed judge of the federal court of Australia, and president of the Australian Trade Practices Tribunal. He held both these positions until 1982, when he was made a justice of the high court of Australia, a post from which he retired in November 1995. He was appointed Knight of the British Empire in 1982 and a Companion of the Order of Australia in 1988.

Sir William Deane is married and has one son and one daughter.

Thomas **Klestil**

Thomas Klestil has been federal president of Austria since 1992, serving a six-year term in this post which is chosen by direct election but which is largely ceremonial in its functions. The president may have a maximum of two consecutive terms of office. Klestil, a former career diplomat who was elected as the candidate of the Austrian People's Party (ÖVP), succeeded as president the former UN secretary-general Dr Kurt Waldheim, whose tenure of office had been unusually controversial due to persistent allegations that he had been guilty of war crimes in the Balkans as a German army officer during the Second World War.

Klestil was born in Vienna on 4 November 1932. He attended school in Vienna and then enrolled in the city's University of Commercial Studies, where he gained the degree of *Diplomkaufmann* and then in 1957 a doctorate in economics.

From 1957 he worked in the office for economic co-ordination of the federal chancellery, before joining the diplomatic corps in 1959. His first appointment was as a member of the Austrian mission at the Paris-based Organization for Economic Co-operation and Development (OECD). In 1962 he was posted to the Austrian embassy in Washington, before taking up an appointment in 1966 as aide to the ÖVP federal chancellor Josef Klaus, a position he held until 1969. From 1969 to 1974 he was Austrian consul-general in Los Angeles. On his return to Vienna he was appointed head of the department of international organisations in the federal ministry for foreign affairs. He held this post until 1978. In 1978 Klestil was appointed permanent representative of Austria at the United Nations in New York. He remained in this post until 1982, when he became Austrian ambassador to the United States and to the Organization of American States (OAS) in Washington. Between 1987 and 1992 he was general secretary for foreign affairs.

Klestil was elected federal president on 24 May 1992, when he secured 56.9 per cent of valid votes cast in a second round of voting. He obtained a majority in every federal province over his Social Democratic Party of Austria (SPÖ) opponent, Dr Rudolf Streicher. Klestil was sworn in on 8 July 1992 as the republic's seventh post-war president.

The resumption of more normal diplomatic relations in the post-Waldheim era was signalled by a visit from the then Israeli foreign minister Shimon Peres in December 1992, while Klestil paid a state visit to Israel in November 1994, the first by an Austrian president.

Thomas Klestil is married with three children.

Heydar **Aliyev**

Maj.-Gen. Heydar Aliyev became acting president of Azerbaijan in June 1993 after a rebellion had forced the incumbent Abulfaz Elchibey to flee the capital, Baku. Aliyev was later elected president by 98.8 per cent of voters in an election in October 1993. His term of office as president and commander-in-chief of the armed forces of Azerbaijan is five years. During the Soviet period Aliyev had headed the KGB security service in the Azerbaijan republic in the late 1960s, then became first secretary of the republic's communist party, and sat on the politburo of the Communist Party of the Soviet Union (CPSU) from 1982 to 1987.

Born on 10 May 1923 in Nakhichevan, an Azeri-populated enclave surrounded by the territory of Armenia, Turkey and Iran, Heydar Alirza oglu Aliyev was the fourth of eight children. He began studies at the Azerbaijan Industrial Institute's department of architecture in Baku, but these were interrupted by the Soviet entry into the Second World War in 1941. He later successfully completed a history degree at the Teachers' Training Institute of Azerbaijan, while in his military career he was promoted to the rank of major-general.

A member of the CPSU from 1945 to 1991, Aliyev was an official of the security forces and a member of the council of ministers of the Nakhichevan Autonomous Republic from 1941 to 1949. In 1949 he became part of the staff of the ministry of foreign affairs and the committee of state security (KGB) of the Azerbaijan Soviet Socialist Republic, rising to become vice-chairman, then chairman of the Azerbaijan KGB between 1967 and 1969. In July 1969 he was elected first secretary of the central committee of the communist party of Azerbaijan.

In 1982 he became a member of the politburo of the CPSU and also first deputy chairman in charge of transport in the Soviet Council of Ministers. However, in 1987 he retired from the CPSU politburo following disagreements with Mikhail Gorbachev, the then general secretary of the party. Aliyev opposed the Soviet reassertion of control in Baku in January 1990, which followed increasing unrest after the 1988 outbreak of hostilities with neighbouring Armenia over the status of Nagorny Karabakh.

In October 1990 Aliyev was elected to the Azerbaijan Supreme Soviet but in 1991, the year of Azerbaijan's declaration of independence, he resigned from the CPSU. The following year he founded the New Azerbaijan Party (NAP) and became its chairman.

On 15 June 1993, following the ousting of Elchibey, the *Milli Majlis* (unicameral national assembly) elected Aliyev as chairman of the Supreme Soviet of the Azerbaijan Republic and he assumed the duties of state president. Following an August referendum supporting the removal of Elchibey, presidential elections were held on 3 October 1993. Aliyev won 98.8 per cent of votes in a turnout of 97 per cent. However, no major opposition candidates had stood for election, while human rights monitors described the poll as undemocratic and said that the media had been closely controlled by Aliyev throughout. Aliyev was sworn in on 9 October 1993.

In March 1995 Aliyev foiled a coup attempt by the interior ministry's militia. That August, an assassination attempt against him was uncovered. Aliyev's New Azerbaijan Party secured an overwhelming majority of seats in legislative elections to a new 125-seat parliament in November 1995. International observers recorded irregularities in the voting, while certain opposition parties, which had not been allowed to field candidates, refused to recognise the new assembly.

Heydar Aliyev was married to an ophthalmologist, Zarifa-khanum, who died in 1985. He has two children, a son and a daughter.

Sir Orville **Turnquest**

Sir Orville Turnquest has been governor-general of the Bahamas since January 1995. In this post he represents the monarch, Queen Elizabeth II, as titular head of state. His appointment came after a long career spanning private legal practice, political leadership and church affairs. As governor-general, Orville Turnquest has interested himself particularly in youth issues and education, announcing that he planned to visit every school in the Bahamas.

Born on 19 July 1929 at Grant's Town, Orville Turnquest was educated locally before entering the Government High School in 1942. He studied law from 1947 until 1953, when he began his private practice, which lasted until 1992. He pursued further legal studies at London University in 1957, and after returning to the Bahamas in 1959 became a stipendiary and circuit magistrate and a coroner. In 1960 he was admitted to the English Bar. The rest of his career was marked by continued involvement in legal matters: he chaired the Bahamas Bar Council (1970–72) and served as a member of the Bahamas law revision committee.

Turnquest's first significant political position was that of secretary-general for the Progressive Liberal Party (PLP) from 1960 to 1962. He sat as an MP for the south central constituency of New Providence from 1962 to 1967, and from 1972 to 1979 was the leader of the opposition in the Senate, representing the Free National Movement (FNM). He became a member of parliament for the Montagu constituency in 1982, and was appointed deputy leader of the FNM in 1987.

After the FNM's general election victory in 1992 he served as attorney-general, minister of justice, minister of foreign affairs and deputy prime minister until his resignation from active politics in 1994.

Turnquest was a delegate at the constitutional conferences in London in 1963 and 1972, and has represented the Bahamas at the Commonwealth Parliamentary Association Conference, as a delegate in New Delhi in 1976, as an observer at the Nairobi conference in 1983, and as chair of the Nassau conference in 1992. He has also served as chancellor of the Anglican Diocese of Nassau and the Bahamas, and is a member of the diocesan council and the diocese finance committee.

Shaikh **Isa** bin Sulman al-Khalifa

Shaikh Isa bin Sulman al-Khalifa has been ruler of Bahrain since 1961, steering his territory through independence in 1971. A member of the Sunni Muslim dynasty which has held power for over two centuries, he oversaw the introduction of Bahrain's first constitution in 1973, but he dissolved the legislature two years later. As amir he retains effectively total control over the government, in which his eldest brother is prime minister. The amir rules mainly by decree, although in 1993 he appointed a consultative council.

Born in Al-Jasrah, Bahrain, on 3 June 1933, and educated privately at the Royal Court, Shaikh Isa was appointed in 1953 to the Regency Council, represented his father at the coronation of King Faisal II of Iraq in 1954, and was named crown prince on 5 July 1957. Between 1956 and 1961 he chaired the Manama Municipal Council, and has also been chairman of the Irrigation Council, head of the Khalifa Council, and vice-chairman of the board of administration.

Shaikh Isa succeeded to the throne in November 1961 on the death of his father Shaikh Sulman. Under his leadership the country became independent in August 1971, when he decreed that his title, "Ruler of Bahrain", be changed to "Amir of the State of Bahrain". Having gained independence, Bahrain became a member of the UN and of the Arab League. Helped by its location, it has become a leading banking and communications centre in the Arab world; although oil and gas production continue to dominate the economy, oil refining, aluminium smelting and plastics industries have also been built up. The Amir has also distributed thousands of homes in pursuit of his goal that every citizen should be a home-owner. Since the 1979 Iranian revolution his regime has encountered some fundamentalist agitation from elements within Bahrain's majority Shi'ite population. The government has taken security measures with growing frequency against those accused of fomenting or carrying out acts of violence, and withdrew its ambassador from Iran between June 1996 and March 1997.

Shaikh Isa is married with five sons and four daughters, the eldest son and heir apparent being Shaikh Hamad bin Isa al-Khalifa, born in 1950.

Shahabuddin **Ahmed**

Shahabuddin Ahmed has been president of Bangladesh since October 1996, serving a five-year term in this post which, since the restoration of the parliamentary system of government in 1991, is a primarily ceremonial role. A former high court judge and the country's chief justice from 1990 to 1995, as well as its interim president for ten months following the resignation of Gen. Ershad in late 1990, Ahmed has also been influential in a variety of important commissions and helped shape amendments to the Bangladeshi constitution.

Shahabuddin Ahmed was born in 1930 in Mymensingh district, the son of a social worker and philanthropist. Graduating from Dhaka University in 1951 with a degree in economics, and completing his higher education at Lahore Civil Service Academy and Oxford University, he worked in the Pakistan civil service until 1960, when he transferred to the judicial branch. Having served as district and sessions judge in Dhaka and Barisal, he had become registrar with the high court of East Pakistan by 1971, the year of the conflict which resulted in East Pakistan becoming independent as Bangladesh. From 1972 to 1974 he attended numerous conferences and commissions, both in Bangladesh and abroad, on subjects relating to labour legislation. He was president of the Bangladesh Red Cross from 1978 to 1982.

In 1980 Ahmed entered the Appellate Division of the Supreme Court of Bangladesh as a judge. In 1990 he was appointed chief justice of Bangladesh, retiring in February 1995. In international judicial circles he is notable as a critic of authoritarian governments in the Third World for negating constitutional rule and for violating human rights.

From December 1990 to October 1991 he served as acting president of Bangladesh following the resignation of Gen. Ershad. He was not a candidate in the presidential election of October 1991, but stood in 1996 and was elected unopposed by the parliament as a non-party candidate on 23 July; he was inaugurated on 9 October 1996 for a five-year term.

Sir Clifford **Husbands**

Sir Clifford Husbands has been governor-general of Barbados since June 1996. He represents the monarch, Queen Elizabeth II, as titular head of state. A British-trained barrister, he was a Supreme Court judge before his appointment as governor-general.

Clifford Straughn Husbands was born on 5 August 1926 at Morgan Lewis Plantation in St Andrew parish. He was educated locally at Harrison College, before travelling to Britain to begin his legal training. He was called to the Bar in 1952, and later that year was admitted to practise in Barbados, working in private practice from 1952 to 1954. For the next six years, he practised in Barbados, Grenada, Antigua, Montserrat and elsewhere before returning to Barbados in 1960 to work in the attorney-general's chambers.

In 1967 Sir Clifford was appointed Director of Public Prosecutions, a year later becoming a Queen's Counsel. In 1976 he was appointed a judge of the Supreme Court in Barbados, and he has held the position of justice of appeal since 1991; he acted as chief justice of Barbados on a number of occasions. He also acted as governor-general for a brief period in 1990, before his formal appointment as governor-general on 1 June 1996.

Sir Clifford has been chairman of the Community Legal Services Commission and the Penal Reform Committee, and also a member of the Judicial and Legal Services Commission. He received the Gold Crown of Merit in 1986, and was made a Companion of Honour of Barbados in 1989. Sir Clifford was created a Knight of St Andrew in 1995 in recognition of his outstanding legal and judicial service to Barbados, and upon becoming governor-general in 1996 was made a Knight Grand Cross of the Most Distinguished Order of St Michael and St George.

Aleksandr **Lukashenka**

Aleksandr Grigorjevich Lukashenka was elected as the first president of Belarus in July 1994, and has since had his powers increased by referendum and his term of office extended to 2002. As head of state he holds executive power and appoints the chair of the council of ministers, although it is the latter who is designated formally as the head of government. Manager of a collective farm in the Soviet and immediate post-Soviet era, Lukashenka continues to favour a considerable degree of state regulation of the economy, and at the international level he has made close relations with Russia the centrepiece of his presidency.

Aleksandr Grigorjevich Lukashenka was born on 30 August 1954 in the village of Alaksandryna in the Mogilev oblast (region). He graduated from the history faculty of the Mogilev Pedagogical Institute in 1975. He also has a degree in agricultural and industrial economics from the Belarussian Agricultural Academy (1985). During his military service in 1975 and 1977, he worked as a political propagandist with the Soviet border troops in Brest and then in 1977/78 in Komsomol, the Communist Youth League. From 1980 to 1982 he rejoined the army as a deputy company commander but then moved to various positions within the command economy. He rose to the post of deputy chair of the collective farm in Shklov and then deputy manager of a construction materials factory in the same town. In 1987 he became head of the Harazdiec farm in the Mogilev region, a post he held until 1994.

In July 1990 Lukashenka was elected as a deputy to the Supreme Soviet of the Belarus Soviet Socialist Republic and founded a "Communists for Democracy" deputies' group. At the time of the short-lived coup against Soviet President Mikhail Gorbachev in August 1991 he supported the "national emergency committee" which briefly seized power in the Kremlin. In December of the same year he was the only deputy in the Belarus Supreme Soviet to vote against the formation of the Commonwealth of Independent States (CIS).

Lukashenka subsequently built up his popularity as chair of the Supreme Soviet Commission for the Struggle against Corruption, a post to which he was appointed in April 1993. The Commission's allegations played a key role in ousting the reformist Stanislau Shushkevich as chair of the Supreme Soviet in January the following year. A new constitution providing for a presidential form of government opened the way for direct presidential elections held in two rounds in June and July 1994. In an unexpected result, Lukashenka was elected president for a five-year term, polling 44.8 per cent of the vote in the first round and 80.1 per cent in the second.

During his term of office Lukashenka has promoted increasingly close political relations with Russia. A treaty of friendship and co-operation was signed in February 1995, followed by a customs union in May of the same year and a treaty of union with Russia, signed in April 1997.

Domestically Lukashenka has come increasingly into conflict with parliament, the judiciary, the media and the wider public, as he has strengthened his hold on power. In August 1996 he announced that a nationwide referendum would be held on proposals to change the 1994 constitution in order to strengthen his presidential position still further. In this referendum, on 24 November, the results were recorded as an 84 per cent turnout and a 70.4 per cent "yes" vote for establishing a bicameral parliament and extending Lukashenka's term of office to the year 2001 (a term extended further to 2002 in June 1997). The opposition denounced the vote as a "farce" designed to legitimise a dictatorship, but Russian premier Victor Chernomyrdin, who had sought to mediate between the opposing sides, congratulated Lukashenka on a "real victory".

Aleksandr Lukashenka is married with two sons.

King **Albert II**

Albert II took the constitutional oath and ascended the Belgian throne on 9 August 1993 after the death of his brother, Baudouin I. He is the sixth king of the Belgians and, while playing no direct political role as head of state, he is regarded as a key unifying figure in a country with three distinct linguistic and cultural heritages: that of French-speaking Wallonia, Flemish-speaking Flanders, and the small German-speaking minority.

Albert was born prince of Liège in Brussels on 6 June 1934, the son of Léopold III and Queen Astrid. He studied harbour management and transport policy, and as prince of Liège (i.e. before his accession to the throne) he held several related posts, as a vice-admiral of the navy, and as honorary president (from 1962) of the Belgian office of foreign trade. In this capacity Albert has presided over almost 90 economic missions abroad, seeking to win foreign investment for Belgium. Between 1954 and 1992 he also served as president of the Caisse Générale d'Epargne et de Retraite. He was president of the Belgian Red Cross from 1958 until 1993, and set up the Prince Albert Fund for the Training of Foreign Trade Experts in 1984. This fund was designed to award grants to young Belgian graduates or executives to undergo training in the branches of Belgian companies located outside western Europe.

In the political sphere, Albert has fulfilled a variety of roles, especially after 1967 when he began to carry out projects in the fields of town planning, housing, environmental protection and management. In 1969 he was appointed president of the conference of European ministers responsible for the preservation of cultural heritage. He represented Belgium at the 1972 UN environmental conference in Stockholm, Sweden, and has presided over the Belgian committee for the European "year of the renaissance of the city".

Albert II is extremely interested in sport. He married Donna Paola Ruffo di Calabria in 1959. They have two sons and a daughter.

Sir Colville **Young**

Sir Colville Young has been governor-general of Belize since November 1993, representing the monarch, Queen Elizabeth II, as titular head of state. His background is in linguistics and education. The governor-general has few real powers, being required on most issues to act in accordance with the advice of the prime minister and the government.

Colville Norbert Young was born in Belize City on 20 November 1932, and was educated at St Michael's College (1946–50) before going on to obtain a first class teacher's certificate in 1955. He studied for a degree in English at the University of London and then at the University of the West Indies, graduating in 1961. He gained a doctorate in linguistics from York University in 1973, his thesis being based on a study of the creolised English spoken in Belize. Young followed a career in education, and was principal of St Michael's College from 1974 to 1976. Having spent a decade as lecturer in English and general studies at the Belize Technical College, he became president of the University College of Belize in 1986. From 1990 until 1993 he was one of its lecturers. He presented papers at the 1980 and 1990 conferences of the Society for Caribbean Linguistics, and received a citation from the prime minister in 1988 for his contribution to Belizean culture.

Young was awarded an MBE in 1986, and was appointed governor-general in November 1993, after the prime minister had requested his predecessor's resignation. He is also a trustee of the Belize Urban Development Corporation. Young has written a number of books, including *Creole Proverbs of Belize* (1980), *Caribbean Corner Calling* (1988), *Language and Education in Belize* (1989) and *From One Caribbean Corner* (poems) (1983). He was a founding member of First Belizean Steel Band and of the Beltek Steel Orchestra, and has composed music including *Missa Caribeña*, the first Belizean setting of the mass.

Sir Colville Young is married to Norma Trapp and they have three sons and one daughter.

Mathieu (Ahmed) **Kérékou**

Gen. Mathieu (Ahmed) Kérékou returned to power as president of Benin in 1996, when he won the country's second multiparty presidential election in March. He is currently serving a five-year term, renewable once only. A French-trained army officer, Kérékou had originally seized power in 1972 and installed an ostensibly Marxist–Leninist single-party regime. In 1991, however, having returned the country to multiparty democracy, he had become the first former dictator in mainland Africa to hand over power after losing a presidential election.

Born on 2 September 1933 in Natitingou in the north of Dahomey (now Benin), Kérékou was educated initially in Mali and Senegal. He then enrolled at the Saint-Raphael military school in France, and served in the French army until 1961 when he was appointed second lieutenant in the army of newly independent Dahomey. He was an aide-de-camp to President Hubert Coutoucou Maga between 1961 and 1963. In 1967, when his cousin Maj. Maurice Kouandeté led a military coup, Kérékou became chair of the Military Revolutionary Council. He returned to French military schools between 1968 and 1970, when he became commander of the Ouidah paratroop unit and deputy chief of staff.

In October 1972, following five years of coups and political crises, Maj. Kérékou led a military coup which ousted President Justin Ahomadegbé. On coming to power he declared the country a Marxist–Leninist state and appointed a military revolutionary government of army officers who were all under the age of 40, assuming for himself the positions of president, head of government and minister of national defence. He executed some of his political opponents, imprisoned others, dismissed senior army officers and has been accused of human rights abuses. In 1975 he changed the country's name from Dahomey to Benin. Four years later at a time when his power base was sufficiently strong for him to retain the presidency he staged elections, nominally returning the country to civilian rule.

During nearly two decades in power he nationalised private business and expanded government control but by the late 1980s began to be accused of destroying the economy, while public pressure grew for him to introduce reforms reversing these policies. In 1989 he dropped Marxism for multiparty politics in the face of further mass protests and demonstrations as well as pressure from the French government to introduce reforms. A national conference in February 1990 appointed former finance minister Nicéphore Soglo as interim prime minister and Kérékou reluctantly agreed to hold free elections. In the ensuing March 1991 presidential election he won only 32.2 per cent of the vote. Conceding victory to Soglo, Kérékou stepped down in what was the first example in mainland Africa of a former dictator relinquishing power following a democratic election. Kérékou was given immunity from prosecution, made a public apology for the mistakes and abuses of his term, and was allowed to remain active in politics.

In the next presidential election, in March 1996, Kérékou was returned to power. Although he polled only one-third of the total vote and trailed Soglo in the first round, he picked up support from the eliminated candidates and won 52.49 per cent of the vote in the second round on 17 March. Soglo, whose popularity had suffered both from his perceived autocratic attitudes and his economic austerity policies, contested the result before the constitutional court, but conceded defeat when the court on 24 March formally declared Kérékou the winner.

King **Jigme** Singye Wangchuk

King Jigme acceded to the throne of Bhutan in July 1972 at the age of 16 on the death of his father, Jigme Dorji Wangchuk. As king he has followed the cautious modernising approach of his father, although he remains firmly rooted in Bhutan's traditional heritage, which he has sought to protect against being overwhelmed by outside cultural influences.

Jigme Singye Wangchuk was born in Dechen-chholing Palace, Thimpu, on 11 November 1955. He was initially educated by private tutors, and later at St Joseph's School in Darjeeling, India. He studied in England from 1965 to 1969, returning to Bhutan in 1970 to complete his education at the Wangchuk Academy in Paro. He was named crown prince in March 1972, after which he began participating in cabinet meetings, and was appointed chairman of the planning commission. Installed formally as crown prince on 5 May 1972, he acceded to the throne as *Druk Gyalpo* (the Dragon King) only just over a month later, on 24 June, on the sudden death of his father. His coronation ceremony took place in June 1974.

As king of Bhutan, he chairs the council of ministers and is commander-in-chief of the armed forces. He has also retained the chairmanship of the Bhutan Planning Commission and regularly tours the country, attempting to combine the ideals of technological development with principles of continuity in a traditional society. He has, however, taken a strong stance against the growth of political opposition in the country, especially from those of Nepalese descent in the banned left-wing Bhutan People's Party. In 1988 he imposed a code of conduct, and his attempt to forge a new national identity has alienated the ethnic Nepalese of the south, inspiring a fierce minority rights campaign. Partly to counter the threat of cross-border dissident activity, he has worked to promote diplomatic links with India (from which Bhutan receives most of its aid) and with China.

King Jigme has participated in summit meetings of the non-aligned movement every year since 1976, and since 1985 has also attended the annual summits of the South Asian Association for Regional Co-operation. He has been instrumental in the very gradual opening up of Bhutan to economic development and to strictly limited tourism.

Hugo **Banzer**

Hugo Banzer became president of Bolivia for the second time in August 1997, having being elected by the Congress to serve a non-renewable five-year term. The executive presidency combines the roles of head of state and head of government. Gen. Banzer, a cavalry officer, had first held a government post under a military government in the mid-1960s and took power himself in a 1971 coup, heading for seven years a military government notorious for its brutal suppression of opposition.

Born on 10 May 1926 in Santa Cruz, Hugo Banzer Suárez was educated at the military college in La Paz. Previously commander of a cavalry regiment, he was minister of education and culture from 1964 to 1966 and then went as military attaché to Washington and then Buenos Aires. Shortly after the death of President Barrientos in a helicopter accident in 1969, he was appointed director of the La Paz Military College. He was forced into exile in Argentina from January to August 1971 as a known opponent of the coup which brought the leftist-backed Gen. Juan Torres to power in late 1970.

With the support of the right-wing Nationalist Revolutionary Movement (MNR) and the Bolivian Socialist Falange (FSB) as well as the army, Banzer mounted a coup on 22 August 1971 (the 193rd coup since the country became independent in 1825) and deposed Torres. Despite having initially promised to return the country to civilian rule, Banzer's regime had eliminated all civilians from the government by mid-1974, tightening his control against attempts to mount coups against him, and declaring that elections were to be postponed indefinitely. Widespread unrest in 1976 brought the eventual promise of elections in July 1978. These were declared void after allegations of fraud, but Banzer was ousted in a military coup by the armed forces candidate shortly afterwards.

Banzer became leader of the right-wing Nationalist Democratic Action (ADN) Party in 1980, but in 1981 he again went into exile in Argentina, after being accused of plotting against the then current military regime.

Bolivia finally returned to civilian rule in October 1982 and Banzer thereafter took part in a succession of presidential elections as the ADN candidate, narrowly losing his first bid for election in a second-round run-off in 1985. In 1989 he pulled out after the first round to back an unlikely coalition with the Movement of the Revolutionary Left (MIR), which made him a "power behind the throne" in the ensuing four years of coalition government and chair of a joint Political Council of Convergence and National Unity, possibly the real point of power. The 1993 elections saw him again finishing runner-up.

In 1997 he won the first-round popular vote on 1 June but without gaining an absolute majority. A congressional coalition between his party and four other parties then secured the presidency for him. Sworn in on 6 August, he pledged to combat the ongoing drugs problem, appointing a former US Green Beret, Guillermo Canedo Patino, as the interior ministry's new social defence secretary, in charge of coca leaf eradication.

Hugo Banzer Suárez married Yolanda Prada in 1962. They have two sons and three daughters.

Alija **Izetbegovic**

Alija Izetbegovic has been president of Bosnia-Herzegovina since December 1990. Initially he was chair of the collective presidency of the republic, in the last 15 months before its declaration of independence from the disintegrating former Socialist Federal Republic of Yugoslavia. He remained titular Bosnian president, but in practice he was the embattled leader of the Bosnian Muslims, in the civil war which tore the country apart after independence in March 1992. Under the 1995 peace agreement the Republic of Bosnia-Herzegovina has a tripartite collective presidency, consisting of directly elected representatives of each of the three ethnic groups (Bosniaks or Bosnian Muslims, Bosnian Croats and Bosnian Serbs). Following his election and that of the Croat and Serb representatives in September 1996, Izetbegovic took office as chair of the collective presidency, the chair being due to rotate every two years.

Alija Izetbegovic was born on 8 August 1925 in Bosanski Samac in northern Bosnia. He studied law in Sarajevo, but was sent to prison for three years by the post-war communist government of Yugoslavia in 1946 when his writing for a Muslim newspaper was denounced as pan-Islamic activity. After his release he completed his studies and worked as a legal consultant. An "Islamic declaration" which he published in the late 1970s led to his arrest once again in 1983 and a conviction for disseminating Islamic propaganda. He had served five years of his 14-year sentence when he was released in 1988.

Yugoslavia moved in 1990 to introduce a pluralist political system amid a growing crisis of competing nationalist aspirations. A strong performance in elections that November by the Party of Democratic Action (PDA), a Muslim nationalist organisation which Izetbegovic had founded in May, made it the largest party in the Bosnian republic's legislature. He was himself elected at the same time to the seven-member republican collective presidency. The strength of the PDA and of counterpart Serb and Croat nationalist parties left the communists in a minority, and Izetbegovic was chosen in December as president of the collective presidency.

The rapid disintegration of the Yugoslav federation, with Croatia, Slovenia and Macedonia all declaring independence in 1991, overtook the efforts even of the politically adroit and inventive Izetbegovic to find a formula for Bosnia to remain a multi-ethnic republic in a wider Yugoslav context. A referendum on Bosnian independence, held in March 1992, was boycotted by Serbs now seduced by the prospect of belonging to a "Greater Serbia", while both Bosnian Muslims and Bosnian Croats voted heavily in favour. Left with little option but to declare independence, Izetbegovic then saw the state of which he was president torn three ways by civil war.

Izetbegovic stood down as PDA president in December 1992, in a forlorn attempt to boost the idea that the state president could stand apart from ethnically based politics, but he resumed the party leadership in March 1994. Throughout the three years of bitter fighting he insisted repeatedly that his position be respected as the lawful head of state, rather than as leader of one of the warring parties. In reality, however, he commanded the allegiance only of the Muslim community, and even this was challenged at one stage by his old rival in the northwest, Fikret Abdic.

Izetbegovic was a signatory of the eventual Dayton peace accord in November 1995, under which the fighting was halted after NATO intervention, and the task of rebuilding national institutions resumed. The Dayton accord opened the way for elections on 14 September 1996 for the various state institutions, including the three-member collective presidency. Izetbegovic topped by a huge margin the poll for the Bosniak (Muslim) representative, winning 80 per cent of the vote against seven other candidates. Despite a recent history of heart problems, he was formally sworn in on 5 October 1996 to take the first two-year term as chair of the presidency, at a ceremony boycotted by the Bosnian Serbs.

Under the 1995 peace agreement there are two entities within the state, namely the Federation of Bosnia-Herzegovina and the Republika Srpska, which are in effect separate governments for, respectively, the Bosniaks and Croats on the one hand, and the Serbs on the other. Each has its own president and prime minister, their presidents being respectively **Ejup GANIC** and **Biljana PLAVSIK.**

Ejup Ganic, a Muslim born on 3 March 1946, was a professor of engineering in the USA from 1975 to 1982 thereafter an adviser to the Bosnian government, based in Sarajevo. He was a member of the presidency from 1990 and throughout the civil war, and vice-president to Izetbegovic from 1992. He became vice-president of the Bosniak-Croat entity, the Federation of Bosnia-Herzegovina, when it was formally set up in May 1994, retaining this post until late 1997 when he became its president by rotation with his Croat counterpart.

Biljana Plavsik, a Serb from Tuzla in the north, was born in 1930, graduated from university in Zagreb (Croatia) and spent two years studying in the USA, before becoming a professor of biology at Sarajevo University. She joined the hardline nationalist Serbian Democratic Party in 1990, took over in June 1996 as Republika Srpska president when her party's leader, the indicted war criminal Radovan Karadzic, was forced out by international pressure, and was confirmed by the elections in September of that year. The following year her position was threatened as a bitter rivalry developed between her supporters and those of Karadzic, whom she now identified as a major obstacle to coming to terms with the 1995 peace settlement. From her base in Banja Luka she called fresh elections to the Serb legislature, and their successful completion by the end of 1997 appeared to strengthen her credibility.

Sir Ketumile **Masire**

Sir Ketumile Masire has been president of Botswana since the death of Sir Seretse Khama in 1980, and as such is both head of state and head of government. He was most recently voted a further term of office by the National Assembly following the general election in October 1994. Sworn in for a five-year term later that month, he has announced his intention of stepping down in March 1998. A veteran of African nationalist politics in what was then Bechuanaland, Masire co-founded the Botswana Democratic Party with Seretse Khama in 1962 and was the country's vice-president for 16 years from independence in 1966.

Born on 23 July 1925 in Kanye in the south of the country, Ketumile (Quett) Masire was the eldest son of a minor chieftain of the Bangwaketse ethnic group. He was educated at local schools while working as a herdsboy, before training to be a teacher in South Africa. After graduating in 1949 he started a secondary school in Kanye where he taught for seven years. He farmed for a couple of years, while writing as a journalist. Then in 1958 he became director of the *African Echo*. At this time he was also elected to the Bangwaketse tribal council. In 1961 he was elected to Bechuanaland's new legislative council for Kanye South.

Masire and Seretse Khama founded the Botswana Democratic Party (BDP) in January 1962, with Seretse Khama as leader and Masire as secretary-general until 1980. He was editor of the BDP newspaper *Therisanyo* for the party's first five years. He was a member of the National Assembly and became deputy prime minister of Botswana in 1965, during which time he was deeply involved in the negotiations for independence. When this was achieved in 1966 he was appointed vice-president and minister of finance and development planning. As such he promoted investment in mining, transforming the economy from one based on subsistence, to become the world's third largest producer of diamonds. Masire lost his seat at the 1969 general election but was appointed as one of four "special elected members" of the National Assembly. He was subsequently elected to the National Assembly in 1974 and again in 1979 as the member for Ngwaketse-Kgalagake.

In July 1980, following the death of Seretse Khama, Masire was elected president by a secret parliamentary ballot, to serve the remaining four years of the presidential term (coinciding with the life of the current parliament). He also took over as BDP party leader. He has been re-elected for full five-year terms in 1984, 1989 and 1994.

Masire has twice been chairman of the Southern African Development Community, taking an independent stance *vis-à-vis* neighbouring South Africa. He is also chancellor of the University of Botswana.

In recent years there has been a decline in support for Masire's BDP as a result of corruption scandals, economic problems, and the increased urbanisation of the population. Support for the BDP fell in the legislative election held on the same day as the presidential poll on 17 October 1994, although the party (which has been in power since independence) still retained an absolute majority of seats in parliament. In November 1997 Masire announced that he planned to step down at the end of March 1998, leaving vice-president Festus Mogae to complete the remaining 18 months of his current term of office.

Masire is married to Gladys Olebile Molefi. They have three daughters and three sons.

Fernando **Cardoso**

Fernando Cardoso has been president of Brazil since January 1995, having been elected in October 1994 for a four-year fixed term. In June 1997 the Senate finally approved a constitutional amendment for which Cardoso had been pressing, to remove the prohibition on an incumbent president standing for re-election. The executive presidency combines the functions of head of state and head of government. Cardoso, a sociologist with an international academic reputation, has been actively involved in politics with centrist parties since the early 1980s, and claimed credit as saviour of the economy after the success of his "Real Plan" as economy minister in 1993/94.

Fernando Henrique Cardoso was born on 18 June 1931 in Rio de Janeiro, the son of a general. He gained a doctorate from the University of São Paulo in 1961, and in 1962/63 studied industrial sociology at the University of Paris. Becoming known as a leading young leftist academic in Brazil, he was forced into exile in 1964 when the military dictatorship took power, but he continued teaching abroad, while writing critical articles about the military regime. During this period he was professor of developmental sociology in Chile and deputy director of the CEPAL centre for economics and planning (1964–67) and then taught sociological theory at the University of Paris-Nanterre (1967/68).

On his return to Brazil in 1968 he set up a social sciences think-tank, and took over the directorship of the department of social sciences at the University of São Paulo (1968/69). During this period his research centre was bombed by right-wing terrorists, and he was banned from teaching in 1969, arrested, and interrogated by military intelligence agents. In 1972 he left Brazil again for a lengthy period, holding professorships notably at Stanford (1972), Cambridge (1976/77) and Paris (1977 and 1980/81). From 1973 until 1976 he was a member of the Latin American committee of the New York-based Social Science Research Council, and from 1976 onwards a member of the governing body of the Institute for Latin American Studies at Santiago, Chile.

In 1980 Cardoso revived his São Paulo think-tank, the Brazilian Centre for Analysis and Planning (CEBRAP), of which he was president until 1982. Also in 1980 he helped found the Christian Democratic centrist Party of the Brazilian Democratic Movement (PMDB), which pursued a broad pro-democracy campaign, and in 1982 he entered the Brazilian senate as a PMDB senator for the state of São Paulo. After the end of the era of military rule, and the PMDB's success in the 1986 elections, Cardoso rose to the position of government leader in the Senate, and took part in the work of the National Constituent Assembly to frame the more liberal 1988 constitution.

Cardoso resigned as leader of the PMDB in June 1988 in order to found (with others) the new Brazilian Social Democratic Party (PSDB), which condemned the then President Sarney for clinging to office without a real mandate and for indulging in what Cardoso called "corruption with impunity". After several years in opposition, and the eventual impeachment of Sarney's successor President Collor, Cardoso was appointed by his successor Itamar Franco as minister of foreign affairs in October 1992. Moving over to become minister of finance and economy in May 1993, and thereby accepting what many in his party believed was an impossible brief, Cardoso made his political reputation with the success of his plan to regain control over the economy, tackling Brazil's rampant inflation and implementing a currency reform, the so-called Real Plan.

In the presidential elections of 3 October 1994 he overcame a strong challenge from the Workers' Party candidate, who had a massive early opinion poll lead, and took over 54 per cent of the vote in the first round. His three-party centrist coalition also established a strong position in the concurrent legislative elections.

Cardoso was sworn in as president on 1 January 1995. He vowed to democratise the country, to limit human rights abuses within the police force and to reduce the sharp disparities of wealth currently characteristic of Brazilian society. His free-market economic philosophy has made him an enthusiastic proponent of the privatisation of state-run monopolies and the removal of trade restrictions, but his social welfare promises have run into difficulties, and on human rights and environmental protection his government has made limited real progress beyond the framing of policies and programmes.

Cardoso has retained an active interest in the study of political and sociological issues and alternative paths to development, having first established his reputation internationally in the late 1960s as co-author of *Dependency and Development in Latin America.* He is president of several foundations and has been a member since 1990 of the New World Dialogue initiative at the World Resources Institute in Washington D.C.

Fernando Cardoso is married to Ruth Corrêa Leite and they have three children.

Sir Hassanal **Bolkiah**

Sir Hassanal Bolkiah succeeded to the throne as Sultan of Brunei on 5 October 1967 following his father's abdication, and was crowned as the 29th Sultan and Yang Di-Pertuan *on 1 August 1968. He is both head of state and head of government, and rules by decree with an appointed legislative council. Sultan Bolkiah is frequently cited as one of the richest people in the world, thanks to his tiny country's oil wealth, and has travelled widely in Asia, Europe and the USA. He has placed increasing emphasis in recent years on Brunei's Islamic identity, putting behind him his earlier image as something of a "jet-setter" and playboy.*

Sultan Bolkiah was born on 15 July 1946 in Brunei Town, and was educated privately in Brunei and in Kuala Lumpur, Malaysia. In 1961 he was installed as the crown prince and heir apparent. From 1963 he attended the Royal Military Academy, Sandhurst, as an officer cadet and gained his captain's commission in 1967, before succeeding to the throne.

In 1978 Sultan Bolkiah led a diplomatic mission to London to discuss with the British government a change of status for Brunei. A Treaty of Friendship and Co-operation was drawn up, whereby the British government relinquished its responsibilities for the conduct of Brunei's foreign affairs and its defence. The treaty confirmed that Brunei would, at the end of 1983, "assume its full international responsibilities as a sovereign and independent state".

On the day Brunei formally became fully independent, 1 January 1984, Sultan Bolkiah appointed himself prime minister and minister of finance and home affairs, and in 1986 he also became minister of defence. He is advised by the Privy Council, the Religious Council, the Council of Cabinet Ministers and the Council of Succession.

Sultan Bolkiah has ten children by his two wives: four sons and six daughters.

Peter **Stoyanov**

Peter Stoyanov has been president of Bulgaria since 20 January 1997, having defeated the candidate of the governing Bulgarian Socialist Party (BSP) in direct nationwide elections the previous November. He is serving a five-year term. The president is head of state, whereas the head of government is the prime minister, and until the April 1997 elections Stoyanov had to "cohabit" with a BSP government. A lawyer who speaks fluent German and is an advocate of integration with western Europe, Stoyanov only entered politics in 1989 when the former communist regime was forced to concede to a new multiparty system. He remained relatively unknown until he was chosen unexpectedly as the Union of Democratic Forces (UDF) candidate for the 1996 elections.

Peter Stoyanov was born in Plovdiv on 25 May 1952. He was educated at Sofia University, and graduated from the law faculty of the Kliment Ohridski University in Sofia in 1976. He practised as a lawyer from 1978 to 1989, during which time he never joined the ruling Bulgarian communist party (later re-formed as the BSP).

Stoyanov only became politically active in 1989, when the political upheavals began which were to bring down the communist government. He joined the newly formed UDF and became its spokesperson in Plovdiv as the first multiparty election approached in June 1990. In 1992 Stoyanov entered the first non-communist government since 1944 as deputy minister of justice. However, this government, formed by the UDF and led by Filip Dimitrov, collapsed in late 1993. In the 1994 general election, which returned the BSP to power, Stoyanov was re-elected as a UDF deputy and also became deputy chair of the parliamentary committee on youth, sports and tourism. In 1995 Stoyanov became deputy chair of the UDF with responsibility for domestic policy.

As the 1996 presidential election approached, the main group of opposition parties agreed to field a single candidate. In US-style primaries held in June 1996 Stoyanov won the nomination ahead of incumbent president Zhelyu Zhelev. In the presidential election itself a so-called "business bloc" candidate split the anti-BSP vote but Stoyanov nevertheless headed the first-round ballot on 27 October with just over 44 per cent of the vote, going on to take 59.9 per cent in the second round to defeat Ivan Marazov of the BSP. At his first official press conference he promised to focus attention on the economic crisis, and committed the country to closer integration with "European and Euro-Atlantic structures".

Stoyanov was sworn in as president on 20 January 1997. Although initially he had to cohabit with BSP prime minister Zhan Videnov, since the April 1997 general election he has been able to work with fellow UDF member Ivan Kostov, who became prime minister in May 1997.

He is married to Antonina Stoyanova, a former diplomat. They have two children.

Blaise **Compaoré**

Capt. Blaise Compaoré has been president since the 1987 military coup which overthrew his former fellow officer Thomas Sankara. Compaoré's military regime gave way to a multiparty system in 1991, when a new constitution was approved by referendum, and he was elected in December 1991, under controversial circumstances, for a seven-year presidential term. According to the 1991 constitution, executive power is vested jointly in the president and in the council of ministers, headed by a prime minister whom the president appoints.

Born on 3 February 1951 in Ouagadougou, Compaoré joined the army and was sent as a parachute trainee to the Yaoundé military school in Cameroon, where he first met fellow trainee Sankara. He graduated as an officer in 1978, going on to become a commander at the National Commando Training Centre in the town of Po in southern Burkina. When Sankara took power in a 1983 coup, establishing an avowedly Marxist–Leninist government, he appointed Compaoré as minister of state to the presidency and as a member of the National Revolutionary Council. Compaoré subsequently became minister of justice, holding this post from 1984 to 1987.

In October 1987, following disagreements with Sankara, Compaoré mounted his own coup. Together with up to 100 others, Capt. Sankara was killed in fighting in the capital during the struggle. Compaoré declared himself chairman of the Popular Front and head of state, and formed a new government on 31 October. Over the succeeding years he followed policies of "rectification" which, although nominally socialist, in fact featured economic reforms including the privatisation of state-run industry. In 1989 he founded the Organisation for Popular Democracy-Labour Movement (ODP-MT).

In June 1991 Compaoré retired from the army under public pressure and announced multiparty elections. On 1 December he was elected president in a direct election in which he was the sole candidate. Opposition parties boycotted the contest (the turnout was only 28 per cent) after the breakdown of tripartite talks, complaining of the lack of any prospect of a national conference. Violent protests followed, and a leading opposition figure was killed in a bomb explosion.

Condemning this violence as the work of the enemies of democracy, Compaoré postponed legislative elections due in January 1992 and announced that a national reconciliation forum would be convened forthwith to consider democracy, human rights and development. When the legislative elections did take place, in May 1992, opposition parties claimed that massive fraud had taken place. Compaoré's ODP-MT won three-quarters of the seats, and repeated this success five years later, having in the meantime absorbed several opposition groupings and restyled itself as the Congress for Democracy and Progress.

Than Shwe

Senior Gen. Than Shwe has been both head of state and head of government of Burma (officially known under the military regime as Myanmar) since 1992. A career soldier, he is head of state by virtue of his office as chairman of the ruling military council which seized power in 1988.

Born on 2 February 1933, in Kyaykse, Mandalay Division, Than Shwe attended secondary school before becoming a postal clerk. Joining the military officers' training school in 1953, he rose to the position of army general. In 1985 he became deputy commander-in-chief of the army under Gen. Saw Maung. After Saw Maung seized power in 1988 and became chairman of the State Law and Order Restoration Council (SLORC), Than Shwe became deputy chairman and commander-in-chief of the army.

Than Shwe took over the defence ministry in March 1992 and was appointed on 23 April of that year to head the ruling military council in succession to Saw Maung, who was replaced on grounds of health. Than Shwe was in addition named as prime minister the following day. He is generally seen as a hardliner, although in recent years he has ordered the release of a number of political prisoners, including members of the National League for Democracy (the victorious party in general elections in 1990, the results of which the SLORC refused to recognise). Than Shwe has promised to hold open talks with insurgent groups, and in 1994 he met Aung San Suu Kyi, the leader of the pro-democracy movement and winner of the 1991 Nobel Peace Prize. Increasingly pragmatic in his approach, Than Shwe realises that Burma can only receive foreign aid if it is willing to make some changes, and has recently redesignated SLORC as a State Peace and Development Council (SPDC). By accepting the need for some reform, however, his regime faces stronger opposition from pro-democracy supporters. In the meantime, with a military government and no officially recognised opposition party, most government opposition is met with heavy repression.

Pierre **Buyoya**

Maj. Pierre Buyoya has been president of Burundi since July 1996, when troops loyal to him overthrew the government of interim President Sylvestre Ntibantunganya in a bloodless coup. A member of the Tutsi ethnic group, and a former career soldier who had already seized power once before, in 1987, Buyoya justified his latest military intervention as a move to avert ethnic violence between majority Hutus and minority Tutsis.

Buyoya was born on 24 November 1949. Pursuing a military career, he trained in Belgium, at the Royal Military Academy in Brussels, and in France and West Germany, before returning to become an officer in Burundi, where successive military regimes had been in place since 1966. In 1982 Buyoya became a member of the central committee of the ruling and sole party, the ostensibly left-wing Union for National Progress (Uprona). He rose to the rank of major, but was nevertheless little known until September 1987, when he led the military coup in which President Bagaza was deposed.

For the next five years Buyoya ruled as head of the Military Commission of National Redemption. Relying on the support of the small Tutsi élite, he nevertheless attempted to aid Tutsi–Hutu reconciliation, releasing hundreds of political prisoners and appointing Hutus to ministerial posts.

In March 1992 Buyoya approved a constitution providing for the country's first multiparty elections. The resulting June 1993 presidential election saw his defeat by Melchior Ndadaye, who thus became Burundi's first Hutu president.

As ethnic tension persisted, with clashes between the largely Tutsi army and Hutu militants, Ndadaye and several of his ministers were murdered in a Tutsi coup attempt in late 1993, and his Hutu successor, Cyprien Ntaryamira, was killed in a helicopter crash in April 1994. (It was the death of the Rwandan president, a passenger in the same helicopter, which precipitated the attempted genocide by Hutus against Tutsis in neighbouring Rwanda.) Inter-ethnic tension continued to bedevil the supposed four-year transition period which was then initiated under a power-sharing interim government formula.

Buyoya's second coup, on 25 July 1996, was followed up by the suspension of the parliament and a ban on political parties. These measures were lifted two months later, while the civilian cabinet appointed by Buyoya featured members of the rival parties and a Hutu prime minister. However, Buyoya's attempts to establish democratic credentials (with presidential and legislative elections scheduled for June 1998) were dealt a serious blow when a United Nations report named him and other senior army officers as instigators of the murder of Ndadaye in 1993.

King **Sihanouk**

King Norodom Sihanouk has headed the Cambodian government since the 1991 UN-sponsored peace agreement, and took up in 1993 the title of king which he had already held from 1941 to 1955. Between 1955 and 1991, as Prince Sihanouk, he had been prime minister; he was head of state through the 1960s until the Lon Nol coup of 1970; nominal head of the Khmer Rouge regime briefly in 1975/76; and head of an anti-Vietnamese coalition government in exile from 1982. Real power lies with the government, headed (nominally as joint prime minister) by rival faction leader Hun Sen. Sihanouk. Although elderly, ill and distant, he nevertheless retains significance as a durable expression of Cambodian national identity.

Norodom Sihanouk was born on 31 October 1922 in Phnom Penh, the capital of Cambodia, then under French rule. His early education was in Paris and he completed his secondary schooling in what was then Saigon in Vietnam, later also receiving military training in France.

Upon the death of his grandfather, Sihanouk was proclaimed King of Cambodia for the first time on 26 April 1941, with the support of a French Vichy government which anticipated being able to manipulate the new young king. However, Sihanouk proved to be no mere jazz-loving playboy but a subtle and astute political operator, and increasingly significant as a national independence leader. In 1953/54 he mounted a protest against French rule by going into exile, returning only when independence was achieved. By abdicating the throne in favour of his father in 1955 he freed himself to play an unfettered political role. Retaining the title of prince, he effectively controlled internal affairs through his political movement Sangkum, while holding office as prime minister and minister of foreign affairs until 1956, and then ambassador at the UN.

On his father's death in 1960 he became once again head of state, but declined to take up the title of king. A participant at the founding conference of the non-aligned movement in Belgrade in 1961, he demonstrated great skill in getting aid from both superpowers at the height of the cold war, but ultimately was unable to keep Cambodia isolated from the region's dominant confrontation, the Vietnam war.

In 1970 he was driven into exile by Lon Nol's US-backed right-wing military coup, the US government suspecting him of complicity with the North Vietnamese and of allowing them the use of Cambodian territory. Controversially, as Cambodia was being shattered in what the US military cynically regarded as a "sideshow" to their Vietnam war, Sihanouk then allied himself with the Cambodian communist Khmers Rouges. Concluding a national unity front agreement (FUNK) in Beijing, he became a figurehead in their insurgency, and was named head of state of

Democratic Kampuchea when they took control of Phnom Penh in 1975. Virtually a prisoner in the royal palace, however, Sihanouk resigned the following year, finding to his enduring shame that he had no power to restrain the Pol Pot government's genocidal policies. Among perhaps 1–2 million Cambodians killed by the Khmers Rouges were five of Sihanouk's own children.

Sihanouk managed to flee in 1979 when the Khmers Rouges were ousted by intervention from Vietnam. He spent the next decade in exile, living mainly in Beijing and in the North Korean capital Pyongyang. The Khmers Rouges, driven out of Phnom Penh, struck back at the new regime from border areas, in an uneasy alliance with non-communist guerrillas. To Sihanouk, the Vietnamese domination of his country was so great an evil that he was tempted back into the expediency of alliance with the Khmers Rouges once again. Accordingly, if reluctantly, he agreed in 1982 to join a tripartite anti-Vietnamese coalition, the so-called "Coalition Government of Democratic Kampuchea" (CGDK). The exiled government over which he presided received wide international recognition, with Western backing, notwithstanding the fact that the Khmers Rouges were militarily its strongest element.

During this period Sihanouk worked to build up the credibility of his own guerrilla forces, founding a National United Front for an Independent, Neutral, Peaceful and Co-operative Kampuchea (known by its French acronym as Funcinpec). In 1989 the CGDK was superseded by a so-called National Government of Cambodia, with Sihanouk again its president.

In 1991 a UN-brokered peace accord was concluded between the three anti-Vietnamese factions and the Hun Sen government in Phnom Penh, Vietnam having pulled its forces out in 1989. Sihanouk took on the presidency of a new Supreme National Council (SNC) of Cambodia, and elections went ahead in 1993 despite a Khmer Rouge withdrawal from the peace process. The June polls were dominated by Sihanouk's royalist supporters on the one hand, and the former Phnom Penh government led by Hun Sen on the other, an outcome which Sihanouk recognised by putting together a power-sharing agreement between them. A vote in the parliament approved a proposal to restore the monarchy, and Sihanouk thus became king once again, on 24 September 1993.

The power-sharing formula created a joint premiership between Hun Sen and Sihanouk's son Prince Norodom Ranariddh, with the king, now old and ill, a distant figure living mainly in Beijing. Suspecting that royalists were promoting reconciliation with the remaining Khmer Rouge rebels to tilt the balance of power, Hun Sen in mid-1997 tightened his own grip in what was effectively a coup, driving out Ranariddh and naming a replacement himself. King Sihanouk's response was equivocal, neither outright condemnation nor acquiescence. Once again his behaviour reflected his appreciation of the realities of power. His readiness to see events in a long-term perspective, over more than 50 years of turmoil, has repeatedly proven to be a means of preserving his unique influence, giving him some claim to moral authority however much he may have been forced to compromise.

Sihanouk has married six times and has fathered, by his count, 14 children.

Paul **Biya**

Paul Biya has been president of Cameroon since November 1982. He took office on the resignation of Ahmadou Ahidjo, whom he had previously served under as prime minister. Having overseen a transition from single-party rule to multiparty politics in the early 1990s, he was elected for further presidential terms in 1992 and again for a seven-year term in 1997. However, his swearing-in ceremony on 3 November 1997 was boycotted by opposition deputies in a protest over what they alleged was massive electoral fraud. The president is head of government as well as head of state, and appoints the council of ministers, including the prime minister.

Paul Biya was born on 13 February 1933 in Mvomekaa, in the southern province of Cameroon. He was educated at local Catholic schools and at the Lycée Général Leclerc in Yaoundé, before going to France in 1956 to study for a degree in public law at the University of Paris. Graduating in 1960, he spent the subsequent two years at the Institut d'Etudes Politiques and at the Institut des Hautes Etudes d'Outre-mer. He returned to Cameroon in 1962, going into the post-independence civil service as a *chargé de mission* in the department of foreign aid (1962/63). In 1963 he obtained a postgraduate diploma in public law. From 1964 to 1967 he moved to the ministry of national education, youth and culture. Biya also served on a goodwill mission to Ghana and Nigeria.

In December 1967 he was appointed director of the civil cabinet of Cameroon. Early the next year he was also made general secretary to the president, and in 1970 he became a minister of state in the president's office. He was appointed prime minister in June 1975, but was regarded as still having a relatively low-profile advisory role until November 1982, when Ahidjo stepped aside for health reasons and handed over the presidency to Biya as his designated successor.

The appointment of Biya, a francophone Catholic from southern Cameroon, directly challenged the political hegemony of the northern Muslims. Several revolts seriously threatened his rule in 1983/84, the first of them blamed on Ahidjo himself, who fled the country and resigned his remaining post as head of the ruling party, the Cameroon National Union (UNC). Biya consolidated his position, taking over the party leadership himself and having his role as president confirmed by an overwhelming majority in the January 1984 election. Promising some gradual steps towards greater democratisation, he restyled the ruling party in 1985 as the Cameroon People's Democratic Movement (CPDM), and initiated some measures of social and economic liberalisation.

Presidential elections in April 1988 were held on the basis that he was the sole candidate, producing the required near-unanimous endorsement, but pressure for political pluralism ultimately led to the drafting of a new constitution, which was formalised in November 1990 and opened the way for multiparty elections. When these took place in 1992 the CPDM won most seats, but not an overall majority, in the legislature. Biya himself only narrowly won the presidential poll in October, claiming almost 40 per cent of the vote against almost 36 per cent officially credited to John Fru Ndi of the Social Democratic Front (SDF).

Thereafter the SDF mounted a sustained campaign for an all-party national conference and an interim government to supervise fresh elections. Biya refused to cede authority from his own government in this way, but his re-election as president on 17 May 1997, when he was recorded as having won 92.5 per cent of the vote, was marred by opposition claims of fraud, and a low turnout in the north and west of the country in response to boycott calls.

Biya married his second wife in April 1994, and is the father of three children.

Roméo **LeBlanc**

Roméo LeBlanc was appointed governor-general of Canada on 22 November 1994, taking office on 8 February 1995. The role is primarily a ceremonial one, representing the monarch, Queen Elizabeth II, as titular head of state, and commander-in-chief of the Canadian armed forces. His appointment followed two decades in teaching and journalism, a ministerial career in which he was particularly identified with the defence of the interests of the Canadian fishing industry, and a seat from 1984 onwards in the Senate, of which he was latterly the speaker.

LeBlanc was born in L'Anse-aux-Cormier, Memramcook, New Brunswick, on 18 December 1927. He was educated at l'Université St-Joseph in Memramcook, where he graduated in the arts and education. He later studied French civilisation in Paris, returning to Canada and taking up a high school teaching appointment in 1951. Between 1955 and 1959 he was at the teachers' college in Fredericton in his native New Brunswick.

In 1960 LeBlanc became a journalist for Radio Canada, spending two years working as a correspondent in Ottawa, then three years in the UK and two in the USA. He was the founding president of the Radio Canada Correspondents' Association in 1965. From 1967 to 1971 he worked as press secretary successively to prime ministers Lester Pearson and Pierre Trudeau, followed by a year as assistant to the president and director of public relations at the University of Moncton.

LeBlanc entered politics in his own right as a successful Liberal candidate at the 1972 general election, representing a New Brunswick seat. He was minister of fisheries from 1974 to 1979, and from 1980 to 1982, holding the environment portfolio as well from 1976 to 1979. Canada's longest-serving fisheries minister, he was involved during this period with measures to improve conservation and resources management, establishing Canada's 200-mile fishing limit, and developing the International Law of the Sea. He held the post of minister of public works from 1982 to 1984.

Leaving office with the defeat of the Liberal government in 1984, he was elected as a senator for Beausejour, New Brunswick, a seat he retained until 1995. From 1993 until his appointment as governor-general he was speaker of the Senate.

Roméo LeBlanc is married and has four children.

António **Mascarenhas Monteiro**

António Mascarenhas has been head of state since 1991, having won a convincing victory in the country's first free presidential election that February against the incumbent President Pereira, the country's leader since independence in 1975. Mascarenhas, a former head of the Supreme Court, was re-elected for a second five-year term in February 1996, in an election in which he was the sole candidate. As president he is head of state, and wields significant power, although the head of government is a prime minister chosen by the parliament.

António Manuel Mascarenhas Monteiro was born on 16 February 1944 in Santa Catarina on Santiago Island. He completed his early education in Cape Verde, and went initially to Portugal to study law at the university in Coimbra but fled to Belgium to avoid military service and completed his law degree at the Catholic University of Louvain. A Marxist in his youth, he joined the African Party for the Independence of Cape Verde (PAICV), the principal force in the island's struggle for independence from Portugal, in 1969, but left in 1971. He worked at the University Centre of Public Law, Belgium, from 1974 until 1977.

In 1977 he returned to Cape Verde, becoming secretary-general of the People's National Assembly of Cape Verde. In 1980 he became president of the Supreme Court and for the next ten years headed most of the delegations which represented Cape Verde, including the conferences which drafted and approved the 1981 African Charter on Human Rights and People's Rights drawn up by the Organization of African Unity (OAU).

In 1990/91 there was a peaceful transition to a multiparty system, the PAICV having been relatively tolerant of criticism during single-party rule. In the presidential poll on 17 February 1991 Mascarenhas stood as the candidate of the Movement for Democracy (MPD), the organisation through which the mainly Lisbon-based opponents of the PAICV regime had successfully pressed for the introduction of multipartyism, and which had defeated the PAICV in legislative elections the previous month. Mascarenhas won 73.5 per cent of the vote as against 26.5 per cent for Pereira, and was inaugurated as president on 22 March 1991. As head of state he has backed a programme of economic reform, including privatisation of key sectors. He has also undertaken a number of international commitments, notably as a member of the OAU "mission of goodwill" to Angola in 1992, and as president of the permanent inter-state committee on drought control in the Sahel (CILSS) from 1994 to 1997.

On 18 February 1996 he was returned to office as the sole candidate in a presidential election marked by a high rate of abstention. The MPD had secured an absolute majority of votes in a general election the previous December.

Mascarenhas is married and has three children.

Ange-Félix **Patasse**

Ange-Félix Patasse has been president of the Central African Republic (CAR) since September 1993, when his election marked the end of the military dictatorship of Gen. André Kolingba. A former agronomist and one-time communist militant, whose turbulent political career includes a spell as prime minister under the notorious regime of self-styled Emperor Bokassa, Patasse was founding president (in exile) of the Movement for the Liberation of the Central African People (MLPC) in 1979 and spent most of the 1980s in detention or in exile. As president, serving a six-year term, he holds executive authority although formally the head of government is a prime minister chosen by him.

Born on 25 January 1937 in Paoua, Patasse was educated at the higher school of tropical agriculture in Nogent-sur-Marne in France. An agricultural inspector in from 1959 to 1965, he then began a political career, initially as director of agriculture, then as minister of development in 1965. The following year Jean-Bédel Bokassa seized power in a military coup, ousting David Dacko as president and dominating the country until Dacko was reinstated in 1979.

In 1969, after several years out of government, Patasse returned to the cabinet, and held a variety of positions under the Bokassa regime. These included ministerial responsibility for transport and power, for development and tourism, and for agriculture, forests and hunting. From 1970 to 1972 he served as minister of state for transport and commerce, becoming in 1972 minister delegate for rural development. There followed the respective posts of *chargé de mission*, minister of state for health and social affairs in 1973/74, and for tourism, waters, fishing and hunting from 1974 to 1976.

In 1976, after these many often short-lived ministerial appointments, Bokassa appointed Patasse as prime minister. Later in the year, when Bokassa declared himself emperor, Patasse's post was restyled "vice-president of the Council of the Central African Revolution", a new body which took the place of the government. However, within two years he had fallen out of favour with Bokassa, who dismissed him in 1978, ostensibly for embezzlement of public funds.

Having fled to Paris, where he founded the MLPC in 1979, Patasse returned when Bokassa was ousted by Dacko with the help of French troops in September of that year. However, he was immediately put under house arrest, and although he escaped he was soon recaptured and detained for a further year. In 1981 he was a candidate in the presidential election, but lost to Dacko, who was ousted by Gen. Kolingba a few months later. Patasse, accused in April 1982 of plotting against Kolingba, took refuge in the French embassy before fleeing to Togo.

Patasse remained in exile for the next ten years before returning to the CAR, when as the MLPC candidate he successfully contested the presidential elections held in two rounds in August and September 1993. Sworn in on 22 October, he ruled in conjunction with a government in which a number of parties accepted representation (the MLPC having failed to win an overall Assembly majority in the legislative elections), but significantly increased his own powers under constitutional amendments introduced from the beginning of 1995.

Despite the 1993 elections being held under French supervision, French officials later expressed dissatisfaction over corruption and ethnic bias in Patasse's administration. A member of the Baya ethnic group himself, Patasse has faced particular opposition within the Yacoma-dominated military, and he has had to rely on intervention by French troops (garrisoned in the CAR) on several occasions to restore order when civilian strikes have been followed by army mutinies.

Idriss **Deby**

Idriss Deby has been in power in Chad since his 1990 coup, and was most recently elected president for a five-year term in July 1996. A French-trained soldier, he was the leader of the forces which enabled his fellow Muslim, northerner Hissène Habré, to take power in the capital, N'Djamena, in 1982. He turned against Habré in 1989 and subsequently mounted a successful Libyan-backed invasion from bases in Sudan. As president he is head of state and dominates the political scene, although formally the head of government (whom the president appoints) is the prime minister.

Deby was born in 1952 in Fada, Ennedi, in eastern Chad, into the Muslim Zaghawa tribe. He trained as a soldier, attending the Aeronautic Institute in Amaury-le-Grange in France in from 1976 to 1978. He quickly rose to become chief of staff in 1982 of the Armed Forces of the North (FAN), the supporters of Habré. In the ongoing civil war Deby led the FAN forces and captured N'Djamena, declaring Habré head of state in June 1982. Habré then promoted him to colonel and appointed him commander-in-chief of the armed forces and his military adviser. In 1985 Deby returned to France, this time attending the higher military academy in Paris.

Deby tried unsuccessfully to oust Habré from power on 1 April 1989, subsequently escaping into Sudan, where he founded a Patriotic Salvation Movement (MPS) and launched a number of attacks into Chadian territory. In November 1990 he led a successful invasion backed by Libyan troops, putting Habré to flight and proclaiming himself head of state and chair of the interim council of state. He was inaugurated as president in March 1991, as fighting continued against troops loyal to Habré and against other tribal groups.

Since taking power Deby has sought progressively to bring the many rival factions in Chad into a "national reconciliation" process, as part of which he eventually conceded the introduction of a multiparty system. A new constitution was approved by referendum in March 1996, which is secular in form (ostensibly to avoid closing the door to reconciliation with southern-based Christian opponents), although Deby's regime has in practice introduced many elements of Islamic sharia law.

In the first round of presidential elections on 2 June 1996 Deby won 44 per cent of the vote against 14 other candidates, and in the run-off on 3 July he won 69 per cent. His new term of office was inaugurated on 8 August 1996. He suffered something of a setback when his MPS failed to win an overall majority in legislative elections in early 1997. Deby again managed, however, to bring in more former opposition groups to support his regime, which has been greatly bolstered by the prospect of exploiting the country's enormous recently discovered oil resources. A harsh policy of shooting criminals on sight, and other human rights violations, has brought criticism from abroad, with European countries becoming increasingly attentive to the Chadian situation.

Eduardo **Frei**

Eduardo Frei Jr has been president of Chile since 11 March 1994, having won the elections the previous December as the candidate of his Christian Democratic Party (PDC). The executive president combines the roles of head of state and head of government, and under a 1994 constitutional amendment is limited to a single six-year term. Frei, a civil engineer before he entered politics at the end of the period of the Pinochet military dictatorship, has a reserved and non-confrontational manner, but has energetically pursued a liberal economic agenda during his presidency to make Chile attractive to foreign investment. He is the son of the PDC's founder Eduardo Frei Montalva, who was himself president of Chile from 1964 until 1970 and a prominent opponent of the left-wing Allende regime overthrown by Gen. Pinochet in 1973.

Eduardo Frei Ruiz-Tagle Jr was born in Santiago on 24 June 1942, the fourth son in a family of seven. Educated at the Instituto Luis Campino school and the University of Chile, he graduated with a degree in civil engineering, specialising in hydraulics, before studying administration and management techniques in Rome. In 1958, Frei joined the PDC, and accompanied his father on his presidential campaign of 1964 as a spokesman. He worked as a civil engineer with a prominent Chilean building firm, Ingenieria Sigdo Koppers S.A., from 1969 until 1988.

Following the death of his father in January 1982, Frei helped set up the Frei Foundation, a political and academic institution which he chaired until April 1993.

Although he was a long-standing critic of the Pinochet dictatorship, Frei did not enter politics proper until 1988, when he became a member of the Committee for Free Elections, and travelled over much of Chile promoting the "no" campaign for the 1988 plebiscite in which Gen. Pinochet unsuccessfully sought a mandate to extend his military-based presidency. In the 1989 legislative elections Frei was elected a senator for Santiago. As a member of the PDC he was the president of the party's finance and budget committee and its citizen safety committee from 1991 until 1993. He was also a member of the housing committee and the committee on citizen violence and safety.

Frei was elected PDC party president on 23 November 1991, and by mid-1993 had obtained the endorsement of his party and the broader Coalition for Democracy (CPD) alliance for his candidacy in the forthcoming presidential election. The result of that election, held on 11 December 1993, was a convincing victory for Frei, with almost 58 per cent of the vote against six other candidates. Meanwhile a dispute over the length of the presidential term, and whether it should be renewable, was eventually resolved by a compromise agreement in the Congress (not formally ratified until February 1994) on a six-year non-renewable term.

Frei had campaigned on a platform promising increased public spending to offset the impact of free-market economic policies, but also demanded the restoration of the presidential power to appoint and remove senior military officers. In August 1994 he set out a series of proposed reforms of the 1981 constitution, focusing in particular on reforming the Senate to remove the entrenched position of the pro-military right-wing parties. These intentions foundered, however, against the sustained opposition of the Senate, where eight non-elected members held the balance of power. As of December 1997 the Frei government had still not secured a final agreement on the departure of Gen. Pinochet as army commander. Pinochet had retained this post for himself under the terms of his transfer of power in 1990, and Frei had agreed, against some pressure to the contrary, to respect this provision until the end of 1997.

Eduardo Frei is married to Marta Larraechea and they have four daughters.

Jiang Zemin

Jiang Zemin has been president of the People's Republic of China since March 1993, when he succeeded Yang Shangkun as head of state. The president is elected by the National People's Congress for a five-year term. Jiang Zemin has also been since June 1989 the general secretary of the ruling Chinese Communist Party (CCP), a post to which he was most recently re-elected at the 15th congress in September 1997, and he is in addition president of the party's central military commission. He has established himself as the leading political figure in the country, although formally the head of government is the premier (currently Li Peng). Regarded as a reformist, Jiang Zemin has identified himself with the rapid opening-up of the economy to private enterprise. Described officially as at the centre of the third generation of Chinese communist leaders, he came up gradually through the party as holder of a series of posts in industrial plants, and was mayor of Shanghai in the mid-1980s, before his rise to the top in the party and government under the patronage of "elder statesman" leader Deng Xiaoping.

Jiang Zemin was born on 17 August 1926 in Yangzhou City, west of Shanghai, in Jiangsu province, which remained under Japanese occupation until 1945. The adopted son of a communist revolutionary martyr, he attended an American missionary school, joined the party himself in 1946, and graduated with a degree in electrical engineering from Jiaotong University in Shanghai in 1947. He took up the post of party secretary in a Shanghai food factory, then in a Shanghai soap factory (1949–1955), before going to Moscow as a trainee and working in the Stalin Automobile Plant. Returning in 1956, he soon moved into the power industry and machine-building, rising through a series of party posts to membership of the central committee in 1982. That year he also became a first deputy minister of electronics, and he was promoted in 1993 to the rank of minister in the same department, holding the portfolio for two years.

Jiang Zemin first came to wider public notice as mayor of Shanghai, a post he held from 1985 to 1989, and he also became a member of the party politburo during this period (in 1987). When Zhao Ziyang was dismissed as party general secretary and from all his other party posts as a dangerous liberal, in the clampdown which accompanied the June 1989 Tiananmen Square massacre, Jiang was picked to replace him. This was partly on the strength of his own handling of student demonstrations in Shanghai in December 1986, when he had taken a firm line but defused the situation without recourse to military force. He had also endeared himself to the hardliners by taking a firm position in April 1989 against allowing the Beijing student demonstrations to develop, while impressing others in the party by his record of effective economic management in the relatively go-ahead environment of Shanghai. In November

1989 and April 1990, when Deng stepped down as chairman of the central state and party military commissions, Jiang's appointment confirmed his status as Deng's unofficial heir apparent. He was elected (with the usual unanimity) by the People's National Assembly on 27 March 1993 for a five-year presidential term.

Jiang's ascendancy, *vis-à-vis* the more conservative faction associated with Li Peng, has been established in the context of China's rapid economic growth and a reduction in inflation. His promotion of market reforms, including far-reaching privatisation measures approved by the 1997 congress, has been accompanied by a firm line against dissident activity, and a campaign against corruption. Following the death of Deng in February 1997, Jiang Zemin also paid particular attention to his relationships with the army, where his ascendancy is apparently less firmly founded than among party cadres. At the 1997 congress, however, he announced plans to cut the armed forces by 500,000 men. He has also given cautious backing to the holding of village-level elections in which independents can run against party officials, without departing from the Chinese leadership's effective consensus about maintaining tight political control through the period of rapid economic reform.

Jiang Zemin is married to Wang Yepin. They have two sons.

Ernesto **Samper**

Ernesto Samper Pizano has been president of Colombia since August 1994. His four-year non-renewable term as head of state and government has been dominated by charges that he received campaign financing from drug barons, fatally compromising his government in the overriding national issue of the "war on drugs". From a background in finance and banking, Samper first entered politics in 1981, holding various posts from 1981 to 1984 including that of Liberal Party (PL) secretary-general. Wounded in an assassination attempt in 1989 during his unsuccessful bid for the party's nomination as its presidential candidate, Samper joined President Gaviria's government in 1990 as minister of economic development, and then went as ambassador to Spain, before returning to domestic politics and successfully contesting the 1994 elections.

Samper was born on 3 August 1950 into a prominent family in the capital, Bogotá. Educated at the local Gimnasio Moderno in Bogotá, he graduated in 1973 from Bogotá's Javeriana University in law and economics, while also working in economic research at the Bank of Bogotá and teaching at Bogotá Central University. In 1974 he pursued his studies in economics at the University of Mexico, specialising in capital markets. Returning to Colombia, Samper distinguished himself in the role of president of the National Association of Financial Institutions (ANIF) from 1975 to 1981, while pursuing a busy academic career. He received a master's degree from Columbia University, New York, in 1979 and lectured at Javeriana University and elsewhere until 1991.

Samper's direct involvement in national politics dates from 1981 to 1982, when he left ANIF to take on the role of co-ordinator of the presidential campaign of the PL candidate, former President Alfonso Lopez Michelson. The election, in May 1982, was won unexpectedly by the Conservative candidate, but the new President Betancur nevertheless chose Samper, then aged only 32, as extraordinary ambassador to the United Nations General Assembly.

The PL was left in some disarray by its election defeat, with a dissident New Liberalism faction pressing for the development of a broad centre-left movement. Samper played an important role in the ensuing period, as founder and director of the Institute for Liberal Studies think-tank, and as party secretary-general from 1982 to 1984. In 1984 he was elected to the local assembly for the Cundinamarca department assembly and to the Bogotá city council, and in 1986 he won a seat in the Colombian Senate. Identifying himself with the project of reforming the PL from within, he was elected as party president at the 1987 national convention, and campaigned for the reintegration of the New Liberalism faction and the democratisation of party structures.

On 3 March 1989 Samper narrowly survived an assassination attempt at Bogotá airport. Shot 11 times in one of a series of high-profile attacks blamed on drug-related "narco-terrorism", he recovered in time to campaign for his party's presidential nomination. The favourite, Luis Carlos Galán, was himself killed by narco-terrorists, but the eventual nomination went not to Samper but to César Gaviria. Gaviria, after his May 1990 election victory, then brought Samper into what was effectively a "government of national unity".

As minister of economic development until late 1991, Samper was identified in particular with the provision of family allowances for social housing, measures to open up the economy, the promotion of international trade, and regional integration, with Venezuela and other Andean Pact countries. In late 1991 he was appointed as ambassador to Spain.

Leaving his ambassadorial post in 1993, he announced in May of that year that he would again seek nomination as PL candidate for the 1994 presidential elections. Having secured this nomination, he narrowly topped the first-round poll on 30 May 1994 and went on to win the 19 June run-off with 50.37 per cent of the vote. He assumed office on 7 August 1994.

Samper's presidency began with a pledge to tackle social problems and generate one-and-a-half million new jobs, while maintaining an overall free-market orientation and an emphasis on economic growth. He also committed himself to ending the long-running war with left-wing insurgents. However, he has struggled since the outset to deal with allegations that he accepted US$5 million in campaign financing from the powerful Calí drugs cartel. The US administration regards his government as compromised and insufficiently committed to the "war on drugs", and both the Colombian opposition and prominent members of Samper's own party have called on him to resign over this issue, although parliament has ruled that there is insufficient evidence to bring proceedings against him.

Samper is married and has three children.

Mohamed Abdoulkarim **Taki**

Mohamed Abdoulkarim Taki has been president of the Comoros since March 1996. Under a revised constitution introduced by him in October 1996 the president's executive powers have been increased substantially, and the presidential term set as six years with no limit on re-election. Taki, a veteran of the country's turbulent and coup-ridden post-independence political scene, was an unsuccessful candidate for the presidency in 1990, and spent part of the following five years in exile or in hiding, interspersed with a short-lived experiment in a national unity government. Since taking office he has reinforced the Muslim character of the Comoros (which is officially a federal Islamic republic).

Taki was born on 20 February 1936 in Mbeni, went to secondary school in Madagascar and completed his education at the University of Paris with a civil engineering diploma at the Ecole des Arts et Métiers. Returning to the Comoros, he was employed in the public works department under the French colonial administration from 1964 to 1967 and sat in the local assembly from 1965 to 1969.

A minister in the first government after independence in 1975, Taki later fell out with the leftist revolutionary regime of President Ali Soilih and was imprisoned in 1977/78. Released after the first of the mercenary-backed coups led by Col. Bob Denard in 1978, he was elected in December to the National Assembly, and was its speaker until 1984, holding his own seat at elections in December 1982. An opponent of President Ahmed Abdallah Abderrahman's increasingly dictatorial regime in the late 1980s, Taki returned from temporary exile after Abdallah's assassination to contest the first-ever presidential elections, held in March 1990. As the candidate of the National Union for Democracy in the Comoros (UNDC), which he had led since 1984, Taki was runner-up in the second-round ballot and complained that the election victor, incumbent interim President Said Mohamed Djohar, had defeated him only by widespread ballot-rigging.

Accused by Djohar of complicity in a coup attempt in August 1990, Taki spent over a year in exile but succeeded in creating an opposition coalition and, at a meeting with Djohar in Paris in November 1991, in negotiating his return to launch a national reconciliation process. This produced a set of constitutional proposals, approved by referendum in June 1992, and a new cabinet, headed by Taki, which was announced in May 1992 but then dismissed on 4 July. After another failed coup in September, and with Taki now in hiding, the UNDC boycotted legislative elections in November 1992 (and boycotted parliament after further elections were blatantly manipulated by Djohar's supporters the following December).

When a Denard-backed coup ousted Djohar in September 1995, an attempt was made by the coup leaders to transfer power to Taki and another opposition figure as joint civilian presidents, but this proved abortive as French forces mounted an effective intervention. When presidential elections took place in March 1996, Taki as the UNDC candidate emerged as the victor, receiving 64 per cent of the vote in the run-off on 16 March, with support from all but one of the 13 candidates eliminated in the first round. He was sworn in as president on 25 March 1996.

At first distrusted by the French, who feared that he was a fundamentalist Muslim linked with Iran, Taki had been sufficiently conciliatory before the election to ensure that France would not be overtly hostile to his candidacy. He afterwards confirmed the acceptance of a French military presence in the Comoros, and in the first months of his presidency appeared to court Western business involvement, although he has latterly placed more emphasis on traditional Islamic social values and sought to strengthen links with Arab states.

New constitutional arrangements, with stronger presidential powers and no limit on the number of terms a president might seek, were approved by referendum in October 1996. The constitution also provided for the banning of political parties not represented in the parliament, allowing Taki to outlaw the main opposition Forum for National Recovery (FRN) after it boycotted elections held in December 1996. Those elections produced an overwhelming parliamentary majority for a newly formed pro-presidential National Rally for Development (RND), with opposition confined to one small fundamentalist Islamic party.

The main challenges to Taki's government were mounted not in parliament but in response to continuing and deepening economic problems. Civil servants, alienated by non-payment of salaries, launched strikes and protests. In August 1997 a fresh crisis erupted, over an attempted secession by the islanders on Anjouan – apparently an economically motivated bid to have the island redesignated (like neighbouring Mayotte) as a French overseas territory. Taki dissolved the government in September following a disastrous attempt to reimpose central control by force. He established a new State Commission of Transition, acting not only as president but also as prime minister – a post transferred to a presidential appointee in December.

Taki is married with children.

Denis **Sassou-Nguesso**

Gen. Denis Sassou-Nguesso has been president of the Republic of Congo (Congo-Brazzaville) since October 1997. A career soldier and a prominent member of the military committee which took over the running of the then Marxist regime in 1977, Sassou-Nguesso was president from 1979 to 1992, under a single-party structure, but was then defeated in the country's first multiparty elections and took his party (and its militia) into opposition. His return to power in 1997, after years of unrest, was assisted by Angolan forces in a decisive military offensive which ended five months of effective civil war.

A member of the Mboshi ethnic group, Sassou-Nguesso was born in 1943 in Oyo in the territory then known as the Middle Congo, which was part of French Equatorial Africa. He joined the army of the newly independent Republic of Congo and as a young junior officer he supported the self-declaredly Marxist regime established after a military coup in 1968 by Gen. Ngouabi, who set up the ruling Congolese Labour Party (PCT). Regarded as strongly pro-Soviet, Sassou-Nguesso headed the political police from 1974, and in late 1975, when he had reached the rank of major, he was appointed to a nine-member ruling council of state.

The military leadership sought to tighten its grip on the party after the assassination of Ngouabi in March 1977, and Ngouabi's successor, Gen. Yhombi-Opango, set up a military committee in which Sassou-Nguesso was first vice-president "responsible for co-ordinating PCT activities" as well as minister of defence. Using his party role as a power base, however, Sassou-Nguesso was able to challenge Yhombi-Opango for power within two years, forcing him to resign when he criticised the PCT in February 1979. A newly formed PCT presidium thereupon appointed Sassou-Nguesso as interim president. He was confirmed in this post, as well as becoming party chairman, at a special PCT congress on 27 March.

Although the single-party structure ensured Sassou-Nguesso's unopposed re-election at five-year intervals (in July 1984 and 1989), economic difficulties led his regime to turn increasingly away from state socialism, and towards free-market policies which could satisfy the criteria for attracting International Monetary Fund support. In October 1990 an extraordinary party congress (at which Sassou-Nguesso was elected president of a new central committee) formally abandoned Marxism–Leninism and endorsed the creation of a multiparty political system.

A national conference was convened from February 1991, and by June of that year had secured the role of interim head of government for the prime minister rather than the president. Legislative elections in June/July 1992 established a recently formed Pan-African Union for Social Democracy (UPADS) as the leading party, and when presidential elections were held in August 1992, Sassou-Nguesso as the PCT candidate was knocked out in the first-round ballot, finishing third with under 17 per cent of the vote. Conceding defeat with what he claimed to be "serenity", he thereupon called on his supporters to vote for the UPADS leader Pascal Lissouba, who won the run-off and was sworn in on 31 August.

In the five years of the Lissouba regime, however, Sassou-Nguesso maintained a high profile within a series of alliances which combined parliamentary opposition with extra-parliamentary protest and militia activity. Talks on a possible all-party coalition, and the integration of rival militias into the national army, produced a short-lived agreement in late 1994 on ending hostilities, and a similarly unimplemented peace pact a year later. With the approach of presidential elections due in July 1997, Lissouba tried unsuccessfully to disarm the PCT militia, and large-scale fighting broke out in the capital, Brazzaville, in June of that year. Attempts at external mediation failed to resolve the conflict, and were rendered irrelevant when a successful offensive by Sassou-Nguesso's forces, backed by Angola, left him in full control by mid-October.

Sassou-Nguesso was inaugurated as president on 25 October 1997. He named a cabinet on 3 November and also announced plans to create a transitional "national forum for unity and democracy". Sassou-Nguesso is well connected in France and has a long association with Jacques Chirac, the French president, with whom he held a long meeting at the francophone summit in Hanoi, Vietnam, in November 1997, at a time when his takeover was still not widely accepted. Both men are members of a French Masonic order.

Sassou-Nguesso is the father of five children and is married to Marie-Antoinette née Loemba, his second wife. He has one older brother, Maurice.

Laurent **Kabila**

Laurent-Desiré Kabila became president of the newly renamed Democratic Republic of the Congo in May 1997, his seven-month military campaign having brought about the collapse of the Mobutu regime in what was then known as Zaïre. A lifelong revolutionary and former supporter of Patrice Lumumba, the country's left-wing leader at the time of independence, Kabila emerged from obscurity after decades as a minor guerrilla leader based in eastern border areas. As president he has sought to reassure prospective foreign-aid donors and investors, alarmed that he might retain his Marxist orientation, and has tried to avert accusations of authoritarianism, promising elections within two years. Under the current transitional regime the executive president combines the functions of head of state and head of government.

Kabila was born in Shaba province, in the southern part of what was then the Belgian Congo, on 1 January 1939. A member of the Luba tribe, brought up as a Christian and reputedly a teetotaller, he studied political philosophy in France, became a Marxist and returned to his native country just as it was becoming independent in 1960. He has also attended military school in China and studied at the University of Dar es Salaam, Tanzania.

Elected as a member of the Katanga regional assembly in the southeast, Kabila was identified as a supporter of Lumumba, who became the country's first prime minister. When Lumumba was killed in a coup, Kabila and other supporters of Lumumba fled into the jungles of eastern Zaïre and, supported by the Soviet Union and China, launched successive rebellions against the government subsequently formed by the US-backed coup leader Gen. Sese Seko Mobutu.

In 1964, at the time of the Stanleyville rebellion, forces led by Kabila in the Ruzizi area near Uvira were crushed by Mobutu's troops with the aid of mercenaries and Belgian paratroopers. Forced out of the country, the group continued to launch guerrilla raids from Tanzania. Kabila, who was reportedly associated in the mid-1960s with the Latin American revolutionary Che Guevara, set up his own People's Revolutionary Party (PRP) in 1967. Based near Lake Tanganyika, and obtaining Chinese support as well as attracting recruits from among exiled Rwandans of the minority Tutsi ethnic group, the PRP set up its own leftist mini-state in Uvira district. Financed by gold mining and a trade in diamonds and ivory, the party ran collective farms, health clinics and schools. In 1975 Kabila's forces kidnapped three US students and a Dutch researcher, demanding ransom money and weapons, but later released them after receiving an undisclosed payment.

In 1977 Mobutu's troops once again forced Kabila out across the border into northern Tanzania. The interrelationships between left-wing rebel movements in the region brought him into contact with the forces of future Ugandan leader Yoweri Museveni and with the Rwandan Tutsi leader Paul Kagane, but when his guerrilla group disappeared from view in 1988 it was generally thought that Kabila was dead.

Kabila re-emerged as a rebel leader in October 1996, however, backing a Tutsi struggle against efforts by the Mobutu government to remove them from their land. Leading an Alliance of Democratic Forces for the Liberation of Congo (AFDL) which he had apparently put together four years beforehand, he mounted an insurgency which gathered momentum as Mobutu's forces crumbled before it, and by May 1997 had reached the capital, Kinshasa. South African mediation helped avert large-scale violence at this point, although Kabila showed himself uncompromising in insisting on the departure of Mobutu. Kabila was sworn in as president on 29 May 1997.

Kabila's AFDL, the dominant element in his subsequent coalition government, itself consists of four groups originally brought together with the purpose of overthrowing the Mobutu dictatorship. These are Kabila's own PRP, the National Council of Resistance for Democracy, the Tutsi-dominated People's Democratic Alliance, and the Revolutionary Movement for the Liberation of Congo-Zaïre.

A major focus of international concern about Kabila's attitude to human rights has been his resistance to a United Nations investigation of the allegation that his forces were implicated in a massacre of many thousands of Rwandan Hutu refugees in 1996 in eastern areas under their control. Kabila has also been criticised for appointing too many of his Tutsi allies to positions of power, and for insensitively echoing Mobutu's despised nepotism by appointing his own cousin as foreign minister and putting his son in charge of his northern military campaign.

José María **Figueres**

José María Figueres took office in May 1994 for a four-year term as president of Costa Rica. He was the candidate of the National Liberation Party (PLN), founded after the 1948 revolution by his father, former Costa Rican president, José "Pepe" Figueres Ferrer. His election vow was to modernise the welfare state, also created by his father.

José María Figueres Olsen was born on 24 December 1954 in San José. He went to the USA for his further education, gaining a degree in engineering from the West Point Military Academy in 1979. He returned to the USA just over ten years later when he studied at the Kennedy School of Law and Government, Harvard University, receiving a master's degree in public affairs in 1991.

Figueres made his career in business after graduating, initially as general manager of Central American Fibres, and from 1984 as president of the Agroindustrial Society of San Cristobal. In 1987/88 he was also vice-president of the board of directors of the Costa Rican Railway Institute.

Between 1988 and 1990 he was a member of President Arias's PLN government as minister of foreign trade and minister of agriculture and livestock. The party's defeat in the 1990 elections, on a platform determined by its more conservative wing, and the death of his father in June of that year, left something of a leadership vacuum within the PLN. Figueres, identified at this stage with the more social democratic strand in the party, emerged as its candidate for the 1994 elections as part of a process of rejuvenation. In the polling on 6 February 1994 he obtained a narrow majority over the Social Christian Unity Party's candidate.

Beginning his term of office in May 1994, Figueres came under pressure from international creditors and financial organisations to reduce the budget deficit. He accordingly introduced severe economic austerity measures, which contrasted sharply with his campaign platform of more state intervention and support for the welfare state. Confronted by a wave of strikes and protest demonstrations, and with his "approval rating" down to an unprecedentedly low 10 per cent in opinion polls in 1996, he responded by "relaunching" his presidency with a renewed programme of infrastructural investment and promises of improved welfare provision.

Figueres is married to Josette Altmann; they have two children.

Henri **Konan Bédié**

*Henri Konan Bédié has been president of Côte d'Ivoire since December 1993. He is only the second holder of this post, having taken office on the death of "father of the nation" Félix Houphouët-Boigny. A French-educated former diplomat, he is also leader of the free enterprise-oriented Democratic Party of Côte d'Ivoire (*Parti Démocratique de la Côte d'Ivoire – *PDCI). His current five-year term commenced in 1995, following an election in October of that year which was boycotted by most of the opposition parties. The president is not only head of state but also wields considerable executive power and appoints the prime minister and other members of the cabinet, although it is the prime minister rather than the president who is formally designated head of government.*

A southerner and member of the Baoulé ethnic group, from a rich plantation-owning family, Henri Konan Bédié was born on 5 May 1934 in Dadiekro, in the Daoukro department. He went to primary school in Daoukro and secondary school in Guiglo and Dabou. According to the established pattern for young members of the educated élite under French colonial administration, he went to university in France after passing his baccalaureate, in his case studying law and economics in Poitiers. He obtained a degree in law, a diploma in further studies in political economy and economic science, and ultimately a doctorate in economic science. In 1959 he joined the French diplomatic service, working as an adviser in the French embassy to the USA from 1959 and as a member of the French permanent mission to the United Nations.

After the independence of Côte d'Ivoire in August 1960, he established the new country's first embassy in Washington, where he was ambassador from 1961 to 1966 (also accredited as ambassador to Canada from 1963 to 1966). Returning to Côte d'Ivoire in 1966 he was made minister of economic and financial affairs, a post he held until 1977. During this time he held the presidency of the IMF-World Bank development committee (1974–76), and in 1978 he became a special adviser at the International Financial Corporation (IFC) in Washington D.C.

In 1980, having been elected to the National Assembly as a member of the PDCI (the sole party until 1990), he was chosen as the Assembly's president (speaker) and retained this post following the elections of 1985 and 1990. Although the "old guard" in the PDCI successfully resisted the suggestion that the elderly President Houphouët-Boigny should stand aside in 1990 to let Konan Bédié win the presidency, a constitutional amendment confirmed him as next in line of succession in his capacity as parliamentary speaker. When Houphouët-Boigny eventually died on 7 December 1993 he accordingly assumed presidential powers, warding off any attempt to transfer authority instead to Prime

Minister Alassane Ouattara, his main rival and leading Muslim within the ruling party.

Konan Bédié was elected unanimously as chair of the ruling PDCI in April 1994. He used his party's dominance of the legislature to push through later that year a set of amendments to the electoral code which imposed strict nationality and residency requirements on presidential candidates, thus effectively debarring Ouattara from standing against him. This measure, coupled with the refusal to appoint an independent electoral commission, and the repression of protest demonstrations, led most opposition parties to join a boycott of the presidential election held on 22 October 1995. Konan Bédié was duly elected, being credited with over 96 per cent of the vote, and commenced his new term of office on 27 October. The following month, after a military coup attempt had been thwarted, elections took place for the National Assembly, again producing a legislature heavily dominated by the PDCI.

Henri Konan Bédié is married to Henriette Koinzan Bomo. They have four children.

Franjo **Tudjman**

Franjo Tudjman has been president of Croatia since May 1990. He was first elected, indirectly, after the victory of his right-wing nationalist Croatian Democratic Union (HDZ) in multi-party legislative elections held within the Yugoslav federal context. He thus led Croatia in its breakaway from Yugoslavia, and won overwhelming support in direct presidential elections in 1992. He was re-elected in June 1997 for another five-year term. Tudjman is a former Titoist partisan and Yugoslav army general, whose historical research and growing interest in Croat nationalism led to his expulsion from the communist party in 1967. After two decades of dissident activity and imprisonment, Tudjman founded the Croatian Democratic Union in 1989. He was the dominant Croat nationalist figure throughout the period of conflict which followed the collapse of Yugoslavia, and has been accused of increasing authoritarianism with particular respect to the press and broadcasting media. As president he wields real power, although the prime minister, appointed by the president, is designated as head of government and is responsible to the parliament.

Tudjman was born on 14 May 1922 in the village of Veliko Trgovisce, in Zagorje. His father was a leading figure in the Croatian Peasant Party. His mother died when he was seven. He attended school locally, before going to high school in Zagreb from 1934 to 1941, tutoring other students in order to support himself.

His father founded the wartime anti-fascist movement in his native region, and Franjo Tudjman joined the Titoist partisans in northwest Croatia, where his brother was killed in 1943 in the resistance against German occupying forces and against the Croat collaborationist Ustasa regime. In January 1945 he became a Croatian representative at the Belgrade headquarters of the National Liberation Army and the Movement for the Liberation of Yugoslavia.

Shortly after the war and the establishment of Tito's communist government in Yugoslavia, Tudjman's father was killed by the secret police, his wartime record apparently affording him no protection against being targeted as a critic of the new regime. Franjo Tudjman spent the next few years in Belgrade, working for the defence ministry, studying at the higher military academy between 1955 and 1957, and reaching the rank of general in the Yugoslav national army by 1960. Throughout this time he studied and published papers on history and politics, attending and speaking at conferences and growing increasingly absorbed in his academic work. Resigning his army commission in 1961, he founded the Institute of the History of the Workers' Movement in Zagreb, becoming its director until 1967. In 1963 he was appointed a professor of political science at the University of Zagreb, teaching Marxist analysis and contemporary national history. Two years later he was awarded a doctorate.

In 1967 he was expelled from the communist party because of his controversial writings, in particular his claim that the war crimes of the Croatian Ustasa regime had been exaggerated, and because of his support for the recognition of Croat as a separate national language. He was forced to resign from all his positions, and three years later his passport was confiscated. In 1972 he was imprisoned, along with other Croatian dissidents, but released after serving nine months of a two-year sentence. Arrested again in 1981 for pro-nationalist comments in interviews with foreign journalists, he was imprisoned again until 1984.

When his passport was returned in 1987, Tudjman travelled to North America and Europe, raising support among Croatian emigrés for the 1989 launch of his Croatian Democratic Union (HDZ). In Croatia's first multiparty elections, in April/May 1990, the HDZ won a large majority of parliamentary seats and on 30 May the new parliament elected Tudjman as president. On the basis of a new constitution approved in December, Croatia declared itself independent in 1991. Bitter fighting followed as the Serb-dominated federal army moved in to support Croatian Serbs in resisting this secession, but by January 1992 the new state had won international recognition, albeit with a quarter of its former territory in Serb hands. As the hero of independence, Tudjman was returned to power with nearly 60 per cent of the vote against seven other candidates in presidential elections held in August 1992.

The conflict in the neighbouring republic of Bosnia from 1992 to 1995, in which ethnic Croats were one of three warring groups, raised the temptation of a "Greater Croatia", which might include parts of Bosnia, just as a "Greater Serbia" might swallow up the Serb-held areas. Ultimately, Tudjman became a firm supporter of alliance between Bosnian Croats and Muslims, turning his back on any implicit (or even explicit) deal with the Serbian leader Slobodan Milosevic. Supporting the Bosnian Croat–Muslim federation did give Tudjman the eventual opportunity of recovering Serb-held areas of Croatia. His army achieved this in a series of offensives when Serb forces were overstretched across Bosnia in August and September 1995. Many thousands of Serb refugees were sent streaming eastwards, such "ethnic cleansing" having already become appallingly familiar in the region's four years of conflict. Tudjman was a signatory of the Dayton peace agreement at the end of 1995, and also signed an accord with the rump Yugoslavia the following August, after talks with Milosevic, to resolve the outstanding issue of the last Serb-held enclave in eastern Slavonia.

The military successes of 1995 helped Tudjman's HDZ win a majority in the legislative elections that October, although rivals made some headway by focusing on complaints of authoritarianism, and the party was denied the two-thirds majority needed for constitutional amendments. As the HDZ candidate in the presidential elections held on 15 June 1997, Tudjman was returned to office with 61.4 per cent of the vote, and sworn in for a further five-year term, despite being in poor health, reportedly with cancer of the stomach.

Franjo Tudjman is married to Ankica Zumbar and they have two sons and one daughter.

Fidel **Castro**

Fidel Castro Ruz has been in power in Cuba since 1959, longer than any other current non-hereditary ruler. He came to power as leader of the Cuban revolution against the dictatorial Batista regime, with the title of prime minister until 1976, and since then formally as head of state as well as president of the council of ministers. He was most recently re-elected (unopposed) by the parliament in March 1993 for a further five-year term. Targeted as an object of particular hatred by successive US administrations, Castro still presents himself in spite of his age as the fatigues-clad bearded revolutionary, although the collapse of communism elsewhere has left his regime isolated.

Fidel Castro Ruz was born on 13 August 1926 in Birán in the Oriente region of southeast Cuba. His father, who had arrived as an immigrant farm labourer from Galicia in Spain, owned a 23,000-acre plantation. Fidel had a strict upbringing in a large Catholic family, although he was later to be excommunicated. He attended Jesuit schools in Santiago and Havana, and graduated in law from the University of Havana in 1949. He practised as a lawyer in Havana, and planned to stand for parliament, until Gen. Batista seized power in 1952.

After first attempting unsuccessfully to use the law to oppose Batista, by bringing a suit against the dictator for contravening the constitution, Castro became involved in underground resistance. On 26 July 1952 he led an assault on the Moncada barracks in Oriente. Half of his force were killed and both Fidel Castro and his brother Raúl were captured and sentenced to 15 years in prison, but released under a general amnesty in May 1955. Defending himself at the trial, Castro closed his defence with the much-quoted words "History will absolve me".

Fleeing to Mexico after his release, and then on to the USA, Castro returned to Cuba aboard the *Granma* on 2 December 1956 as leader of an 82-man group of Cuban exiles calling themselves the 26 July Revolutionary Movement. Batista's troops killed 70 of them soon after they landed, leaving the Castro brothers, Che Guevara and just nine others to form the nucleus of a guerrilla movement in the mountainous Sierra Maestra region. Gathering strength over the next two years, the guerrilla army marched on Havana and put Batista to flight on 1 January 1959. The USA recognised Castro's government on 7 January and on 16 February Castro declared himself prime minister.

It was the expropriation of US-owned firms which underlay the rapid deterioration in relations with the USA. Castro responded to Soviet overtures by concluding deals on trade, oil, food and credit, while the USA retaliated on the expropriation issue by imposing an economic embargo. Fearing a Marxist and pro-Soviet state "in its back yard", the new Kennedy administration in the USA gave the go-ahead for a disastrous attempted invasion of Cuba by CIA-backed Cuban exiles, who were wiped out at the Bay of Pigs in April 1961. In 1962 Castro agreed to a Soviet nuclear weapons base being established on the island. Global nuclear war seemed imminent as the USA imposed a naval blockade to stop the missiles reaching their new base. Superpower negotiation between Presidents Kennedy and Khrushchev ended the crisis, with the Soviet ships turning back with their cargo of missiles, but from then on Castro's government was viewed with even more hostility by the USA and several attempts were made to assassinate Castro.

Castro had declared Cuba a communist single-party state in December 1961, the year in which he was awarded the Lenin Peace Prize. His regime pressed ahead with the nationalisation of industry, setting up farm collectives and appropriating property from the wealthy or from foreigners. Thousands of opponents of his regime were imprisoned or executed and many of the middle and upper classes left Cuba, forming a substantial community of exiles in Miami.

In 1963 Castro became first secretary of the United Party of the Cuban Socialist Revolution (PURSC) which became the Cuban Communist Party in 1965. He did not formally join the party's politburo, however, until 1976. In that year, when Cuba approved its first constitution, Castro officially became head of state and government as president of the council of state and the council of ministers. Since then he has been re-elected to the presidency a number of times and retains the leadership of the party as its first secretary. In 1992 he also became chair of the national defence council.

From the 1960s until the 1990s Castro governed Cuba on strict Marxist lines. Within Cuba he pointed with particular pride to achievements in the national education and health services. Keen to export the Cuban example, he was active in the non-aligned movement and supported revolutions in Latin America, Ethiopia and Angola, with substantial commitments of military hardware, training and troops.

In the 1990s Castro has insisted on maintaining Cuba's Marxist identity, and has come under increasing criticism for the suppression of dissent as well as for his cautious approach on economic reform. The loss of the previously substantial Soviet aid and preferential trade deals has contributed to the problems of the economy, as has above all the maintenance and even tightening of the US trade embargo. There have been some concessions to free enterprise since 1993, such as the introduction of farmers' markets, but in December 1995, during a visit to China, Castro reinforced his own reputation for last-ditch resistance by praising his hosts for holding out against capitalism. In March 1996 a rare meeting of the communist party's central committee was called, at which Castro announced stronger measures to restrict private business ventures, emphasising again his hardline stance.

Fidel Castro Ruz married Mirta Diaz-Bilart. They were divorced in 1955 while he was in prison. The couple had one son.

Glafcos **Clerides**

Glafcos Clerides has been president of Cyprus since 1993. The president is both head of state and head of government, and is elected for a five-year term, with the next elections due in February 1998. The leader of the conservative Democratic Rally (DESY), which he founded in 1976, Clerides is a British-trained barrister and parliamentarian, and a veteran of Greek Cypriot politics since pre-independence days.

Clerides was born in Nicosia on 24 April 1919, the eldest son of a lawyer, and received his early education in Cyprus and in Britain before the outbreak of the Second World War in 1939. He joined the Royal Air Force, was shot down over Germany in 1942 and spent the rest of the war in a prison camp. He then resumed his studies in law at King's College, London, gaining a degree in law in 1948. He was called to the Bar in 1951, after which he returned to Cyprus to practise law (1951–60). During this time he defended numerous fighters of EOKA (National Organisation of Cypriot Combatants) who had been arrested by the British authorities, and also prepared a dossier on British human rights violations in Cyprus, which was submitted to the Human Rights Commission of the Council of Europe.

When agreement on the basis for independence was eventually reached in 1959, Clerides joined the transitional government as minister of justice. He also led the Greek Cypriot delegation in the joint constitutional committee, which drafted the island's new constitution. Following independence in August 1960, Clerides was elected to the House of Representatives and became president (speaker) of the House the same year, holding this post until 1976.

In 1964 he led the Greek Cypriot delegation to the London conference on the Cyprus problem, and from 1968 to 1972 he was the chief Greek negotiator in intercommunal talks between the two halves of the island. As president of the House of Representatives Clerides often acted as deputy to President Makarios, most notably in July 1974 when a coup forced Makarios to flee and Turkish troops invaded the northern part of the island. Clerides acted as head of state until Makarios returned at the end of the year.

Clerides founded the Unified Party in February 1969. He went on to create the more conservative DESY in 1976, drawing members from the Unified Party, the Progressive Front, and the Democratic National Party. Although DESY didn't win any seats in 1976, it has since grown to be the largest party in parliament. Clerides sat in the House of Representatives between 1981 and 1991 as a member for Nicosia, and led the DESY party campaign in general elections in 1981, 1985 and 1991, but failed in his 1983 and 1988 bids for the presidency. However, in the 1993 presidential election, he eventually succeeded in beating his rival, the millionaire businessman and incumbent president Georgios Vassiliou, by a small margin of 2,176 votes in a second round of voting on 14 February. Clerides thus became the first head of state of Cyprus to be elected since independence without the backing of the communist Progressive Party of the Working People (AKEL). He was sworn in for a five-year term on 28 February.

During Clerides's presidency there have been intermittent outbursts of intercommunal violence. United Nations mediation has resulted in direct talks between Clerides and Rauf Denktash, president of the self-proclaimed Turkish Republic of Northern Cyprus, in October 1994 and in July/August 1997. However, there has thus far been no resolution of the long-standing division of the island.

Clerides was the president of the Cyprus Red Cross from 1961 to 1963. He has also been recognised for his services towards the Roman Catholic minority living in Cyprus. He is married, and his daughter, Katherine Clerides, is a member of the House of Representatives.

Rauf **Denktash**

Rauf Denktash is the veteran Turkish Cypriot leader who in November 1983 became the first president of the self-proclaimed Turkish Republic of Northern Cyprus (TRNC). Re-elected for successive five-year terms in 1985, 1990 and 1995, his claim to the status of head of state is recognised only by Turkey, whose military intervention in 1974 partitioned the island de facto *between Greek Cypriot and Turkish Cypriot communities. Denktash is a British-trained barrister whose role in representing the Turkish Cypriots dates back to before the ending of British rule in 1960.*

Rauf Denktash was born in Baf, Paphos, on 27 January 1924 and was educated at the English school in Nicosia and then as a barrister at Lincoln's Inn, London. A teacher from 1942 to 1943, he practised law in Nicosia from 1947 to 1949, becoming a junior crown counsel to the attorney-general's office in 1949, crown counsel in 1952 and then acting solicitor-general from 1956 to 1958.

In 1948 he became a member of the Consultative Assembly seeking Cypriot independence from the UK and a member of the Turkish Cypriot affairs committee. As chairman of the Federation of Turkish Cypriot Associations he attended the UN General Assembly in 1958 and led the Turkish Cypriot delegation at the 1959 London conference, at which it was agreed that Cyprus should be a bi-communal partnership state; the rights of the Turkish Cypriot minority, and the independence of the country as a whole, were to be guaranteed by Greece, Turkey and the UK. Denktash headed the Turkish Cypriot delegation on the constitutional committee drafting the constitution under which Cyprus became independent on 16 August 1960.

As president of the Turkish Communal Chamber from 1960, Denktash led the opposition to Greek Cypriot proposals to modify the constitution, an issue which led to intercommunal conflict (and the interposition of a UN peacekeeping force) in 1964. Exiled from the island for four years, Denktash became interlocutor at intercommunal talks which followed a fresh upsurge of violence in 1967, and was re-elected as president of the Turkish Communal Chamber in 1970. The nominal position of vice-president of Cyprus, to which he was elected unopposed in February 1973, was increasingly irrelevant to the real situation, however, with talks getting nowhere and the Turkish Cypriots focusing instead on organising their own government within the area in which they were the majority population.

A short-lived extreme right-wing coup backed by the Greek military junta on 15 July 1974, and the Turkish response of sending troops to occupy northern Cyprus, crystallised the partition of the island. A Turkish Federated State of Cyprus was proclaimed in the Turkish-occupied north in February 1975. Denktash was designated as its first president, and won an overwhelming victory when presidential elections were held in June 1976, with his National Unity Party (UBP) dominating that year's elections to a Turkish Cypriot assembly. He retained this post until 15 November 1983, when the federated state was replaced by a Turkish Republic of Northern Cyprus (TRNC), whose "declaration of full independence" was recognised only by Turkey.

Although indisputably the leading figure in Turkish Cypriot politics, Denktash has seen his share of the vote fall from over 70 per cent to only just over 60 per cent in successive TRNC presidential elections in 1985, 1990 and 1995. On this last occasion he failed to win outright on the first round, reflecting concern over the deteriorating economic situation in the internationally isolated north, the perceived dangers of being left out of possible Cypriot membership of the European Union, and the absence of any breakthrough in the protracted talks on a negotiated Cyprus settlement. Denktash favours continuing with these talks under UN auspices, although his own involvement has not contributed any real new ideas. The UBP split in 1992 when he rejected the idea of abandoning the talks and formalising the partition, and his supporters set up a breakaway Democratic Party which he subsequently joined; like the UBP it is essentially a centre-right formation, committed to a secularist approach and ostensibly inspired by the example of Ataturk as founder of modern Turkey.

Rauf Denktash is married to Aydin Munir. They have had two daughters and two sons. One of the sons has died; the other, Serdar Denktash, has led the Democratic Party since May 1996 and became deputy prime minister of the TRNC in August of that year.

Vaclav **Havel**

Vaclav Havel was elected on 26 January 1993 for a five-year term as the first president of the Czech Republic following its "velvet divorce" from Slovakia. Havel had been president of Czechoslovakia from the end of 1989 until mid-1992, having helped found and lead the Civic Forum movement in the "velvet revolution" which precipitated the collapse of the communist regime. His moral authority derived from his high profile in the Charter 77 movement as a dissident and campaigner for civil rights, aided by his international stature as a playwright. The Czech president's official functions are mainly ceremonial. Havel, however, is sometimes described as his country's "philosopher king", with an unassuming and informal manner which belies the strength of his influence. His role has been particularly significant in building relations with western Europe, in matters affecting civil rights and in his campaign for what he describes as the deepening of democracy. Moreover, his power to appoint the prime minister took on direct political importance in late 1997, when he insisted on his right to appoint a non-party caretaker head of government, in a crisis provoked by the fall of Vaclav Klaus as prime minister.

Havel was born on 5 October 1936 in Prague. His bourgeois family background (his father was a prominent businessman) meant that the post-war communist regime initially denied him a university place and he worked instead as a chemical laboratory technician, while studying at evening classes and eventually graduating in 1954. From 1954 to 1957 he attended the economics faculty of the Czech Technical University in Prague. He did his military service from 1957 to 1959 and began producing his first literary works.

In 1960 he started working as a stage hand at the Theatre on the Balustrade in Prague, rising to be literary manager and assistant director by 1968 and beginning to make a name as a writer and dramatist. His plays were first performed while he was studying dramatic art theory at the Prague Academy of Performing Arts from 1962 to 1966; he won international acclaim with *The Garden Party* (1963) and later gathered awards for work such as *The Increased Difficulty of Concentration* (1968), *Audience* (1975) and *The Mountain Hotel* (1976).

Havel, like many fellow intellectuals, became caught up in enthusiasm for the promise of a new liberal communism in the so-called "Prague spring" of 1968. He chaired the Circle of Independent Writers, and was a fierce opponent of the invasion by Warsaw Pact forces that August. The subsequent period of repression, the so-called "normalisation", saw his work banned in Czechoslovakia, and he was forced to move to the country, working as a labourer in a brewery.

In addition to his literary work, he began concentrating on more formal expressions of political opposition, organising a petition in 1972 pressing for the release of political prisoners and writing a critical open letter to the president in 1975. On 1 January 1977 Havel was a founding signatory of what became the rallying call of the human rights movement, Charter 77, and spokesperson for the small group of dissident intellectuals behind this original initiative. The following year he helped set up the Committee for the Defence of the Unjustly Prosecuted (VONS), and wrote his influential essay, *The Power of the Powerless.*

Havel's sustained dissident activity led to his frequent arrest between 1977 and 1989. He was held under house arrest in 1978/79, and spent a long period in prison from 1979 to 1983 on a charge of sedition. In January 1989 he was again arrested, with a group of human rights demonstrators, and sentenced to nine months' imprisonment for incitement and obstruction, but international protests embarrassed the regime into releasing him in May.

Despite his ambivalence about direct political involvement, Havel was informally identified as the leader of the Civic Forum which he helped set up in November 1989. Civic Forum and Havel himself were at the forefront of the protest movement and massive popular demonstrations which led to the astonishingly rapid collapse of the communist regime. On 29 December he was elected by the parliament as interim president, pending the holding of general elections the following June; the new Federal Assembly, meeting on 5 July 1990, then confirmed him in office for two years.

The 1990 elections underlined problems which Havel was experiencing in establishing a neutral non-party presidential role, given his close connections with Civic Forum (which nominated him for the presidency), his attendance at their rallies and his controversial comment during the campaign that he would be voting for Civic Forum candidates. During his subsequent presidential term, Havel's relations with Slovak nationalist leader Vladimir Meciar were often difficult, while it was common knowledge that he differed with the finance minister and later Czech prime minister Vaclav Klaus over the speed and uncompromising radicalism of the switchover to a free-market economy.

Havel stood down as president at the end of his two-year term in July 1992, when his federalist constitutional proposals had been rejected and it was becoming increasingly unlikely that any form of Czech and Slovak federation would survive the pull of Slovak separatism. When the separation of the two states had been formalised, the parliament of the Czech Republic elected him unopposed to the presidency on 26 January 1993.

In May of that year several foreign nationals were arrested after a suspected assassination attempt against him. A serious bout of pneumonia in October/November 1997 renewed the concerns about his health (a heavy smoker, he had already had surgery for lung cancer in December 1996), but Havel was nevertheless expected to seek, and win, a further term of office in January 1998.

Havel married Olga Splichalova in 1964, and later wrote her a famous series of letters from prison. Olga died in 1996, and Havel is now married to the acclaimed Czech actress Dagmar Veskrnova.

Queen **Margrethe II**

Queen Margrethe II succeeded to the Danish throne in January 1972 upon the death of her father Frederik IX. An amendment to the Danish constitution, adopted in 1953 through a referendum, permitted female descendants of the reigning monarch to ascend the throne as long as there were no male heirs. As is the rule with Scandinavian monarchs, Queen Margrethe has no personal political power. Her titular roles include that of supreme commander of the Danish defence forces.

Margrethe II was born on 16 April 1940 at Amalienberg. Given the names Margrethe Alexandrine Thorhildur Ingrid, she is the eldest daughter of King Frederik IX (1899–1972) and Queen Ingrid (born 1910). Having completed her secondary education in Denmark at Zahles Skole, she took the philosophy examination at Copenhagen University in 1960, studied prehistoric archaeology at Cambridge University in 1960/61, and later specialised in political science at Aarhus (1961/62), the Sorbonne (1963) and the London School of Economics (1965). In her youth she took part in several archaeological excavations in Greece, Sudan and Rome.

In April 1958 Margrethe II first began attending the weekly meetings of the Council of State between the monarch and the cabinet. Since ascending the throne on 15 January 1972, she has taken an active interest in matters of state, meeting her ministers weekly and representing Denmark abroad.

Margrethe II illustrated Tolkien's *The Lord of the Rings* in 1977 and as an artist she has also worked with handicrafts and textiles and designed seals and calendars, and costumes for television and theatre productions. In 1981, with her French husband, she translated Simone de Beauvoir's *All Men Are Mortal.* She was awarded the Danish Language Society Prize in 1989 and is an honorary member of the Swedish Royal Academy of Science, History and Antiquities.

Margrethe II married on 10 June 1967 the French diplomat Henri-Marie-Jean-André Count de Laborde de Monpezat, who took the courtesy title Prince Henrik of Denmark. They have two sons, Crown Prince Frederick and Prince Joachim.

Hassan **Gouled Aptidon**

Al-Haji Hassan Gouled Aptidon has been president of the Republic of Djibouti since independence in 1977, and was most recently re-elected for a further six-year term in May 1993. He is the country's dominant political figure and, as president, appoints the council of ministers (cabinet), although cabinet meetings are chaired by the prime minister who is formally head of government. A member of the Issa clan, Gouled Aptidon faced armed revolt from an Afar-dominated opposition front in the early 1990s, but gained increased legitimacy from the introduction of a degree of multipartyism, and rival groups now focus more on the succession to the ailing president than on seeking to overthrow him.

Hassan Gouled Aptidon was born in October 1916 at Garissa near Zeila, in what was then known as French Somaliland. The territory was given French Overseas Territory status in 1946 and he represented it in the French National Assembly from 1952 to 1958 and from 1959 to 1962 (with a break in 1958/59 during which he was vice-president of the Territorial Assembly). A member of the territory's internal government from 1963 to 1967 as minister for education, he then broke away to help set up the pro-independence LPAI *(Ligue Populaire Africaine pour l'Indépendance)*, becoming its president in 1975.

In 1977 the LPAI won elections to a constitutional assembly. Gouled Aptidon was elected president by acclamation on 24 June 1977 and declared the country's independence three days later. In 1979 he became chair of the Popular Rally for Progress (*Rassemblement Populaire pour le Progrès* – RPP), which replaced the LPAI as the sole legal party throughout the 1980s. He was re-elected in 1981 by the Chamber of Deputies and, after the institution of direct presidential elections by universal suffrage, for a third term in 1987.

Under growing pressure from the Afar-dominated Front for the Restoration of Unity and Democracy (*Front pour la Restauration de l'Unité et de la Démocratie* – FRUD), which had launched a guerrilla war in the early 1990s, he introduced constitutional changes permitting a limited multiparty system. These were approved in a referendum in September 1992. In the ensuing presidential election in May 1993 Gouled Aptidon was re-elected president for a six-year term with 61 per cent of votes cast in a 49.9 per cent turnout. The poll was boycotted by FRUD, while the four unsuccessful opposition candidates claimed fraud and election rigging.

In December 1994 Gouled Aptidon signed a peace and reconciliation agreement with one of the FRUD factions. Subsequent manoeuvres over the succession resulted in the registration of FRUD as a legal political party in March 1996, and in divisions within the RPP.

The ailing president spent the first three months of 1996 in hospital in France. The apparent decline in the popularity of his regime among its Issa supporters was illustrated at legislative elections in December 1997 by an unusually low turnout, although an RPP alliance with FRUD moderates won all the seats.

Crispin **Sorhaindo**

Crispin Sorhaindo succeeded Sir Clarence Seignoret in the largely ceremonial post of president of Dominica on 25 October 1993, having been elected for a five-year term by the House of Assembly on 4 October. Previously speaker of the House of Assembly, he has had a long career in financial administration and development institutions.

Crispin Anselm Sorhaindo was born in the village of Vieille Case on the northern coast of Dominica on 23 May 1931, and gained his early education at the Dominica Grammar School. In 1956/57 he completed the Oxford University overseas service course and in 1963/64 studied public finance at the Royal Institute of Public Administration. As a member of the Dominican public service from 1952 until 1973, he first served as a clerk of the executive on various legislative councils. In 1963 he served as secretary to the Civil Service Commission on the Proposed East Caribbean Federation. From 1964 to 1973 he was the principal secretary at the ministry of finance, and he also attended international conferences as a member of the Dominican government delegation.

Sorhaindo has chaired a number of development and funding institutions in Dominica, including the Agricultural and Industrial Development Bank and the investment committee of the National Provident Fund, and he sat on the Caribbean Development Bank's board of directors until 1988. He worked on the drafting of the East Caribbean Common Market Agreement, the Caribbean Development Bank Agreement, the Georgetown Accord and the CARICOM Treaty. From 1990 to 1993 he chaired the National Commercial Bank of Dominica. In 1991 Sorhaindo became a member of the executive committee of the Commonwealth Parliamentary Association, and continued to serve with a number of committees involved in the CARICOM Treaty.

In 1988 Sorhaindo became speaker of the Dominican House of Assembly, a position he retained until his election as president in 1993.

Crispin Sorhaindo is married with six children.

Leonel **Fernández**

Leonel Fernández Reyna has been the head of state and government of the Dominican Republic since August 1996, having been elected for a four-year term as the successful candidate of the Dominican Liberation Party (PLD) in June 1996. A student activist in the 1970s and supporter of ex-president and PLD founder Juan Bosch, Fernández combined journalism with a career as a political scientist, and in 1994 stood for vice-president as Bosch's unsuccessful PLD running-mate.

Born on 26 December 1953 in Santo Domingo, he was educated as a child in New York, before enrolling in the Free University of Santo Domingo (UASD). As a student in the faculty of political science and law, he was attracted to Bosch's radical ideas, taking an active part in student politics and protests against the right-wing regime of President Joaquín Balaguer. He was awarded his doctorate in 1978, his thesis subsequently becoming an influential book on media law. He held a succession of professorships at UASD over the next 15 years, in political science, law and media studies, while also attending courses elsewhere. Having completed a journalism course at Columbia University in New York in 1984, he wrote for several Santo Domingo newspapers and ran the international section of the PLD's *Vanguardia del Pueblo.*

A founder member of the PLD, Fernández joined the inner party leadership in 1990 when he was elected to its political committee. By this time Bosch and other PLD leaders were espousing rapid privatisation and the promotion of private enterprise, in marked contrast to the PLD's original stance, and in a major schism in 1992 a number of dissident left-wingers resigned from the party. In 1994 the PLD picked Fernández as vice-presidential candidate in a final bid for the presidency by the veteran Bosch, who resigned his party post after finishing a poor third in the poll in May. The eventual outcome of the controversial 1994 elections was an inter-party agreement on a further short term for the elderly Balaguer, the incumbent president and leader of the conservative Social Christian Reformist Party (PRSC). The PLD backed a subsequent deal to extend this from 18 months to two years, leading up to fresh presidential elections in 1996.

In the first round in May 1996 Fernández finished second with 38.9 per cent, behind the candidate of the Dominican Revolutionary Party (PRD) but well ahead of the PRSC. He then announced a "national patriotic front" electoral alliance with outgoing President Balaguer's PRSC supporters, enabling him to win the 30 June runoff with 51.25 per cent of the vote. Sworn in as president on 16 August, he faced the problem of governing without a majority in the Congress, where his PLD had won few seats at the 1994 election. Among the early decisions of his presidency were the retirement of senior military leaders, and significant salary rises for public officials, as part of a campaign against corruption.

José Alexandre ("Xanana") **Gusmão**

Although East Timor is not recognised as an independent state, its occupation and subsequent annexation by Indonesia following the withdrawal of the Portuguese colonial authorities in 1975 has been contested ever since, mainly by Fretilin (the Revolutionary Front for an Independent East Timor) and the broader-based National Council of Maubere Resistance (CNRM). "Xanana" Gusmão has been leader of Fretilin since the early 1980s and was a founder of the CNRM. He was captured by the Indonesian government in 1992 and is currently in prison. Gusmão has been engaged in the struggle for independence since 1974, during which time he has been both military commander and human rights campaigner.

José Alexandre Gusmão was born in Manatuto, East Timor, on the night of 20/21 June 1947. He attended a Jesuit seminary for his secondary education, and spent the subsequent years either unemployed or in low-grade jobs. In 1974 political tensions in East Timor escalated, as Portuguese sovereignty came increasingly to be questioned and internecine conflict threatened. Gusmão joined Fretilin after the Democratic Union of Timor (UDT) tried to seize power from the Portuguese in August 1975, precipitating a civil war.

In 1975 Gusmão helped organise the Fretilin, later gaining election to the Fretilin central committee. He also helped set up the Falintil, the Revolutionary Armed Forces for the National Liberation of East Timor. On 28 November 1975 Fretilin declared East Timor independent but Indonesian troops invaded on 7 December 1975, decimating Fretilin and leaving Gusmão separated in the far eastern part of East Timor. After this Gusmão was given responsibility for a handful of resistance fighters and set about rebuilding the movement there.

In 1986, Gusmão presided over the formation of the National Council of Maubere Resistance (CNRM). By 1988 he was the commander of a pan-East Timorese underground army, uniting several underground resistance movements, including Fretilin, the UDT, and the youth movement Renetil. During this period he continued to seek a peaceful resolution to the conflict, pushing for negotiations with the Indonesian government and a UN presence. He has also tried to promote international awareness of the political situation in East Timor.

Gusmão was captured in November 1992 in Dili. In 1993 an Indonesian court tried him for rebellion, possession of firearms and causing death to villagers. He was sentenced to life imprisonment, later reduced to 20 years. Gusmão has continued to appeal to the international community from his prison cell, and to demand UN involvement in East Timor. Konis Santana was reported in November 1993 as having taken over as Fretilin's *de facto* military commander.

Xanana Gusmão married in 1970.

José **Ramos Horta**

José Ramos Horta has led the campaign to promote wider international awareness of the situation in East Timor for the past two decades. Exiled since 1975, he has been the main representative at the UN of the Revolutionary Front for an Independent East Timor (Fretilin), and special representative of the more broadly based National Council of Maubere Resistance (CNRM) formed in 1986. A journalist in East Timor before the Indonesian occupation in 1975, he has published several books on the struggle for independence.

José Ramos Horta was born in Dili, East Timor, on 26 December 1949. He took a number of jobs in television, the press and radio from 1969 to 1974. By the time the Portuguese withdrew from East Timor in 1975, Ramos Horta was already a leading member of the Timorese liberation movement and he became effectively the minister for foreign affairs in the Fretilin government which declared independence on 28 November of that year. However, the Indonesian takeover of the territory the following month drove him into exile where he became Fretilin's main representative at the UN, working to expose Indonesian human rights abuses and to promote the claims of the independence movement.

Ramos Horta has addressed a wide variety of international organisations, including the UN Security Council, the UN Special Committee on Decolonisation, the UN Commission on Human Rights, the Non-aligned Movement, and the European Parliament; early in his career he became the youngest diplomat to address the UN. He lived in the USA between 1975 and 1989, where he undertook studies on international relations and world peace. Among his lecturers on international politics was Noam Chomsky at New York University. Ramos Horta has lived in Sydney and Lisbon since 1990 and works both as the executive director of the diplomacy training programme at the University of New South Wales and as an administrator for the Borja da Costa Foundation in Lisbon. More recently he has worked as an expert for the International Service for Human Rights in Geneva.

José Ramos Horta has achieved international recognition, not only for his diplomatic work, but also for academic achievement. In 1996 he was awarded the Nobel Peace Prize together with Bishop Carlos Felipe Ximénes Belo (also of East Timor). His publications include *The Unfinished Saga of East Timor* (1987) and *Tomorrow in Dili* (1994).

Ramos Horta is single and has one son.

Fabián **Alarcón**

Fabián Alarcón Rivera was elected by the National Congress (parliament) in February 1997 as interim president of Ecuador, and thus as both head of state and head of government. He replaced Abdalá Bucaram Ortíz, whom Congress had declared to be "mentally incompetent". Alarcón, a Quito-based lawyer and centrist politician who had hitherto been president (speaker) of the National Congress, was confirmed as state president in a referendum in May 1997. However, his term will not last the usual four years since Congress stipulated that it should last only until 10 August 1998.

Alarcón was born in Quito on 14 April 1947. He received his secondary education at schools in Mexico, Bogotá (Colombia) and Quito, before enrolling at the Pontificia Universidad Catolica de Quito, where he obtained a variety of qualifications in political science and in law. During this time he was president of the law faculty association of the university. At the age of 23 he founded the centrist Patriotic Popular Party (PPP), although he later switched to other parties, including most recently the small Alfarist Radical Front (FRA) which he led from 1994 to 1996.

Alarcón entered politics at municipal level in Quito, where he was successively a municipal town councillor, president of the hygiene commission and president of the commission for public works. He also chaired several legal practitioners' bodies. He further enhanced his influence by involvement in the politics of the central region of Pichincha which surrounds Quito. There, he was director of the commission for a minimum wage and in 1984 presided over the consortium of Ecuador's provincial councils. From 1984 to 1988 he was provincial prefect for Pichincha.

Alarcón was first elected to parliament in 1990 and won election again in 1994. He was director of the civil and penal permanent legislation commission from 1990 to 1994, and in 1990/91 was the Congress representative on the national defence junta. In 1991/92 and again from 1995 to 1997 he was president (speaker) of the National Congress. He headed the national development council from 1992 to 1995 and the council of national security in 1991/92 and again in 1995. Alarcón also deputised briefly for the vice-president in 1992 and 1995. He has served on numerous fiscal and judicial commissions, and was chairman of the tourism commission of the National Congress.

Alarcón's swearing-in as interim president on 12 February 1997 followed a period of popular unrest and constitutional uncertainty. Bucaram, attracting votes in a highly colourful campaign in the 1996 presidential elections, had won the post in the run-off ballot, but lacked congressional support and was viewed with great suspicion by the armed forces. His eccentric behaviour in office rallied his opponents to threaten him with impeachment, and he eventually agreed to step down on 9 February, while accusing the military of intervening to remove him from office. Rosalia Arteaga, the vice-president and former education minister, was thereupon briefly sworn in as the country's first woman president, but she resigned on 11 February, returning to the post of vice-president. Later the same day Alarcón was elected president by over two-thirds of the National Congress.

Alarcón moved quickly to reinstate public employees and teachers whom Bucaram had dismissed, to bring the customs system under the control of the armed forces, and to set up an anti-corruption commission. On 25 May 1997 a referendum confirmed Alarcón's position as president, while also requiring that a national assembly be convened by the end of the year to reform the constitution. Congress passed a resolution to postpone this, but widespread protests obliged Alarcón to agree in August that it should go ahead.

Alarcón is married to Lucia Pena Ochoa. They have two sons and a daughter.

Hosni **Mubarak**

Hosni Mubarak has been president of Egypt since 1981, having come to power following the assassination of President Anwar Sadat by Islamic militants. He was most recently re-elected in October 1993 for a further six-year term. Mubarak rose through the Egyptian air force, taking credit as its commander for successes against Israel in the 1973 war and was for six years Sadat's deputy president. Since becoming president he has been the country's dominant political figure, although lacking the flamboyance and charisma which had been characteristic of Sadat's rule. The president appoints all the members of the council of ministers, including the prime minister, although it is the prime minister who chairs ministerial meetings and is formally designated head of government.

Mohammed Hosni Mubarak was born on 4 May 1928 in Kafr al-Musailha, within the Minuffya governorate. From 1947 until 1949 he studied for a degree in military sciences at the Egyptian military academy. Specialising in aviation sciences, he then attended the air force academy and went on to join the Egyptian air force in 1950. Between 1952 and 1959 he lectured at the air force academy, while he also briefly attended the FROUNZ military academy in the Soviet Union.

In the 1950s and 1960s Mubarak was a successful air force pilot, seeing action in the Yemen civil war as a bomber squadron commander and in the 1967 Arab–Israeli war. Later in 1967 he took up a two-year post as director of the aeronautical academy. He was appointed successively air force chief of staff in 1969 and then commander in 1972 (a post he held until 1975). Acclaimed as a war hero after leading a successful air offensive against Israel in the 1973 war, he was promoted in that year to the rank of lieutenant-general.

Mubarak's subsequent rise to the presidency was rapid. He had first entered politics in 1972 as deputy minister for military affairs. When Sadat made him vice-president in 1975, he was also given special responsibilities for state security. In 1978 he took charge of the organisation of the newly formed National Democratic Party (NDP), acting as vice-president of the party until 1981 and thereafter as its chairman.

A smooth transfer of power to Mubarak took place following Sadat's assassination on 6 October 1981. He was nominated as the NDP's presidential candidate that same day and endorsed by a nationwide referendum a week later with an approval rating recorded as 98.46 per cent.

When he took office Mubarak was seen as a political moderate, who promised a degree of continuity with Sadat's policies. In the event, his presidency has been notable particularly for the gradual rebuilding of relations with the Arab states which had ostracised Sadat over his Camp David accords with Israel. He has maintained a degree of independence in Egypt's foreign policy, despite heavy reliance on US aid. His credit with the US government was boosted by his leading role among Arab states in opposing the Iraqi invasion of Kuwait in 1990 and by his decision to commit Egyptian troops to join the US-led forces in the 1991 Gulf war.

Mubarak has twice been re-elected for further presidential terms, in 1987 and in 1993, despite having earlier proclaimed that no president should serve more than two terms. In each case he has been nominated as the sole candidate by the National Assembly and endorsed overwhelmingly by national referendum.

He described the central themes of his third term as economic reform and the promotion of a free-market system, combating unemployment and fighting terrorism. He has proved uncompromising in his attitude towards Muslim militant groups in Egypt, and there have been several attempts on his life, most notably on 26 June 1995 when he narrowly escaped assassination during a visit to Addis Ababa, Ethiopia. His clampdown on fundamentalist activity, while incurring criticism from human rights groups over reprisal killings, political trials and the use of torture, has not succeeded in doing more than keeping a lid on a situation that remains tense and potentially explosive.

Mubarak is married with two sons.

Armando **Calderón**

Armando Calderón, leader of the extreme right-wing Nationalist Republican Alliance (ARENA), took office as president of El Salvador in June 1994 for a five-year term, combining the roles of head of state and head of government. The 1994 presidential elections were the first to be held in El Salvador since the ending of 12 years of civil war.

Born on 24 June 1948 in San Salvador, Armando Calderón Sol studied law and social sciences at El Salvador University, gaining a doctorate in 1977 and then practising as a lawyer. He began his political career as private secretary to Roberto D'Aubuisson, who founded ARENA in 1981, and had risen to be the party's director of legal and electoral affairs by 1983. In 1985 he became a member of the Legislative Assembly, heading ARENA's parliamentary group and becoming vice-president of ideology on its executive council. He has chaired ARENA since 1990.

In 1988 he was appointed president of the Corporation of Municipalities, and also first president of the Municipal Development Institute. In the same year he was elected mayor of San Salvador, where he was re-elected in 1991.

In the March 1994 legislative elections ARENA won the largest number of seats but Calderón narrowly failed to win an overall majority in the first round of the presidential elections. On 24 April, however, he secured the presidency by winning 68 per cent of the vote in the run-off.

Although sometimes described as a "moderate", Calderón has been linked to death squads in El Salvador during his time as D'Aubuisson's private secretary. His term as president has been dominated by issues relating to the transition from civil war to peace, and by problems of widespread crime and poverty. He owed his strong political position during the mid-1990s to serious splits in the opposition parties – the Farabundo Martí National Liberation Front (FMLN) and the Christian Democrats. His support in the legislature was reduced after the March 1997 legislative elections in which ARENA finished only narrowly ahead of the FMLN.

Armando Calderón Sol is married with three children.

Teodoro **Obiang Nguema**

Brig.-Gen. Obiang has been president of Equatorial Guinea since 1979, when he led a coup against his uncle, Francisco Macías Nguema. He is the founder and leader of the Democratic Party of Equatorial Guinea (PDGE), and the dominant political figure in the country, although formally the prime minister is designated as head of government. He has twice held presidential elections, in 1989 and again in 1996, and on both occasions he was the sole candidate. His current term of office runs until 2003.

Teodoro Obiang Nguema Mbasogo was born on 5 June 1941 in Acoakam, and is a member of the Esangui ethnic group. He went to school in Bata and then received military training at the Saragossa Military Academy in Spain from 1963 to 1965. In 1968 under his uncle's regime he was appointed deputy minister of defence and then military governor of the island of Fernando Po. In the early 1970s he worked in government service, in the planning department and in the ministry of education. From 1975 he was defence minister and aide-de-camp to the president. The 11-year dictatorship of Macías was known for its brutality and Obiang's own brother was among victims who were executed, in his case for complaining about unpaid wages.

On 5 August 1979 Obiang led a coup against Macías, ordered his execution and declared himself president. Despite the release of many political prisoners Obiang continued to rule despotically as his uncle had done. Since 1980 Obiang has also held the position of minister of defence and supreme commander of the armed forces. He survived a number of coup attempts and in 1982 a new constitution was adopted by the government which provided for a handover to civilian rule after a seven-year period during which Obiang was to rule as president.

In 1987 Obiang founded the PDGE as the sole legal political party and, having meanwhile arrested his opponents, was the only candidate for the presidential elections held in June 1989. External pressure, including the withholding of foreign aid and funds from the International Monetary Fund (IMF), eventually induced him to allow a nominal change to multipartyism, with six parties legalised in 1992. Most of the opposition leaders remained in exile, however; those who were allowed back returned only at real personal risk, and there was frequent violent disruption of opposition meetings. In 1993 the USA withdrew its diplomatic representation, citing the government's abuse of human rights. In November of that year the PDGE won 68 of 80 seats in legislative elections which were boycotted by the opposition following more arrests. The results were disputed by the US and Spanish governments and the latter withdrew aid to the country.

Presidential elections were held again in February 1996, three months before the end of Obiang's term. Opposition parties were given only six weeks' notice of the poll. Among the instances of election malpractice was the fact that the electoral list supplied by the United Nations was replaced by a government one, omitting many voters from the register in the areas where opposition groups commanded most support. The poll was boycotted by opposition parties, while the official results, which gave Obiang nearly 98 per cent of the vote, showed many more votes cast than there were registered voters. In June 1997 a coup attempt was foiled and a spate of arrests followed.

Issaias **Afewerki**

Issaias Afewerki is the first president of the state of Eritrea, having been elected for a five-year term by the National Assembly in May 1993 following a referendum which overwhelmingly endorsed secession from Ethiopia. He had come to prominence as a military leader in the three decades of struggle against Ethiopian occupation, helping to found the Eritrean People's Liberation Front (EPLF) under whose leadership the country was liberated when the Mengistu regime in Ethiopia was overthrown in 1991.

Born on 2 February 1946 in Asmara, Afewerki completed one year as an engineering student at the University of Addis Ababa before going underground in 1966 and joining the Eritrean Liberation Front (ELF), which had begun an armed liberation struggle in 1962. Part of his military training was undertaken in China. From 1967 to 1970 he was regional and then general commander of the ELF, which merged with other groups in 1970 to form the Eritrean People's Liberation Front (EPLF). As a founder EPLF member he held various leading positions, becoming deputy secretary-general in 1977 and secretary-general in 1987. Part of his contribution to the liberation struggle was his success in obtaining support for the movement in the Islamic world.

The EPLF's military victories played a major role in the downfall of the Mengistu regime in Ethiopia in May 1991. Afewerki immediately set up a provisional government, and at a conference in London in August he secured recognition of his administration as the legitimate provisional government of Eritrea, while agreeing to hold a referendum on independence within two years. When this took place, in April 1993, there was a 99.8 per cent vote recorded in favour of secession. As a result of the close links maintained between Afewerki and Meles Zenawi, the Ethiopian prime minister, Ethiopia accepted Eritrea's secession on 3 May. A provisional assembly, composed of the EPLF's central committee and an equal number of elected members, confirmed Afewerki as president on 22 May, two days before independence was formally declared.

In February 1994 the EPLF changed its name to the People's Front for Democracy and Justice (PFDJ), since when Afewerki has been chairman of the National Assembly and of the PFDJ. He has made it his priority to develop and modernise the infrastructure of Eritrea and lead the country out of its many years of warfare and famine. A national constitution was adopted in May 1997, but multiparty elections, due to have been held within four years of independence, have yet to be arranged.

Issaias Afewerki is married with two children.

Lennart **Meri**

Lennart Meri was first elected president of Estonia in October 1992 and is currently serving his second four-year term, having emerged as the winner in a protracted indirect election in September 1996. Meri is a former writer and film maker, whose contribution to maintaining Estonian cultural identity during the years of Soviet annexation took on added national significance as the country reasserted its independence in the late 1980s and early 1990s. As head of state he has considerable influence particularly in external affairs, although it is the prime minister who heads the government, and the parliament (which chooses the president) which determines its political complexion.

Lennart Georg Meri was born on 29 March 1929 in Tallinn, son of the diplomat and writer Georg Meri, who represented Estonia in Berlin and Paris before the country's annexation by the Soviet Union in 1940. Lennart Meri thus received some of his primary education in Berlin and Paris, and is fluent in German, French, English, Finnish and Russian. He was deported to Siberia with his family in 1941, only returning in 1946. He graduated in history from Tartu University in 1953.

Initially, Meri made his name as an author and award-winning film maker. One of his best-known works is *Hbevalge* (Silverwhite), an historical, literary, geological and ethnographic reconstruction of Baltic prehistory which was a best-seller in Estonia and in neighbouring Finland. Meri was also an editor for Estonian Radio from 1955 to 1961, editor at the Tallinnfilm Studio from 1963 to 1971, chairman of the Estonian Writers' Union from 1985 to 1987, and founder and director of the Estonian Institute in 1989/90. He has translated works by Remarque, Graham Greene, Vercors, Solzhenitsyn and Boulle into Estonian.

Never a member of the communist party, Meri only entered politics in 1990, the year of Estonia's declaration of independence. On 12 April 1990 he became minister of foreign affairs in the government of Edgar Savisaar and set about thoroughly restructuring the ministry. He played a central role in reviving the Baltic Council, which co-ordinates the foreign policy of the three Baltic states but until 1990 had been non-functional for 50 years. He was also the first public figure in Estonia to protest publicly against a planned Soviet phosphate-mining project in Estonia which would have had a damaging environmental impact on the country. By 1992 his ministry had established a number of Estonian information offices in various European capitals, including Copenhagen, Stockholm, London and Paris. Meri himself took the post of Estonian ambassador to Finland in March 1992.

Meri returned to Estonia later that year to contest the country's first free presidential elections, for which (exceptionally) the first round of voting was by popular vote with a concurrent legislative election. In a field of four candidates Meri received 29 per cent of the vote, well behind the incumbent president, Arnold Rüütel. However, since Rüütel failed to win an absolute majority, the choice passed to parliament, where Meri's right-wing Pro Patria group (*Isamaa*) was the largest faction. The parliament duly voted on 5 October by 59 votes to 31 in favour of Meri.

Despite the country's marked progress in switching over to a free-market economy, and his position as incumbent, Meri faced considerable difficulty in securing re-election in 1996. Opposition to him arose primarily because he was seen as too conciliatory towards Russia on both the main contentious issues, the position of ethnic Russians under new citizenship laws, and Estonia's Western-oriented stance as an aspirant for membership of both the European Union and NATO. He was finally re-elected on 20 September after five rounds of voting, the first three held among parliamentary deputies (in which he repeatedly failed to win the necessary two-thirds majority over Rüütel) and the subsequent rounds held in a wider electoral college also involving local council representatives. In these final rounds he won the deciding run-off by 196 votes to 126. He was sworn in for his new four-year term on 7 October.

Lennart Meri has been married twice and has three children.

Negaso Gidada

Negaso Gidada has been president of Ethiopia since the establishment of the Federal Democratic Republic of Ethiopia in August 1995, serving a six-year term in this essentially ceremonial post. A member of the transitional government set up when the Mengistu regime was driven out in 1991, he was previously a teacher, with an academic background in history, and was active in Ethiopian exile groups during a long period of residence in West Germany from 1974.

Negaso was born in 1943 in the town of Dembi Dolo in western Wollega province, the son of a Protestant preacher. He attended primary school in Dembi Dolo and secondary school in Nazareth and Addis Ababa. Between 1961 and 1971 he studied history at Haile Selassie University in Addis Ababa. After his graduation he worked as a teacher, but went into exile in West Germany in October 1974 after the overthrow of Emperor Haile Selassie.

While in Europe he was secretary, editor and chairman of the Union of Oromo Students from 1976 to 1981. He was also a member and representative of the Oromo Liberation Front (OLF) between 1979 and 1981 and a member of the Ethiopian Discussion Forum (1980–85). From 1983 to 1985 he taught the Oromo language at university in Frankfurt while attending graduate school. He obtained a master's degree in history and social psychology from the University of Frankfurt in 1984, and went on to study for a doctorate in ethnology. In 1985 he was director of the Third World Centre in Frankfurt. He became chairman of the Union of Oromo in Europe in 1986, holding the position until 1991.

In 1989 he became a supporter of the Ethiopian People's Revolutionary Democratic Front (EPRDF), the multi-ethnic coalition of groups opposed to the military regime of Mengistu Haile Mariam, and joined one of its component parties, the Oromo People's Democratic Organisation (OPDO) in 1991. He returned to Ethiopia in the summer of 1991 when Mengistu's Marxist regime was overthrown. As well as becoming a member of the central committee of the OPDO, Negaso was appointed to the post of minister of labour and social affairs, which he retained until 1992. He then became minister of information under the transitional government, which ruled until the inauguration of the Federal Democratic Republic of Ethiopia in August 1995. Although his OPDO only managed to win a handful of seats in the May 1995 legislative election to the Council of People's Representatives, he was elected as the republic's new president on 22 August 1995.

Negaso Gidada is married with three children.

Ratu Sir Kamisese **Mara**

Ratu Sir Kamisese Kapaiwai Tuimacilai Mara was appointed president of Fiji by the Great Council of Chiefs in January 1994, following the death of Ratu Sir Penaia Ganilau. Mara is a veteran politician who was Fiji's first and long-serving post-independence prime minister from 1970 to 1987. Having lost an election in that year, he was reinstated in office shortly afterwards under a controversial republican regime established by military coup leader Sitiveni Rabuka to protect the ascendancy of native Fijians. Having moved across to the presidency, initially on an acting basis during his predecessor's illness, he retained the role of head of state under a new and non-racial 1997 constitution.

Mara was born on 13 May 1920, and was educated at the Queen Victoria School and the Central Medical School in Suva. He attended Otago University before studying at Oxford University and the London School of Economics. In 1950 he joined the British colonial service, serving in Fiji from 1951 to 1961. In 1953 he first became a member of the legislative council (later the House of Representatives), where he sat continuously until 1989, and he was a member of the executive council from 1959 to 1961. In 1965 he became leader of the multiracial (though predominantly Fijian) Alliance Party, which he had helped to found in 1960.

Leader of the Fiji delegation to the Constitutional Conference in London in 1965, he was made chief minister in 1967, after the new constitution was introduced in 1966 which provided for a ministerial form of government and a democratically elected legislature.

Following Fiji's achievement of independence within the Commonwealth in 1970, he took office as prime minister, remaining in that post until April 1987, when legislative elections were won by a coalition of the Fiji Labour Party (FLP) and the National Federation Party. The FLP had been founded two years previously, in the hope of redressing continuing discrimination in land ownership rights against the descendants of indentured Indian workers who had come to outnumber the native Fijians. However, the new government, headed by Timoci Bavadra of the FLP, was overthrown in May 1987 by a military coup led by an army officer, Sitiveni Rabuka. Widespread racial violence followed and Ratu Sir Penaia Ganilau, then the governor-general, brought together Bavadra and Mara to resolve the crisis. In September 1987, however, Rabuka staged a second coup and declared himself head of state, and the Commonwealth heads of government formally declared that Fiji's membership of the Commonwealth had lapsed. Rabuka subsequently resigned as head of state, installing Ganilau as the first president of the Fijian republic, and Mara was reappointed prime minister.

In 1990 a new constitution was promulgated guaranteeing a legislative majority to ethnic Fijians. In 1992 Ganilau was reappointed president by the Great Council of Chiefs, and Mara was elected first vice-president. He became acting head of state for three months in 1992, then again from November 1993, and finally was appointed president in January 1994. Fiji continued to be excluded from the Commonwealth until 1997 when it changed its constitution again to remove the overtly racially biased provisions.

Mara married Adi Lara Mara in 1951; they have three sons and five daughters.

Martti **Ahtisaari**

Martti Ahtisaari has been president of Finland since March 1994, serving a six-year term. The role of the president as head of state is more than a ceremonial one, and includes direct responsibility for foreign affairs, although the head of government is the prime minister who is responsible to parliament. Ahtisaari, a diplomat who was associated particularly with the UN's involvement in bringing Namibia to eventual independence, stood as the candidate of the Social Democratic Party (SSDP) in the 1994 Finnish presidential election and is only his country's fourth post-war head of state.

Martti Ahtisaari was born on 23 June 1937. His birthplace, the port of Viipuri, is now known as Vyborg, having been annexed by the Soviet Union in the Second World War and formally ceded by Finland in 1947. Ahtisaari graduated from teacher training college in the Finnish city of Oulu in 1959 and was a school teacher before joining the diplomatic service in 1965.

In 1972 he became deputy director of the department for international development co-operation at the ministry of foreign affairs. His first ambassadorial posting, and the beginning of his association with southern Africa, came when he went in 1973 to Tanzania, where he was also accredited to Zambia, Somalia and Mozambique. He made his name internationally as the principal representative of the UN in the protracted negotiations on the independence of Namibia, having been appointed as special representative of the UN secretary-general in 1978. Between 1984 and 1986 he returned to Helsinki as under-secretary of state at the department for international development co-operation in the ministry of foreign affairs, but his work for the UN (and his special connection with Namibia) resumed when he was appointed under-secretary-general for administration and management of the UN in 1987. During his term of office, which lasted until 1991, he headed the UN operation (UNTAG) monitoring Namibia's transition to independence (1989/90).

In 1991 he led the working group at the ministry of foreign affairs which prepared the Finnish government's move towards membership of the European Union (EU). In 1992/93 he was chairman of the Bosnia-Herzegovina "working group of the international conference on former Yugoslavia", participating in the peace-making efforts and becoming UN special representative for former Yugoslavia in 1993.

Unexpectedly chosen as the SSDP candidate for the Finnish presidency in 1994, Ahtisaari headed the first-round poll on 16 January, taking 25.9 per cent of the vote against ten other candidates, and won the second-round run-off on 6 February with 53.9 per cent. He took office on 1 March, succeeding Mauno Koivisto, who had been president since 1981. Ahtisaari is the first Finnish president to be chosen entirely by direct election.

Ahtisaari is married with one son.

Jacques **Chirac**

Jacques Chirac has been president of France since his victory in the presidential election in May 1995, the third time he had been a candidate. The president is elected in a nationwide ballot for a seven-year term. The constitution of the Fifth Republic, framed by de Gaulle in 1958, gives the presidency significant political powers, in particular with regard to external relations, holding referendums, issuing decrees and declaring a state of emergency. The president appoints the prime minister and other members of the government, and may preside at cabinet meetings, although the prime minister is designated head of government and is responsible to parliament. Chirac has been a prominent Gaullist politician for nearly 30 years. For much of that time he and Valéry Giscard d'Estaing were rivals for dominance of the right and centre ground in French politics. Chirac has been prime minister twice, first under Giscard and then in "cohabitation" with the socialist president, François Mitterrand. Chirac is strongly identified with Paris, where he was mayor from 1977 to 1995, promoting both its architectural modernity and a new pride in the cleanliness of the streets. He also has a rural stronghold in the Corrèze, the département *for which he was a deputy for decades in the National Assembly (standing down, as required, when he took up government posts).*

Chirac was born in the fifth *arrondissement* of Paris on 29 November 1932, the son of a bank clerk. He received his initial education at two prestigious Parisian lycées, and in 1953 attended Harvard University summer school, going on to study at France's élite political and civil service training institutions, the Institut d'Etudes Politiques and the Ecole Nationale d'Administration (ENA). He served with the French army in Algeria, where he was injured in the fighting with the Algerian national liberation front.

After graduating from ENA in 1959 Chirac began his political career as an auditor in the government's finance office. In 1962 he became *chargé de mission* within the government of Georges Pompidou, soon moving from the government secretariat to a three-year spell as adviser in Pompidou's private office. He became a junior minister in 1967, with responsibility first for employment and, from 1968 to 1971, for economy and finance. He was also public auditor at the Cour des Comptes from 1965, a member of the Corrèze municipal council from 1965 to 1967, was first elected National Assembly deputy for Corrèze in 1967, and was chairman of the Corrèze general council from 1970 to 1979.

Chirac gained ministerial experience in the early 1970s at the ministry of agriculture and rural development (1972–74) and briefly as minister of the interior. When Giscard won the presidency in

May 1974, Chirac at first prospered, as a leading Gaullist in Giscard's centre-right alliance. In addition to the post of prime minister from May 1974, he took on the general secretaryship of the Gaullist party, the Union of Democrats for the Republic (UDR) from December. The two fell out, however, less over policy than because of friction between their two dominant personalities. Chirac resigned from the government in August 1976, and in December established his dominance within the Gaullist movement, transforming the UDR into the Rally for the Republic (RPR) with himself as its president. The following March he won election for the first time as mayor of Paris, using this power base to keep himself in the political forefront; he retained both the RPR leadership and the Paris mayorship until he launched his successful bid for the presidency in the mid-1990s.

In the run-up to the 1981 presidential election, Chirac increasingly distanced the RPR leadership from the Giscard government, seeking to project himself rather than the president as the leader of the centre-right "majority". Standing in the election on the RPR ticket, the first of his three bids for the presidency, he split the centre-right vote on the first round but finished a poor third behind the incumbent Giscard and the eventually successful Mitterrand.

The honeymoon of the left in government soon gave way to acrimonious divisions and a reversal of direction on the economy, and in 1986 the centre-right came back strongly in the legislative elections. Chirac's RPR, its leadership rejuvenated by him in the years in opposition, performed so well that Mitterrand had little option but to make him prime minister. Thus began the first so-called "cohabitation", a two-year test of some hitherto unexplored aspects of the division of powers under the Fifth Republic's constitution. The experiment was made to work, but Chirac's economic policies – based on a radical privatisation programme – proved less successful with the electorate, and his party was divided on how to deal with the challenge of the National Front (FN) from the extreme right, a minority favouring some form of alliance.

Challenging Mitterrand for the presidency in April/May 1988, Chirac this time went through to the run-off, but finished second, with just under 46 per cent of the vote. The general election the following month restored a centre-left majority, while also tilting the balance on the right away from Chirac towards Giscard.

Chirac favoured a "yes" vote in the 1992 referendum on the Maastricht Treaty on European Union. Although his RPR was divided on this issue, it gained fresh momentum in the March 1993 legislative elections, again becoming the largest party in a united centre-right grouping which won a landslide victory. Chirac, preparing himself for another presidential bid in two years' time, put forward fellow party member Edouard Balladur as prime minister for the second "cohabitation" government, little expecting that his loyal colleague would emerge as a rival for the presidency. Balladur's candidacy in the 1995 presidential elections was backed by the centre-right Union for French Democracy (UDF), Giscard having decided against standing himself, but Chirac overtook Balladur by campaigning strongly with populist calls to tackle unemployment and "social exclusion". He took second place in the first ballot in April, with socialist Lionel Jospin unexpectedly leading the poll. Picking up most of the Balladur votes in the second round, which he won with 52.6 per cent on 7 May, Chirac was sworn in as president on 17 May 1995.

In a Gaullist gesture asserting French independence on the world stage, Chirac caused particular controversy soon after taking office with a six-month programme of nuclear tests in the Pacific. On controversial issues such as relations with Iraq, he has shown a marked unwillingness to accept any notion of US leadership. Fundamentally, however, his approach to foreign policy is based around the Franco-German alliance at the core of European Union integration.

Two years into his own presidency, Chirac found himself in a third "cohabitation", this time on the other side, when the pendulum in the legislative elections (called early by Chirac in the hope of a vote of confidence) swung back in favour of the left. With Jospin as prime minister, the new socialist-led government in office since June 1997 has been in the forefront of dealing with tensions over the state of the economy. To some extent this has taken the spotlight off Chirac, who had been criticised for neglecting his presidential campaign promises in pursuit of austerity policies designed to prepare for European monetary union.

Jacques Chirac is married to Bernadette Chodron de Courcel and they have two sons.

Omar **Bongo**

Omar Bongo has been the president of Gabon since 1967. Head of state in a single-party regime for 25 years, he won his current term of office in the country's first multiparty presidential elections, held in December 1993. This term runs to the beginning of the year 2001, having been extended by constitutional amendment from five to seven years. Before becoming president he had held a number of posts in government service and had been a close adviser to his predecessor, President Mba.

Omar Albert-Bernard Bongo was born in Lewai, Franceville, in the southeast of Gabon, on 30 December 1935. He gained a diploma in commerce from Brazzaville Technical College in the Congo. From 1958 he worked briefly in the civil service and was in the French air force for two years prior to independence. In 1960 he entered the ministry of foreign affairs.

Appointed as assistant director in the Gabonese cabinet in 1962, he was director of President Léon Mba's private office by that October. In the succeeding years he held a variety of positions in government administration and became one of the president's closest advisers. In 1965 he entered the cabinet, as minister-delegate to the presidency. By November the following year he was vice-president, and he became president in 1967 following the death of President Mba. In 1968 he founded the Gabonese Democratic Party (PDG), introducing a single-party system.

Bongo was elected to a new seven-year term in February 1973, confirmed in office in 1980, and re-elected to a further term in 1986. His government was generally regarded as pro-Western, maintaining close relations with France in particular. His role in international organisations has included chairing the Organization of African Unity (OAU) in 1977, and he has been active as a mediator in regional disputes.

In 1990, announcing proposals to establish a multiparty democratic system, he stood down as PDG secretary-general. Parliamentary elections took place in late 1990 and early 1991. When the presidential elections were held on 5 December 1993, Bongo topped the poll with 51.18 per cent of the vote, and he was sworn in for his new term on 22 January 1994. Although international observers endorsed the conduct of the poll, dissatisfied opposition supporters formed a "parallel administration"; protracted political disputes led eventually to constitutional amendments and the holding in 1996/97 of fresh elections to the National Assembly and Senate. In March 1997 a constitutional amendment was approved extending the presidential term from five to seven years.

Omar Bongo married Edith Lucie Nguesso, the daughter of the president of the Republic of the Congo, in August 1990, and has four children.

Yahya **Jammeh**

Capt. Yahya Jammeh has held power in The Gambia since his bloodless coup in 1994, and was elected as president in a poll held under controversial circumstances in September 1996. As president he acts as both head of state and head of government. Before taking power he was a military police officer, trained in part in the USA.

Yahya A.J.J. Jammeh was born on 25 May 1965 in Kanilai village in Foni Kansala district, and educated locally at the Kanilai and Bwaim primary schools and then at Gambia high school. Joining Gambia's national gendarmerie in 1984, he was promoted to sergeant two years later. Then, in 1989, he was commissioned as an officer and was put in charge of the presidential escort of the presidential guard. He joined the military police unit in 1991. Promoted to lieutenant in 1992, he became commander of the national military police that year and was made a captain in 1994. His military training has taken him abroad to the USA, where he attended the military police officers' basic course in Fort McClellan, Alabama.

In July 1994, he led a coup organised by a small group of five young army lieutenants aged between 25 and 30. The coup ousted the veteran President Dawda Jawara, who had headed a succession of democratically elected governments since independence in 1965, and suspended the constitution. Jammeh assumed the title of president and headed a five-member Armed Forces Provisional Ruling Council.

Under pressure both from within the country and from abroad, Jammeh drew up a revised constitution providing for a return to civilian rule and multiparty politics, which was approved in a referendum in August 1996. However, within a week of the referendum, Jammeh banned the three main opposition parties and announced that anyone who had held presidential or ministerial office in the 30 years preceding the 1994 coup would not be permitted to stand in the forthcoming presidential election. Foreign observers refused to attend the poll because of the circumstances under which it was being held. When it took place, on 26 September, Jammeh was elected president with 56 per cent of the vote. The Alliance for Patriotic Reorientation and Construction (APRC), which Jammeh had formed in August to back his presidential candidacy, won 33 of the 45 elected seats in the new National Assembly the following January.

Eduard **Shevardnadze**

Eduard Amvrosiyevich Shevardnadze has been Georgia's head of state since 1992. Under the new 1995 constitution he was elected to a five-year presidential term in a nationwide ballot in November 1995. As president he is both head of state and head of government, appointing the council of ministers. Shevardnadze is best known internationally for his role as Soviet foreign minister under Mikhail Gorbachev. He was chosen for that post despite his lack of experience in foreign affairs or central government, having risen through the communist hierarchy to the position of first secretary in his native Georgia via the police and the interior ministry. After the collapse of the Soviet Union he returned to newly independent Georgia, where open conflict between nationalist factions was threatening to destroy a country that was already in serious economic disarray. He has pursued a policy of co-operation with Russia, making himself a target for some nationalist hostility and a car bomb assassination attempt. Since the conclusion of a ceasefire in the war with Abkhazian separatists, however, he has had some success in tackling chronic instability, amid signs of economic recovery.

Shevardnadze was born on 25 January 1928, the son of a teacher in the village of Mamat in the Lanchkhuti region of Georgia not far from the Black Sea. Heavily involved in youth work and as a teacher and activist in the Komsomol, the communist youth league, he became first secretary of the Komsomol at republic level in Georgia in 1957. Two years later he was first elected to the Supreme Soviet in the republic, and also in 1959 completed a correspondence degree in history at the Kutaisi Pedagogical Institute.

Drafted into the civilian police (MVD) in Georgia, he began to make a name for himself as head of the republic's ministry of public order from 1965 onwards, tackling both unrest and corruption, and clamping down on self-enrichment by government and party officials. He was promoted to minister of the interior and, from 1972, became first secretary of the Georgian communist party. He held this post, the top leadership position in Georgia under Soviet rule, for over a decade and was noted among other things for a relatively sympathetic attitude towards Jews seeking to emigrate to Israel.

Shevardnadze was a member of the central committee of the Communist Party of the Soviet Union (CPSU) from 1976. However, his rapid elevation at central level in 1995, to the CPSU politburo and simultaneously to the post of foreign minister, came as a result of his political association and growing personal friendship with the new party general secretary Gorbachev.

Over the next five years Shevardnadze worked as Gorbachev's right-hand man in transforming

Soviet foreign relations. Beginning with the bilateral Soviet–US summits of 1985 and 1986, the new Soviet leadership backed away progressively from the economically ruinous effort to sustain the superpower rivalry of the cold war. Soviet troops had pulled out of Afghanistan by 1989, while a series of agreements on arms control and arms reduction coincided with a loosening of the Soviet grip on what had been the communist bloc. The crowds who welcomed the collapse of communism across the countries of central and eastern Europe hailed Shevardnadze, like Gorbachev, as a hero of democratisation.

At home, however, Shevardnadze felt the growing danger of a military and hardline backlash. Resigning as foreign minister in December 1990, he delivered a dramatic speech warning that "dictatorship is coming", and the August 1991 Moscow coup attempt proved his warnings justified. Joining in efforts to rally support for Gorbachev, he returned briefly to the post of Soviet foreign minister as the Soviet Union was disintegrating in 1991.

He returned to Georgia in March 1992 to be appointed within four days as chair of a military-dominated State Council and was thus pitched into a period of overt conflict with the ousted former president Zviad Gamsakhurdia and more seriously with secessionists in Abkhazia, which bordered Russia on the Black Sea coast. On 11 October 1992, he was elected chairman of the parliament of Georgia, and a referendum endorsed him as head of state and commander-in-chief of the armed forces.

In February 1994 Shevardnadze and Russian president Boris Yeltsin signed a treaty of friendship and co-operation, which was especially controversial in that it allowed for the continuing existence of Russian military bases on Georgian soil. His pro-Russian line, and his decision to take Georgia into the Russian-dominated Commonwealth of Independent States (CIS), reflected his perception of how vulnerable Georgia's position had become. Rebel forces had gained the upper hand in Abkhazia (where he himself came under heavy shelling during one visit), creating a flood of ethnic Georgian refugees. The stabilisation of that situation, with a Russian-backed ceasefire in March 1994, still left economic problems so acute that Shevardnadze was forced to announce unpopular food rationing measures later that year.

On 29 August 1995 Shevardnadze survived an attempted car-bomb assassination while leaving the Georgian parliament building on his way to sign the country's new constitution. The attack, attributed to right-wing nationalists, was followed by another in a series of crackdowns as the government fought to control the private armies of various nationalist leaders.

Under the new constitution the office of president was reintroduced, with executive powers, and Shevardnadze was elected for a five-year term in a nationwide ballot on 5 November 1995. He won more than three-quarters of the votes cast, ahead of the former communist party first secretary and four minor candidates, and welcomed the outcome as showing that "democracy and reforms have triumphed". Shevardnadze is also chair of the Citizens' Union, which he founded in 1993 as a pro-democracy and free-market-oriented alliance with a strong environmentalist element and which won a large majority in the November/December 1995 legislative elections.

Shevardnadze is married to Nanuli Shevardnadze. They have a son and a daughter and four grandchildren.

Roman **Herzog**

Dr Roman Herzog is the seventh president of the Federal Republic of Germany and has held office since July 1994, serving a five-year term. His role as head of state, elected by the Federal Assembly, is primarily a ceremonial one. A Bavarian-born Protestant and former university professor, Herzog is a member of the Christian Democrat Union (CDU) and a long-standing friend of federal chancellor Helmut Kohl, and was president of the constitutional court before his election to the presidency.

Roman Herzog was born on 5 April 1934 in Landshut, and studied law at the University of Munich, acquiring a doctorate and working as a research assistant from 1958 to 1964. He became a university lecturer in 1964, and professor of public law and politics at the Free University of Berlin in 1966, moving on to become a professor, then president of political science and politics at the College of Administrative Sciences in Speyer in 1969. Between 1973 and 1978 he was the official representative of the *Land* (federal state) of Rhineland-Palatinate at the seat of the federal government in Bonn, during which time he established his close friendship with Kohl, then minister president of the Rhineland-Palatinate.

From 1978 to 1980 Herzog was minister of education, cultural affairs and sport in the *Land* of Baden-Württemberg. In 1979 he was elected to the CDU's federal executive committee. Elected in 1980 as a member of the state parliament in Baden-Württemberg, he was minister of the interior for Baden-Württemberg from 1980 to 1983, relinquishing the post when he was appointed vice-president of the federal constitutional court (*Bundesverfassungsgericht*). From 1987 to 1994 he was president of the constitutional court.

Since 1972 Herzog has been a full member of the synod of the Protestant church of Germany and for nine years (1971–80) was chairman of its chamber for public responsibility. He was also national chairman of his party's Protestant working group between 1978 and 1983. As an academic, he has a number of publications and honorary doctorates.

Herzog was elected federal president in a third round of voting on 23 May 1994 by the Federal Assembly (*Bundesversammlung*), a constitutional body comprising representatives from both houses of parliament which convenes only for the purpose of electing the head of state. Herzog won 696 votes against 605 for Johannes Rau, the Social Democrat candidate and minister president of North Rhine-Westphalia. He was sworn in on 1 July, succeeding two-term president Richard von Weizsäcker.

Herzog is married with two sons.

Jerry **Rawlings**

Jerry John Rawlings has been in power in Ghana since 1981. He seized control in a coup in December of that year (having already led a 1979 coup by junior officers, but then swiftly handed power over to an elected government). He implemented a reform programme and economic restructuring, and ultimately organised a transition to civilian rule, resigning his military commission and winning election as president in November 1992 as candidate of the National Democratic Congress (NDC). He retained office for a further four-year term in the December 1996 elections. As president he is the leading political figure, and is both head of state and head of government, chairing the council of ministers whose members he appoints.

Rawlings was born on 22 June 1947 in Accra, the son of a Ghanaian mother and a Scottish father (a mixed racial origin which some opponents have tried to use against him). He was educated at Achimota school and then enlisted as a cadet in the Ghanaian air force in August 1967. In 1969 he became a pilot officer and in 1978 a flight lieutenant.

In May 1979 Flt.-Lt. Rawlings was charged with leading a mutiny of junior officers and men of the Ghanaian armed forces. On 4 June, however, he was freed by his supporters and led a revolt which ousted the ruling Supreme Military Council. Rawlings set up the Armed Forces Revolutionary Council (AFRC) as an interim ruling body, while ensuring that general elections could go ahead under the programme already set in motion before his June coup. The elections were duly held in September, and the AFRC handed over to a civilian government formed by the People's National Party (PNP) under President Hilla Limann.

On 31 December 1981, denouncing the corruption of the civilian regime, Flt.-Lt. Rawlings once again led a revolt within the armed forces, replacing the Limann government with a Provisional National Defence Council, composed of both civilian and military members, under his own chairmanship. He became the head of state in January 1982 and chief of the defence staff in November 1982.

In power, Rawlings has placed particular emphasis on avoiding the charges of corruption and self-enrichment levelled against his predecessors. His leftist orientation was reflected in some of his reforms of the administration and the judiciary, and also encouraged him to plan for union with neighbouring Burkina Faso until his kindred spirit Thomas Sankara was ousted from power in that country. Ghana's long transition to civilian rule under Rawlings's leadership was accompanied in the latter stages by a programme of economic reform and adjustment, backed by the World Bank, which resulted in its being widely cited as a rare example of a "success story" among African states.

Lifting the ban on political activities on 1 May 1992, Rawlings resigned his air force commission, as stipulated in the new constitution, in order to contest the presidency. Standing as the candidate of his recently formed NDC party, he won 58.34 per cent of the votes cast on 3 November. He was re-elected for a second four-year term on 7 December 1996, winning 57.2 per cent of the vote to defeat two other candidates. This election, and the simultaneous legislative election, in which an NDC-led alliance won 130 out of 200 seats, were hailed as the most free and fair ever experienced in Ghana.

Rawlings is married to Nana Konadu Agyeman Rawlings, who herself is a political figure of some significance as leader of a women's movement. They have four children.

Constantinos **Stephanopoulos**

Constantinos (Costas) Stephanopoulos has been president of Greece since March 1995, having been elected by the parliament to this largely ceremonial post as head of state for a five-year term. A former lawyer, he was a cabinet minister in the 1970s and founded the short-lived Democratic Renewal (DIANA) grouping in 1985 as an offshoot from the conservative New Democracy party. His election as president was made possible, however, by support from deputies of the Panhellenic Socialist Movement (PASOK).

Stephanopoulos was born on 15 August 1926 in Patras. He graduated from the University of Athens with a law degree and practised law in Patras from 1954. In 1964 Stephanopoulos was elected a member of parliament for Achaia, representing the National Radical Union Party. He spent the seven years of the colonels' dictatorship (1967–74) in exile in Paris. Returning to Greece in 1974, he became deputy trade minister in the government of national unity which was formed after the fall of the military regime. In subsequent elections in 1977, 1981 and 1985 he stood successfully for parliament as a New Democracy candidate in Achaia.

Stephanopoulos held three cabinet posts during the latter half of the 1970s, that of the interior from 1974 to 1976, of social services in 1976/77, and of minister of state from 1977 to 1980. After two failed attempts to win the leadership of New Democracy, he resigned from the party in 1985, setting up his own splinter group, DIANA, on whose platform he won a seat in parliament representing Greater Athens in the 1989 general election.

In 1994 Stephanopoulos dissolved DIANA, after it had failed to win any seats in the European Parliament elections of that year, and withdrew from active politics. He co-authored a work entitled *The National Interest and Security Policy* in 1995.

An uncharismatic but respected figure, Stephanopoulos was nominated to stand for the presidency in 1995 by the small right-wing Political Spring party, but with the support of PASOK. He was eventually elected in a third round of voting on 8 March 1995, polling 181 votes out of 300. He was sworn in on 10 March, succeeding the 88-year-old Constantinos Karamanlis.

Stephanopoulos is a widower with two sons and one daughter.

Sir Daniel **Williams**

Sir Daniel Williams has been governor-general of Grenada since August 1996, representing the monarch, Queen Elizabeth II, as titular head of state. A former teacher and lawyer, he was a member of parliament and government minister from 1984 to 1989.

Born on 4 November 1937 in Grenada, Daniel Charles Williams began his working life early, teaching in a school in Grenada from 1952 to 1958, during which time he was promoted to deputy principal. Moving to London in 1959, he was briefly an assistant machine operator before joining the civil service, working from 1960 to 1964 as a postal and telegraph officer. Entering further education, he became a student at London University and graduated in law in 1967. He then entered Lincoln's Inn to train as a barrister, and was called to the Bar in Grenada in 1969, when he started in private practice. He served as a magistrate in St Lucia between 1970 and 1974 and then returned to private practice for the next ten years. After his political career he returned to practising law, becoming a Queen's Counsel in 1996.

Williams first entered politics in 1984, after the US intervention and the removal of the left-wing revolutionary government, as a successful New National Party candidate in the legislative elections of 3 December. Between 1984 and 1989 he served as minister for health, housing and the environment, for community development and women's affairs, and for legal affairs and as attorney-general. In 1988 he acted briefly as prime minister, deputising for the ailing Herbert Blaize.

Following his appointment as governor-general, he was made a Knight Grand Cross of the Most Distinguished Order of St Michael and St George. He has published several works on law and public affairs. He also founded the Grenada, Carriacou and Petite Martinique Foundation for Needy Students, registered in 1996.

Sir Daniel Williams is married with four adult children.

Alvaro **Arzú**

Alvaro Arzú was elected president of Guatemala for a four-year fixed term in January 1996 and is both head of state and head of government. He was a prominent conservative businessman in Guatemala City, and leader of the National Advancement Party (PAN). He is the third popularly elected president of Guatemala since military rule ended in 1986.

Alvaro Enrique Arzú Irigoyen was born in Guatemala City on 14 January 1947. He traces his ancestors back to 17th-century Russia. Before his entry into politics he was a successful businessman and public administrator, and had gained a reputation for conservatism and efficiency. As a businessman he was interested in the promotion of trade and tourism, and from 1978 until 1981 was director of the Guatemalan Tourist Commission under the dictatorship of Fernando Lucas García.

Arzú became the mayor of Guatemala City in 1986, the year in which military rule came to an end. Here he enjoyed support especially among the business community, and gained a reputation for fighting corruption. He set up the PAN in 1989 as a centre-right, pro-business party.

He remained mayor until 1990, when he made an unsuccessful bid for the presidency, although his candidacy was regarded favourably by both Guatemalan business interests and the US government. Arzú was named foreign minister in the new government, and his party was also given the communications, transport and public works portfolios. In September 1991 Arzú resigned his post in the government in protest against the president's decision to establish diplomatic relations with Belize. From this date until June 1995 he was in opposition, as general secretary of PAN.

As the PAN candidate in the January 1996 presidential election, he defeated the lawyer Alfonso Portillo, candidate of the far-right Guatemalan Republican Front (FRG). In a second round of voting Arzú polled 51.2 per cent of votes compared with 48.8 per cent for Portillo.

One of his first moves as president was to meet with commanders of the Guatemalan National Revolutionary Unity (URNG) in Guatemala City, the first such meeting since the early 1970s. A general peace agreement, ending the 35-year-old civil war, was ultimately signed on 29 December 1996. Arzú has also outlined plans to reduce the political power of the army, and to tackle crime, poverty and corruption. He has pledged to continue the neo-liberal economic policies of his predecessor to reinvigorate and modernise the economy.

Alvaro Arzú is married to Patricia Escobar Dalton de Arzú and they have seven children.

Lansana **Conté**

Maj.-Gen. Lansana Conté has been president since April 1984, following a military coup. He was confirmed in office at elections in December 1993, and was sworn in for a five-year term on 29 January 1994. As president he is both head of state and head of government, appointing the members of the council of ministers including the prime minister. A soldier in the French army prior to Guinea's independence in 1958, he had risen through the Guinean armed forces to be chief of army staff by 1975, and took power nine years later following the death of the country's leftist and increasingly dictatorial leader since independence, President Sekou Touré.

Lansana Conté, who is from the Soussou ethnic group, was born in 1934 in Koya. He went to military schools in Bingerville (Côte d'Ivoire) and Senegal, where he graduated from the St Louis military school, joining the French army in 1955. After Guinea's independence in 1958 he rose to become regional commander in the north and northwest, was promoted to the rank of colonel in 1975, and for the next nine years was chief of army general staff.

In April 1984, ten days after the death in office of President Sekou Touré, Lansana Conté and Col. Diarra Traoré led a successful bloodless military coup, Lansana Conté assuming the presidency and the portfolios of defence and security, while Traoré became prime minister. They abolished the constitution and set up the military committee for national rectification (CMRN) with Lansana Conté as its chairman. Hundreds of political prisoners were released and freedom of speech was restored.

By December 1984 disagreements between Lansana Conté and Traoré led to the latter's demotion. Conté's popularity fell amid resentment of tough austerity measures which he had introduced at the instigation of the World Bank and International Monetary Fund, and in July 1985 Traoré took advantage of his absence abroad to denounce the regime and try to seize power. The coup was halted within a day, however, and over 200 prisoners were taken. Traoré and other leaders were executed, although this was not officially confirmed for two years. Those prisoners who survived were released in 1988.

In October 1988 Lansana Conté agreed to the drafting of a new two-party constitution which would return the country to civilian rule and this was overwhelmingly approved by a referendum in December 1990. Meanwhile he promoted himself to general and in February 1991 a new transitional committee of national recovery (CTRN) was established under his chairmanship. More parties were legalised in 1992 but unauthorised public meetings were banned to avoid further violence.

Presidential elections were set for late 1993 and were eventually held on 19 December after riots had resulted in their postponement by two weeks. Lansana Conté secured 51.7 per cent of the vote, in a poll marred by violence, at least 12 fatalities, and opposition claims of widespread irregularities. In June 1995, in the country's first multiparty legislative elections, Conté's Party of Unity and Progress won 71 out of 114 seats, although opposition parties again alleged electoral fraud.

Lansana Conté is married and has two sons.

João Bernardo **Vieira**

Brig.-Gen. (retd) João Bernardo Vieira has been president of Guinea-Bissau since 1980 and is both head of state and head of government, appointing the members of the council of ministers including the prime minister. He is currently serving the five-year term to which he was elected in July 1994 in the country's first multiparty election, having belatedly responded to pressure to end the single-party rule of the African Party for the Independence of Guinea and Cape Verde (PAIGC). Vieira had risen within the party as a military commander during the struggle for independence from Portugal. His coup in 1980 removed the senior Cape Verdeans from the leadership, and he soon turned the country away from its leftist orientation to encourage private enterprise, foreign investment and Western aid.

Born on 27 April 1939 in Bissau, Vieira started out as an electrician but then trained as a soldier in China. He joined the PAIGC in 1960, studying at the party school in Conakry, Guinea, where his teacher, Amílcar Cabral, was the leader and founder of the party. The following year he was appointed military commander of Catió and political commissioner. In 1964 he was made a member of the PAIGC's political bureau, commander of the southern front in the war for independence from Portugal, and a member of the war council; he was vice-president of the war council from 1965, and assumed overall responsibility for military operations in 1970.

Upon independence in 1974, the PAIGC under Luís Cabral (half-brother of Amílcar Cabral who had been assassinated in 1973) formed a single-party government. Vieira, then aged 35, was commander-in-chief and minister for the armed forces, president of the National Assembly, and permanent secretary of the party central committee. After elections in 1977 he was also appointed vice-president of the republic, and in August 1978 he added the post of prime minister.

On 19 November 1980 Vieira seized power in a coup, capitalising on the resentment of those from mainland Guinea-Bissau who felt that there were too many Cape Verdeans (like Cabral) in the government, and also claiming that Cabral was failing to follow the socialist ideals of the party. The coup was welcomed by the government of neighbouring Guinea, which held hopes of a "Greater Guinea". Vieira, as chair of a new Revolutionary Council of Guinean Officers, also retained for himself the portfolios of defence and the interior.

In May 1984 Vieira re-established the National Assembly, replaced the Revolutionary Council with a Council of State, of which he was unanimously elected president, and also took on the post of prime minister. By this stage he was already turning the country away from left-wing policies followed since independence, instead encouraging private enterprise, foreign investment and Western aid. Internal opposition was reflected in a number of coup attempts, one of which ended with the execution of the vice-president, Col. Paulo Correia, and five co-conspirators.

Elections to the National People's Assembly were held in 1989, but still with a single PAIGC list, while Vieira was re-elected to the presidency.

By 1992 pressure from both within and outside the PAIGC for multiparty elections led Vieira to promise these would be held later in the year, but they were postponed many times and did not take place until 1994. Vieira resigned from the army so as to be eligible to stand. He did not obtain an absolute majority in the first round on 3 July, but won the run-off on 7 August even though all the opposition parties rallied behind a single candidate. In the concurrent legislative election the PAIGC secured 62 of the 100 seats, providing Vieira with a secure majority. He was sworn in for a five-year presidential term on 29 September.

Vieira has latterly sought to improve relations with neighbouring countries. In 1997 Guinea-Bissau replaced the peso with the CFA franc.

Janet **Jagan**

Janet Jagan was elected on 15 December 1997 as president of Guyana, to begin a five-year term in January 1998. The executive president is head of state and the country's main political leader, appointing the members of the cabinet, although the prime minister is nominally head of government. Janet Jagan stood in the election as the candidate of the People's Progressive Party (PPP), and had been prime minister and vice-president since the death in March 1997 of her husband Cheddi Jagan. His death had created a vacancy in the presidency, to which he had been elected in 1992; the then prime minister and vice-president Sam Hinds had stepped up temporarily to be head of state, and was expected to revert once again to being prime minister following Janet Jagan's election.

Janet Jagan was born Janet Rosenberg on 20 October 1920 in a Jewish family in Chicago, USA. She was educated at the University of Detroit, Wayne University and the Cook County School of Nursing. She met her future husband when he was studying dentistry in Chicago, married him in August 1943, and returned with him that year to what was then British Guiana. They worked as left-wing activists together in the British Guiana Labour Union, with rural labourers who were mainly, like Cheddi, of Indo-Guyanese origin. In 1946 Janet Jagan co-founded the Women's Political and Economic Organisation, and she and her husband helped mobilise the East Coast Demerara sugar strike in 1948. In 1950 they co-founded the PPP, then a left-wing Marxist–Leninist party, of which she was general secretary until 1970. Also in 1950 she became the first woman to be elected to the city council in the capital, Georgetown.

In 1953, following a PPP general election victory in April, Janet Jagan became the first woman deputy speaker of the House of Assembly. However, the British colonial authorities, claiming that a communist dictatorship was imminent, dismissed the PPP administration. The 1953 constitution, which had introduced universal suffrage and paved the way for the PPP's election victory, was suspended, while Janet Jagan was sentenced to six months' imprisonment. In 1957 she was returned to the legislature, however, and she was appointed minister of labour, health and housing from 1957 to 1961, and minister of home affairs in 1963/64.

Guyana attained its independence in 1966 under a People's National Congress (PNC) government, whose support was strongest among the Afro-Guyanese rather than Indo-Guyanese population, and whose policies were regarded by the British as less alarmingly left-wing than those espoused by the Jagans in the PPP. The PNC monopolised power for nearly two decades, securing repeated re-election in what were widely considered to be rigged ballots, but was finally ousted at the October 1992 elections by a PPP–Civic Alliance coalition led by the charismatic Cheddi Jagan.

The PPP had by this stage abandoned its Marxist rhetoric and advocated free-market policies designed to maximise foreign investment and growth; it was thus distinguished from the PNC less by ideology than by personalities and along ethnic lines.

The results of the December 1997 elections were not declared until four days after the poll, amid growing opposition accusations of vote-rigging. Janet Jagan was recorded as winning 54.8 per cent of votes cast, against 45 per cent for PNC leader Desmond Hoyte, while the PPP won a majority in the parliament elected simultaneously.

Janet Jagan is the author of a number of publications, including *History of the People's Progressive Party* (1971), *Army Intervention in the 1973 Elections in Guyana* (1973), and four books of stories for children. She was the editor of the PPP's quarterly *Thunder* from 1950 to 1956, and at one time was president of the Union of Guyanese Journalists.

Janet and Cheddi Jagan had one son and one daughter, and at the time of her election as president she had five grandchildren.

René **Préval**

René Préval, president of Haiti since February 1996, is only the second democratically elected president since independence in 1804. An engineer and agronomist whose family fled abroad under the regime of "Papa Doc" Duvalier, he was briefly prime minister when President Aristide was first elected in 1991, and returned to Haiti with Aristide when he was restored to power in 1994. The president is head of state, has executive authority over external agreements, and chairs the council of ministers, but nominates a prime minister to head the government; in the latter part of 1997, Préval's nominees were twice rejected by the Chamber of Deputies.

René Préval was born in Port-au-Prince on 17 January 1943, and is one of four children. His educational background was mainly in engineering and geothermics, and he holds a degree in agronomy from the College of Gembloux in Belgium, having left Haiti in 1963 with his family when they came under threat from the regime. After five years living in Brooklyn, New York, he returned to Haiti in 1975, four years after the death of Papa Doc, and began work with the National Institute for Mineral Resources. The lack of natural resources in Haiti prompted Préval to run a bakery fuelled by sugar cane as an alternative energy source.

Préval was active in opposing the perpetuation of the Duvalier regime under Jean-Claude "Baby Doc" Duvalier, and after the fall of Baby Doc in February 1986, he was involved in several public organisations and voluntary agencies, including the Pa Bliye Committee, to seek justice for the victims of Haiti's dictators and to investigate the disappearance of missing persons.

Préval's political career has been relatively short. He was appointed prime minister by President Jean-Bertrand Aristide in February 1991. When Aristide was ousted in a military coup on 30 September, he initially sought refuge at the embassies of Mexico and France. He joined the government in exile in Washington D.C. from 1992 until the restoration of Aristide in October 1994. Having become Aristide's chief adviser in August 1993, he held this post until his own election as president in 1995. In the 17 December poll he won an overwhelming majority of votes cast, as the candidate of the pro-Aristide grouping *Lavalas*. He was inaugurated as president on 7 February 1996.

Préval has maintained many of his predecessor's plans, especially the reform and modernisation of state institutions. He faced difficult choices regarding the privatisation of state-run industries, being himself on the political left, but needing the approval of foreign lenders and investors for the rebuilding of Haiti's desperately impoverished economy.

Carlos **Flores**

Carlos Flores was elected president of Honduras on 30 November 1997, to be sworn in for a four-year term in January 1998, succeeding fellow Liberal Carlos Roberto Reina Idiaquez. The executive presidency combines the roles of head of state and of head of government. Flores was a financial analyst before involving himself in full-time politics at the age of 30, and stood unsuccessfully for the presidency in 1989.

Carlos Roberto Flores Facussé was born in Tegucigalpa on 1 March 1950 into a wealthy family with extensive business interests and a prominent role in politics and the press. He was educated at the Tegucigalpa American School, studied industrial engineering at Louisiana State University in the USA, and stayed on there to obtain a postgraduate degree in international economics and finance. On returning to Honduras he taught at the School of Business Administration at the National University of Honduras and at the Central American Superior School of Banking, and then worked as a financial analyst for the Development Bank. In 1976 the family started *La Tribuna*, which until the end of military rule in the early 1980s campaigned for the holding of democratic elections. Now owned by Flores, it has become one of Honduras's main newspapers.

Flores first entered the National Congress in 1980 and was a minister in the first civilian government which took office in 1982 under President Roberto Suazo Córdova, but he has since denied knowledge of this government's involvement in the disappearance of many unionists, teachers and academics. In 1984 Suazo's endorsement of Flores as his successor deepened already growing rifts within the Liberal Party, and his candidacy for the presidency in the 1985 elections was withdrawn. Two years later he was appointed Liberal Party president, but when he ran for the national presidency in 1989 he lost to the highly popular Rafael Callejas of the National Party.

In 1993, when Carlos Reina Idiaquez regained the presidency for the Liberals, Flores as president of the National Congress was a major figure in his government. He managed to distance himself from Reina when the administration's popularity waned, and spent the year leading up to the November 1997 presidential elections campaigning as the Liberal Party candidate. He refused to give any press interviews during his entire campaign, however, and his critics accused him of being aloof and autocratic. His election pledges included better education and health services, a reduction in crime, and more rights for women. In the poll on 30 November he won almost 53 per cent of the vote ahead of four other candidates, the only other real contender being the National Party candidate Alba Nora Gunera, the widow of a former military dictator.

Flores is married to Mary Flake, a US citizen, and they have a son and a daughter.

Arpad **Goncz**

Arpad Goncz has been president of Hungary since 1990, and was re-elected in June 1995 for a second five-year term in this mainly ceremonial post. A former lawyer who was imprisoned for several years for involvement in the 1956 Hungarian uprising, he then worked as a writer and translator and came into the "democratic opposition" in 1988 as a dissident intellectual. He was a founder member of the Alliance of Free Democrats (AFD) and speaker of the parliament elected in March/April 1990. He has shown his independent-minded character in his presidential role, notably in opposing the government's wish to place its own appointees in top broadcasting posts, and has won respect across the political spectrum.

Goncz was born on 10 February 1922 in Budapest. He went to study law at Pazmany Peter University, qualifying in 1944, and worked briefly with the National Land Credit Institute while becoming involved in resistance to German occupation. After the end of the war he was private secretary to a leader of the Independent Smallholders' Party and edited a periodical, *Nemzedek*, but the party was broken up in 1948 as the communists moved to establish single-party rule. Goncz worked as a welder and pipe fitter, then turned to soil conservation, returning to university in 1952 to study agricultural sciences at Godollo, near Budapest. His involvement in the 1956 Hungarian uprising, resisting the arrival of Soviet troops, led to his arrest and a sentence of life imprisonment, but he was released under a 1963 amnesty.

Having learnt English in prison, he then made his name as a literary translator and writer, becoming president of the Writers' Union in 1988/89 and of the Hungarian Writers' Association in 1989/90.

As Hungary's political system began to open up to the possibility of pluralism, Goncz and other intellectuals of the so-called democratic opposition became involved in the AFD, which was founded in November 1988. He was elected in April 1990 as an AFD member in the first post-communist parliament, and was chosen at the inaugural session on 2 May as speaker, thereby becoming interim president pending a decision on the method of election of the head of state. He was formally elected president by the parliament, unopposed, on 3 August 1990, and re-elected on 19 June 1995. As president he is independent of any political party, but was nominated for re-election in 1995 by the socialists and AFD (by then in government as a coalition) and elected by 259 votes to 76 against one other candidate.

Goncz has been married since 1947. He has two sons, two daughters, and seven grandchildren.

Olafur Ragnar Grimsson

Olafur Ragnar Grimsson has been president of Iceland since August 1996, having been elected for a four-year term in late June. A one-time finance minister and the former leader of the left-wing People's Alliance (PA), he originally made his name as a broadcaster and political scientist. He gave up the PA leadership the year before he stood for the state presidency. This is primarily a ceremonial office and has recently been held by non-party figures, notably Olafur Ragnar's immediate predecessor, four-term president Vigdis Finnbogadottir.

Born on 14 May 1943 in Isafjordur in northwest Iceland, the son of a barber, Olafur Ragnar went to the capital, Reykjavik, to complete his secondary education and then to university in England. He graduated in economics and political science at Manchester University in 1965 and completed a doctorate there in political science, working on a research project on smaller European democracies, while becoming known at home through radio and television work. He then took up a lectureship at the University of Iceland, where he became professor of political science in 1973.

Initially a member of the Progressive Party, he first stood for parliament in 1974 for the Liberal and Left Alliance, whose executive board he chaired in 1974/75. Moving over to a prominent role in the left-wing People's Alliance (PA), he became a PA member of parliament from 1978, first for Reykjavik and then for Reykjanes. Between 1980 and 1983 he chaired the PA parliamentary party and in 1987 he was elected as PA leader, a post he held for eight years but relinquished at the 1995 national convention. From 1988 to 1991 he was a member of the coalition government led by Steingrimur Hermannsson, and as minister of finance was credited with having brought the problem of rampant inflation under control.

He was elected on 29 June 1996 as the fifth president of Iceland, heading the nationwide poll with 40.9 per cent of the vote against three other candidates, and taking office in August.

A member of the parliamentary assembly of the Council of Europe from 1980 to 1984, and again in 1995, he was active particularly on North–South issues. Between 1984 and 1990 he was chairman and later international president of the International Association of Parliamentarians for Global Action (PGA). In this capacity he was actively involved with the "six nations peace initiative", which included amongst others the late premiers Olav Palme of Sweden and Rajiv Gandhi of India. He accepted the Indira Gandhi Peace Prize on behalf of the PGA in 1987.

Olafur Ragnar is married to Gudrun Katrin Thorbergsdottir, the executive director of the Icelandic Post Office Workers' Union. They have twin daughters born in 1975.

Kocheril Raman **Narayanan**

Kocheril Raman Narayanan has been president of India since July 1997, serving a five-year term in this primarily ceremonial post. A graduate of the London School of Economics and the first member of the so-called "untouchable" caste to become president of India, he is a former diplomat and Congress (I) politician, and was elected to his present position upon the completion of a five-year term as vice-president.

He was born on 27 October 1920 into a poor family in the village of Uzhavoor in the southern state of Kerala. Educated at the University of Travancore, where he gained a master's degree in English literature in 1943, he was then sponsored by industrialist J.R.D. Tata to go to the London School of Economics. There he gained a first-class degree in political science in 1948, working in journalism before joining the Indian foreign service in 1949. His career in the foreign service spanned nearly 30 years, culminating in his posting as ambassador to China in 1976. After his retirement in 1978 he was appointed vice-chancellor of Jawaharlal Nehru University, where he had already been a professor during a break from his diplomatic career (1970–72), working on a study of Nehru's non-alignment policies. In October 1980 he relinquished his vice-chancellorship to go to Washington D.C. as India's ambassador to the USA (1980–84).

On his return from Washington in 1984 he entered politics, winning a seat in the *Lok Sabha* (lower house of parliament) for the Ottapalam constituency in Kerala. From January 1985 to December 1989 he held office in Rajiv Gandhi's Congress (I) government as a minister of state, first for planning, then for external affairs and latterly for science and technology. He was elected in August 1982 as vice-president of India (and chairman of the upper house of parliament, the *Rajya Sabha*), serving one five-year term before standing successfully for the presidency.

In the presidential election on 14 July 1997 Narayanan was supported by all the main parties – the United Front, Congress (I) and the Bharatiya Janata Party – and was backed by some 95 per cent of the electoral college (members of parliament and of the state legislative assemblies), and won by a record margin over former chief election commissioner T.N. Seshan. He assumed office on 25 July 1997 succeeding Shankar Dayal Sharma.

Among various other distinctions he has been chairman of the international jury for the Jawaharlal Nehru Award for International Understanding and for the Indira Gandhi Prize for Peace, Disarmament and Development.

K.R. Narayanan is married to Shrimati Usha Narayanan, whom he met while ambassador in Burma, and they have two daughters.

Thojib N. J. **Suharto**

Gen. (retd) Suharto is the second president of Indonesia and has been the country's dominant political figure for over 30 years; he began his sixth full five-year term of office in March 1993. An army officer whose career dates back to the pre-1949 struggle for independence, he emerged gradually as the key figure in the armed forces leadership which took over control of the country from former president Sukarno in 1965/66.

Thojib N.J. Suharto was born on 8 June 1921 in Kemuju near Jogjakarta, on the island of Java, into a peasant family of tenant farmers. He left school in his early teens, and by 18 had enlisted in the colonial Royal Dutch Indies Army. During the Second World War the Japanese encouraged the growth of Indonesian nationalism and sponsored the formation of an Indonesian guerrilla army to fight the Dutch, in which Suharto became a commander. Pursuing the nationalist and anti-colonial struggle after the end of the Second World War, he distinguished himself by leading an attack on Dutch forces occupying Jogjakarta, shortly before independence in 1949. His career flourished in the post-independence Indonesian army; by the mid-1950s he was commanding central Java's Diponegoro division, and in 1962/63, promoted to the rank of major-general, he led the campaign to wrest Irian Jaya from the Dutch. He was then called back to Jakarta and placed in charge of the low-profile army strategic reserve.

Having apparently fallen out with the top armed forces leadership over business dealings, Suharto was not included in a "death list" of those at the centre of power whom communist insurgents planned to assassinate in their abortive October 1965 coup attempt. He led the forces who retook control of strategic locations in the capital, and soon emerged as the key figure in the military leadership, with President Sukarno effectively sidelined.

On 11 March 1966 President Sukarno formally handed executive powers to Gen. Suharto in the so-called "Supersemar" decree, a play on the Indonesian words for 11 March Order and the name Semar, the legendary founding father of the Javanese. Suharto consciously identified himself with the pragmatic side of the Semar folk myth, rather than with the nationalist rhetoric of his predecessor Sukarno, and focused his regime's efforts on providing stability to develop Indonesia's poor but resource-endowed economy.

The communist threat was ruthlessly eliminated in a nationwide purge costing many hundreds of thousands of lives. The dominant political organisation, *Golkar* (the Joint Secretariat of Functional Groups), became under Suharto's leadership a civilian vehicle for the military regime; and from 1973 to 1975, the other political organisations then in existence were required to merge into two new parties to create a formal three-party system, within which all criticism of the government was banned. In 1984 Suharto decreed that all political groups should base themselves upon the official five-point state ideology of Pancasila (monotheism, humanitarianism, national unity, consensus democracy and social justice).

Named acting president in 1967, he was first elected to a full presidential term by the People's Consultative Assembly in 1968, and since then has been re-elected every five years, most recently (unanimously) on 10 March 1993.

Political stability encouraged Suharto in a brief experiment with liberalisation in the early 1990s, but this gave way to renewed controls on the media in 1994. As he approached a possible seventh presidential term from March 1998, the reins were tightened to prevent the emergence of political rivals, and a show of force by the regime helped to engineer the ousting of former president Sukarno's daughter Megawati from the leadership of the Indonesian Democratic Party (PDI). Although the authoritarian system severely restricted the scope for political differences, the June 1997 parliamentary election campaign proved exceptionally bloody, with nearly 300 deaths, and *Golkar*'s landslide win was offset by a strong showing in the capital by the Muslim-based United Development Party (PPP).

Polite, formal and soft-spoken, but autocratic in style, widely recognised as a shrewd operator behind a public image of simplicity, a Muslim but an exponent of the secular state creed of Pancasila, Suharto remains to some extent an enigma to the outside world. Until the 1997 economic crisis, his regime was generally seen as delivering considerable economic success, but allowing rampant corruption to the benefit of his family and friends. The collapse of foreign investor confidence in economies across southeast Asia in 1997 has focused more urgent attention on the need to tackle this "cronyism" in Indonesia, and has even raised the possibility of Suharto being persuaded to bow out in 1998 without a further term in office.

Suharto's government has faced sustained criticism internationally over the annexation of East Timor, the former Portuguese colony occupied by Indonesian forces in 1975, and over its forcible suppression of opposition there. Rebel activity in Aceh and Irian Jaya has also been firmly put down.

Suharto's wife Siti Hartinah (nicknamed Mrs Tien) died in April 1996 aged 72. Reports of Suharto's subsequent depression were augmented by speculation about his health, apparently confirmed when he visited Germany for medical attention in July 1996. Business rivalries among his six children have become more overt, with Mrs Tien no longer there as arbiter in feuds within the so-called "first family". Eldest son Sigit Harjoyudanto and eldest daughter Siti Hardiyanti Rukmana (nicknamed Tutut) are particularly involved in banking, while sons Bambang Trihatmodjo and Hutomo Mandala Putra (nicknamed Tommy) compete fiercely in automobiles and cellular phones while coexisting relatively peacefully in the airline and petrochemical sectors. Four of the six children also ran for office in the June 1997 parliamentary elections under the *Golkar* banner.

Ayatollah Seyed Ali **Khamenei**

*Ayatollah Khamenei was elected by the Assembly of Experts on 4 June 1989 as Iran's new Supreme Spiritual Leader (*Wali-e Faqih*), the office made vacant by the death the previous day of the leader of the Islamic revolution, Ayatollah Khomeini. The* Wali-e Faqih *combines supreme religious power with overall political authority, although there is also a president, chosen by nationwide ballot. The president's role, which was previously ceremonial, was significantly strengthened following the death of Khomeini, and now combines the functions of head of state and head of government. Ayatollah Khamenei has himself served two terms as president.*

Seyed Ali Hoseini Khamenei was born in 1939 in Mashhad, in the northeastern province of Khorasan. He entered a theological school at Mashhad at the age of ten, continuing his studies at Najaf before moving to Qom Theological School in 1964, where he studied religious science under Khomeini. An outspoken opponent of the regime of the Shah, he was arrested six times in the next 13 years, spending a total of three years in prison, and in 1977/78 he was exiled to Iranshahr. From 1978 Khamenei led the anti-government movement in Mashhad.

After the 1979 revolution Khamenei, who had attained the religious rank of *hojatolislam*, was appointed Revolutionary Council representative for the army. He was deputy for, and then head of, revolutionary affairs at the national ministry of defence, becoming commander of the Islamic Revolutionary Guard. Elected in 1980 to the Islamic Consultative Assembly, the *Majlis*, he was a co-founder and secretary-general of the government-sponsored but now defunct Islamic Republican Party (IRP) and was increasingly seen as one of Ayatollah Khomeini's closest associates.

Khamenei was wounded in an assassination attempt in June 1981, part of a spate of terrorist violence affecting the Islamic regime. In October of that year, following the ousting of Bani-Sadr and the assassination of his successor President Radjai, Khamenei was elected to fill the vacant presidency, winning an overwhelming majority against four other candidates in the nationwide poll. He was re-elected, against two opponents, in August 1985. In May 1989 he was made chairman of the secretariat of the Imam (Khomeini), and on 4 June, the day after Khomeini's death, was elected to his present position. He was also given the religious title of ayatollah, as being more compatible with his status than the less elevated title *hojatolislam*.

As a religious authority, Khamenei has written several books on Islam and history, such as *The Role of Muslims in the Independence Struggle of India*. He speaks Farsi, Arabic, Azerbaijani and Turkish. His career has also spanned the foundation of religious associations, such as the Foundation of the Oppressed, and his membership of the Tehran Militant Clergy Association.

Mohammad **Khatami**

*Hojatolislam Khatami was elected for a four-year term as president of the Islamic Republic of Iran in May 1997 and was sworn in on 3 August, in succession to President Rafsanjani who had held office since 1989. Although overall authority lies with the Supreme Spiritual Leader (*Wali-e Faqih*) under the theocratic state created by the Islamic revolution of 1979, the president is both head of state and head of government, and appoints the council of ministers subject to approval by the* Majlis *(parliament). Khatami, who has studied Western philosophy and speaks both English and German, is widely regarded in the West as a moderate. Within months of his becoming president, new initiatives in foreign policy, notably the successful hosting of an Islamic summit in Tehran, had begun to reduce Iran's international isolation.*

Seyyed Mohammad Khatami was born at Ardakan, in the Yazd province, in 1943. His father was a member of the Islamic clergy. He left school in 1961, after which he went to Qom to study theology. In 1965 he moved to Isfahan, and obtained a degree in 1969, followed by a master's degree in education from the University of Tehran (1970). He then returned to the Qom seminary to complete his philosophical studies and courses on *ijtihad* (practice of religious leadership), attaining the religious status of *hojatolislam.*

While a student, Khatami was involved in the anti-Shah campaign. After a period in Germany in 1978/79 as head of the Islamic centre in Hamburg, he returned to Iran in the wake of the 1979 revolution, and was elected in 1980 to the *Majlis,* representing the constituencies of Ardakan and Meibod. In 1981 he was appointed head of the Kayhan Institute and newspaper. From 1982, he held responsibilities variously as minister of culture and Islamic guidance, and as head of the joint command of the armed forces and chairman of the war propaganda headquarters. In 1992, however, he was severely criticised for using his role as minister of culture to promote "decadent" ideas, and the hardline mullahs successfully pressed for his removal from office. Regarded at this time as a "moderate" close to President Rafsanjani, he was appointed instead as the president's cultural adviser and head of the national library, taking a stand in promoting the free circulation of books and films. In 1996 a decree from the *Wali-e Faqih,* Ayatollah Khamenei, made him a member of the High Council of Cultural Revolution. Following the presidential elections of 1997, he now sits as head of this council.

Khatami's election to the presidency, in a nationwide ballot on 23 May 1997, signalled a surprise defeat for the hardline candidate Ali Akbar Nateq-Noori. Khatami won by a considerable margin, receiving 21 million out of 30 million votes, his candidacy having become the rallying point for a wide-ranging coalition supported in particular by industrialists and technocrats, the urban middle classes, students, and women.

Saddam **Hussein**

Saddam Hussein has been in power in Iraq since 1979, when he deposed former president Gen. Bakr. Under the Bakr regime he had already become deputy chairman of the Revolutionary Command Council (RCC) and security chief a decade earlier. He has been president since 1979, was confirmed by an October 1995 referendum, and is currently serving a seven-year term expiring in 2002. He is head of state, head of the RCC, head of government (and prime minister since 1994), head of the party and head of the armed forces. Saddam Hussein maintains a close grip on power, surrounding himself with an élite republican guard and advisers drawn mainly from his own Tikriti clan. From the time of his invasion of Kuwait in 1990, his expansionism and his effort to become the leading radical voice in the Arab world have been countered by US-led military and diplomatic action. He has remained defiantly in power, however, surviving defeat by US-led forces in the 1991 Gulf war, uprisings by southern Iraqi Shi'ite Muslims and by separatist Kurds in the north, plots by dissidents, and international sanctions intended to ensure his compliance with UN resolutions on the dismantling of weapons of mass destruction.

Saddam Hussein is a Sunni Muslim, born on 28 April 1937 in the city of Tikrit, 120 miles north of Baghdad. Accounts of his childhood suggest that a forceful uncle was the strongest adult influence, and that violence was the key to making a mark within his group of cousins. In 1956 Saddam joined the Iraqi branch of the Arab Ba'ath Socialist Party, involving himself over the next decade in its revolutionist activity and being arrested several times for involvement in attempted coups. Sentenced to death for the attempted assassination of Iraqi Prime Minister Gen. Kassem, he fled the country and lived in Syria and Egypt between 1959 and 1963, studying law in 1961 at Cairo University. Arrested again in 1964 for plotting the overthrow of President Aref, he was elected while in prison as a member of the Ba'ath leadership, and in 1966 became deputy secretary of its Iraqi branch.

Saddam Hussein played an active role in the two Ba'athist coups of July 1968 which brought his fellow Tikriti Gen. Bakr to power, and was rewarded with the RCC vice-chairmanship the following year. He built up an elaborate network of secret police, aimed at uncovering and suppressing dissent, but also providing the power base which enabled him to push out Gen. Bakr and take over the presidency and party leadership himself in 1979. Turning on those whom he could not count on for loyalty, he purged any possible opponents from within the ruling circle, and crushed a Kurdish rebellion in northern Iraq, gaining international notoriety by the use of chemical weapons against Kurdish villagers.

The Iran–Iraq war was launched by Saddam Hussein in September 1980 ostensibly in an effort to regain territory occupied by Iran since 1973. It developed, however, into a protracted (and in human terms immensely costly) eight-year struggle for ascendancy between the two principal regional powers, setting his Iraqi Arab nationalism against Iran's Shi'ite Muslim clerical leaders and their Islamic revolution. Of these two, Western countries feared Iran most, and supplied much military equipment to Iraq until the war finally ended in a stalemate.

On 2 August 1990 Saddam Hussein provoked a wider crisis when he ordered the occupation of Kuwait, again based on a dispute over territory but offering the opportunity of extending his country's oil wealth. UN demands for a complete withdrawal were ignored, and a US-led alliance initiated heavy air strikes followed up by a land war. This had wide support from Western countries, Soviet acceptance, and backing in the Arab world not just from the conservative monarchies but also from Egypt, Syria and other governments. Saddam Hussein nevertheless invoked the ideas of Muslim *jihad* or holy war, making much of his defiance of the West, and launching missiles at Israel to substantiate the view of himself as a true supporter of the Palestinian cause.

Iraqi forces were overwhelmingly defeated in the field in the January/February 1991 Gulf war, driven out of Kuwait, but saved from the apparent prospect of annihilation when the US-led alliance declared a ceasefire at the end of February, thus rejecting the temptation to expand their limited war aims and press on to take Baghdad. Saddam Hussein had to accept the conditions stipulated by UN resolutions for the ending of hostilities, including the requirement that his regime disclose and destroy any nuclear, chemical and biological warfare facilities and stockpiles. A UN inspections regime was set up to monitor this, with economic sanctions in place pending the certification of Iraqi compliance. The severe impact of these sanctions on the economy, and on the Iraqi people, were only slightly alleviated by a humanitarian provision agreed in late 1996 under which some Iraqi oil could be sold internationally to pay for imports of food and medicine.

Defeat in the Gulf war left Saddam Hussein apparently vulnerable, but he quickly gained the upper hand against rebellions by the Kurdish population in the north and the Shi'ite so-called "marsh Arabs" in the south, and followed up various government reshuffles with purges and executions of military officers in early 1992 and August 1993. In August 1995 divisions opened up within his own family, apparently prompted by the growing power of his son Udai Hussein. Two of his daughters and his sons-in-law Hussein Kamel and Saddam Kamel sought political asylum in Jordan, and called for the overthrow of the regime. When a supposed reconciliation was effected they returned to Iraq in February 1996, indicating the reassertion of Saddam Hussein's control over any real internal dissent – and shortly afterwards the two sons-in-law were shot and killed by another close family member.

Internationally, Saddam Hussein has on several occasions disputed the right of access of weapons inspectors. The most recent and most serious confrontation, in late 1997, led to the withdrawal of the inspection teams, and a growing crisis over Iraqi non-compliance took the regime back towards the brink of war. US and British air power had already been used from 1992 to enforce "no-fly zones" in southern and northern Iraq, while air strikes had been mounted against the Baghdad intelligence headquarters in 1993, to punish an alleged assassination plot against former US President Bush, and US troops and air power had also been mobilised in quantity in late 1994 to forestall an apparent renewed threat of Iraqi intervention in Kuwait.

Saddam Hussein married Sajida Khairallah in 1963 and has two sons and three daughters.

Mary **McAleese**

Mary McAleese became the eighth Uachtaran na hÉireann *(President of the Republic of Ireland) on 11 November 1997, succeeding Mary Robinson who had held the post since 1990. McAleese, a Belfast-born barrister, broadcaster and academic, was previously pro-vice-chancellor at Queen's University, Belfast, and is the first person from Northern Ireland to be elected as Irish head of state. She was nominated by the conservative nationalist* Fianna Fáil *party and by the Progressive Democrats as a candidate for the presidency, which is a largely ceremonial role, and was sworn in for a seven-year term after topping the poll in the nationwide election in October.*

Mary Lenaghan was born on 27 June 1951 in Belfast, the eldest of nine children in a Catholic family. She attended secondary school on the Falls Road in Belfast and went on to study law at Queen's University, Belfast, graduating with an honours degree in law in 1973. She studied to be a barrister and was called to the Northern Ireland Bar in 1974 where she practised mainly in criminal and family law work. In 1975 she was appointed Reid professor of criminal law, criminology and penology at Trinity College, Dublin. She held this position until 1979 when she joined the Irish national broadcasting corporation, RTE, as a journalist and presenter.

In 1981 she returned to the Reid professorship at Trinity, continuing part-time with RTE. In 1987 she was appointed director of the Institute of Professional Legal Studies, which trains barristers and solicitors for the legal profession in Northern Ireland and is regarded as one of the most pioneering departments in Queen's University. In 1994 she was appointed as a pro-vice-chancellor of Queen's, the first woman in history to hold such a position at the university.

In 1995 she was a delegate to the conference on trade and investment in Ireland held at the White House, Washington, and then to the Pittsburg conference in 1996. She was also a member of the Catholic Church delegation in 1996 to the North Commission on Contentious Parades, and is a founder member of the Irish Commission for Prisoners Overseas. Before becoming president in 1997 she also held the positions of director of Channel 4 Television, director of Northern Ireland Electricity and director of the Royal Group of Hospitals Trust.

Her election as president of Ireland broke the record for the greatest margin of victory when she took 42.24 per cent of votes in the first round and 58.7 per cent in the second round.

Mary McAleese is married to Martin McAleese, a dentist, and they have three children.

Ezer **Weizman**

Ezer Weizman became the seventh president of Israel on 13 May 1993, having been elected by parliament in March for a five-year term. The role of president is primarily a ceremonial one, the elected prime minister being the executive head of government, although Weizman said upon taking office that he wanted to involve the presidency in promoting peace with the Palestinians. Weizman was an air force officer and deputy chief of staff in the 1960s, and a cabinet member in Likud *governments in the 1970s, subsequently founding his own party and then crossing over to join Labour. As head of state he follows in the footsteps of his uncle, Chaim Weizmann, the scientist and Zionist leader who was Israel's first president from 1949 to 1952.*

Ezer Weizman was born on 15 June 1924 in Tel Aviv. From 1948 to 1966 he was an officer in the Israeli air force, of which he was a founder member, and attended the UK Royal Air Force staff college in 1951/52. He was deputy chief of staff of Israel's defence forces from 1966 until 1969, when he retired as air force general.

A member of the *Knesset* (parliament) from 1970 to 1992, Weizman has made something of a political journey across a range of parties, a consistent theme being his emphasis on finding ways to further the prospect of stable peace in the region. He was chair of the executive committee of the *Herut* party from 1971 to 1973, and a member of the *Likud* front from 1973 to 1980, during which period he ran *Likud*'s successful 1977 general election campaign. As minister of defence between 1977 and 1980 he played a major part in the process leading to the 1979 peace treaty with Egypt. In 1980 Weizman resigned his cabinet post, however, due to differences of opinion with the rest of the government over ways of achieving peace, having become convinced of the need for talks with Arab leaders. He became involved in business activities for the next four years.

In 1984 Weizman founded a political party, *Yahad*, arguing that it was time for an Israeli government to talk directly with the Palestine Liberation Organization (PLO). *Yahad* joined the National Unity government of 1984–88, in which he was himself minister for Arab affairs. *Yahad* merged with Labour in 1986 and Weizman ran Labour's 1988 general election campaign, becoming minister of science and technology in the new government (1988–92).

In February 1992 Weizman resigned from the *Knesset*, believing there to be a lack of progress in the Arab–Israeli peace process. His election as president, on 24 March 1993, was backed by Labour and 66 *Knesset* members in total, with 53 voting for the *Likud* candidate.

He is the author of *On Eagle's Wings* (1978) and *The Battle for Peace* (1981).

Ezer Weizman is married with two children.

Oscar **Scalfaro**

Oscar Scalfaro was elected president of Italy in May 1992. A practising Catholic and a lawyer by training, he has been involved in politics as a Christian Democrat since the end of the Second World War, and had been a parliamentary deputy for Piedmont for over 40 years before becoming president. A government minister on several occasions in the 1960s and 1970s, he returned to government office as interior minister in successive socialist-led coalition administrations headed by Bettino Craxi from 1983 to 1987. As president he has reinforced the image of his office as above party politics and maintains a reputation for rectitude and simplicity. The president, primarily a ceremonial role, is elected by parliament for a seven-year renewable term.

Oscar Luigi Scalfaro was born on 9 September 1918 in Novara, west of Milan, was active in Christian youth organisations, and graduated with a degree in law from the Catholic University of the Sacred Heart in Milan in 1942. He was a magistrate during the last years of the war and became a public prosecutor at the court of assizes in Alessandrai, where he remained until 1946.

His political career began when he was elected as a Christian Democrat (DC) member of the constituent assembly in 1946, on the same day that a referendum approved the abolition of the monarchy. Following the establishment of a republic, Scalfaro successfully contested the first general election to the new Chamber of Deputies in 1948. He was re-elected as a DC deputy for Piedmont in successive elections until 1992, was a member of the DC central leadership from 1949 until 1954, and was the party's organisational secretary from 1970 to 1972.

Scalfaro first joined the ranks of government in 1954 when he was appointed under-secretary for labour and social security and a year later he assumed the post of under-secretary of state at the presidency of the council of ministers. Between 1963 and 1966 he was deputy chair of the parliamentary investigative commission on the Mafia, and also chaired the Chamber of Deputies electoral advisory board during the same period.

From 1966 to 1968 and again in 1972 he served as minister of transport and civil aviation. Later in 1972 he moved from transport to become minister of education and from 1976 to 1983 was vice-president of the Chamber of Deputies. Following the 1980/81 earthquakes in the Basilicata and Campania regions he was also chair of the parliamentary investigation commission on emergency reconstruction.

In 1983 he was appointed to the post of interior minister in the coalition government of socialist premier Bettino Craxi and remained in this post until Craxi resigned in March 1987. No longer in the cabinet, Scalfaro became a member of the foreign and European Community affairs committee of the Chamber of Deputies from 1987 to 1992 and from 1989 to 1992 was also president of the bicameral parliamentary inquiry commission.

After the April 1992 general election Scalfaro was elected president of the Chamber of Deputies. This was superseded, however, by his election on 25 May as president of the republic. He emerged as the eventual winner after 16 rounds of voting by an electoral college comprising both houses of parliament and 58 regional representatives. He was supported not only by his own Christian Democrats and the other members of the outgoing ruling coalition but also by the former communist Democratic Party of the Left (PDS) and the Greens. In his inaugural speech he urged that a bicameral commission be established to revise the constitution.

Oscar Luigi Scalfaro is a widower with one child.

Sir Howard **Cooke**

Sir Howard Cooke has been governor-general of Jamaica since August 1991. A teacher by profession, he was a founding member of the People's National Party (PNP) before the Second World War, and a government minister in the 1970s. Appointed on the government's advice by the monarch, Queen Elizabeth II, to represent her as titular head of state, the governor-general is assisted by a six-member privy council, but the duties of the office are primarily ceremonial.

Born on 13 November 1915 at Goodwill in the parish of St James, Howard Felix Hanlan Cooke was educated at Mico College and at London University. During his long teaching career he spent over 20 years at Mico College, was headmaster at Belle Castle All-Age School, Port Antonio Upper School and Montego Bay Boys' School, and was at one time president of the Jamaica Union of Teachers. Cooke has also held various managerial positions in the insurance industry with Standard Life, Jamaica Mutual Life, and the American Life Insurance Company (ALICO).

Cooke's political career began in 1938, when he was a founding member of the People's National Party (PNP). Within the party he has been a member of the national executive, chairman of the regional executive and chairman of the party. He sat in the West Indies federal parliament as the representative for St James from 1958 until 1962, was a senator in the Jamaican parliament from 1962 to 1967, and a member of the House of Representatives from 1972 to 1980. His government posts included ministerial responsibilities for pensions and social security, education, public service and labour. He also served on the executive of the Commonwealth Parliamentary Association.

An accomplished cricketer and footballer in his youth, Cooke has also been group scout master and secretary of the St Andrew Boy Scouts Association. He is a lay pastor, a senior elder of the United Church of Jamaica and Grand Cayman, and a member of the Ancient and Accepted Order of Masons.

Cooke married Ivy Tal in 1939, and they have two sons and one daughter.

Emperor **Akihito**

Emperor Akihito has been head of state since January 1989. The role of emperor, while accorded the highest respect, is primarily a ceremonial one, and in all political matters he acts only as advised by the government. Before his accession Akihito had been crown prince for nearly four decades during the long reign of his father, Emperor Hirohito.

Akihito Tsegu no Miya was born in Tokyo on 23 December 1933. He is the fourth child, and eldest son, of the late Emperor Hirohito and Empress Nagako. His education, interrupted by evacuation to provincial cities during the Second World War, was partly by private tutors. Akihito also attended the Gakushuin school, which covers the whole range from kindergarten to university, and was originally set up specifically for the imperial family and aristocracy, but opened to the public from 1947. He graduated from Gakushuin University in politics and economics in 1956.

In 1952 Akihito was officially named crown prince, and spent the years before his accession engaged in a mixture of official duties and private interests. His public duties included many overseas visits and tours within Japan. In private life a keen ichthyologist, he is a particular expert on the goby fish, and has made numerous contributions to the *Journal of the Ichthyological Society of Japan*; he has also been a research associate at the Australian Museum, and in 1985 he was honorary secretary at the International Conference on Indo-Pacific Fish.

In 1987 Akihito became acting head of state. Acceding to the throne on 7 January 1989, he was formally crowned on 12 November 1990.

In 1959 Akihito married Michiko Shoda, the first non-aristocrat to be elevated to royal status. The couple have three children: Naruhito (born in 1960), Fumihito (born in 1965) and Sayako (born in 1969).

King **Hussein**

King Hussein has ruled the Hashemite Kingdom of Jordan since 1952. The king is head of state and appoints the prime minister, who is designated head of government. He has generally been seen as a pro-Western element in the Arab world, except during the period following the Iraqi invasion of Kuwait in 1990, when he determined that Jordan should remain neutral, and criticised the US-led intervention which inflicted a military defeat on Iraq. A Sunni Muslim like the majority of the population, King Hussein has generally maintained good relations with moderate elements in the Muslim brotherhood, although he has been prepared to clamp down hard on domestic unrest, having already shown particular ruthlessness in dealings with the Palestinians in 1970/71. King Hussein has been the target of a number of coups and assassination attempts.

Hussein ibn Talal was born on 14 November 1935 in Amman. He was educated at Victoria College in Alexandria, Egypt, and in England at Harrow School and the Royal Military Academy, Sandhurst. In 1951 Hussein witnessed the assassination in Jerusalem of his grandfather, King Abdullah, by a Palestinian extremist. On 11 August 1952 he was proclaimed king and head of state, aged 17, after his mentally ill father was forced to abdicate. He formally acceded to the throne of Jordan on 2 May 1953.

King Hussein's Hashemite kingdom is founded on the allegiance of rural tribes of Bedouin origin, but his long reign has been dominated by relations with the Palestinians, who made up much of the population after the refugee influxes of 1948–50 and 1967, and by the wider regional issues centring on the Arab–Israeli conflict. He expelled the Palestine Liberation Organization (PLO) from Jordanian territory in 1970/71, amid bitter fighting, but subsequently repaired relations. He gave valued support to the cause of Palestinian independent statehood when he formally renounced his own claim to sovereignty over the West Bank in 1988, endorsed the 1993 Israeli–PLO agreement (after some hesitation), supported Palestinian claims to east Jerusalem in 1995, and visited Palestinian-run parts of the West Bank in 1996.

Within the broader Arab context, in 1957/58 King Hussein dismissed a leftist-nationalist government and opposed integration into the Egyptian–Syrian project of a United Arab Republic. The Arab–Israeli war in 1967 saw Israel reoccupy territory on the West Bank which Jordan had held since the 1949 armistice, and east Jerusalem, including the old city. The 1973 war with Israel, on the other hand, affected Jordan much less, as only a nominal participant, but allowed King Hussein to restore relations with (and aid from) the Arab world cut off since his expulsion of the PLO. His pro-Iraqi stance in 1990/91, popular at the time domestically but damaging to his international image in the eyes of Western powers, was abandoned by 1993, when he announced his opposition to the continued rule of Saddam Hussein. Gradual normalisation of relations with Israel culminated in a declaration ending the state of war, which King Hussein and Israeli prime minister Yitzhak Rabin signed in Washington D.C. in July 1994, and a formal peace accord three months later.

Pressure for the modernisation of state institutions, and for greater democratisation, led King Hussein to call elections (after a 22-year gap) in 1989, to lift the remaining martial law provisions (in force since 1967) over the subsequent years, and to allow elections on a party basis for the first time in 1993 and again in 1997. The House of Representatives retains, however, a majority of independents loyal to him, confounding some predictions that party politics would greatly strengthen the Islamic fundamentalist movement within Jordan.

Although he is now severely restricted by illness, King Hussein's leisure interests include water sports, karate, flying, driving, fencing and photography, and he is a celebrated amateur radio operator. His autobiography, *Uneasy Lies the Head,* was published in 1962, and *My War with Israel* was published in 1967.

King Hussein married his fourth wife, Lisa Halaby of Virginia, now known as Queen Noor, on 15 June 1978. In all he has 11 children by his four marriages.

Nursultan **Nazarbayev**

Nursultan Nazarbayev became president of what was then the Kazakh Soviet Socialist Republic in 1990; he retained power after the disintegration of the Soviet Union and was elected president of Kazakhstan in a popular vote in December 1991. In a referendum held on 29 April 1995 he was confirmed in office until 2000. An official of the Communist Party of the Soviet Union (CPSU) for over 20 years, and briefly a politburo member in 1990/91, but now an advocate of transforming the economy on free-market lines, he has made himself the dominant political personality of independent Kazakhstan, ruling for substantial periods by decree, although formally the head of government is the prime minister (whom the president appoints).

Nursultan Abishevich Nazarbayev was born on 6 June 1940 in the village of Chemolgan. After attending the higher technology course at the Karaganda Metallurgical Combine, he spent some time in Moscow attending the CPSU's Higher Party School (and joined the CPSU in 1962). When not in Moscow, he worked until 1969 at the Karaganda Metallurgical Combine. In 1969 he began a career as a party functionary, which took him via district level posts to membership of the CPSU central committee in 1986, and appointment in 1989 as first secretary of the central committee of the Kazakh Republic CP. Meanwhile, within the government structure, he was chairman of the Kazakh council of ministers from 1984 to 1989, when he was elected chair of the Kazakh Supreme Soviet.

Nazarbayev was appointed to the CPSU politburo in 1990, but resigned from both the politburo and the central committee in 1991 in protest over the attempted coup in Moscow that August. From 1989 to 1991 he also held a seat in the Chamber of Deputies. He was elected president of the Kazakh Soviet Socialist Republic in 1990, and thus became first president of independent Kazakhstan in 1991, with the endorsement of a popular vote that December.

As president, he has advocated an independent stance while insisting on the importance of relations with Russia, and at the global level has committed Kazakhstan to becoming a non-nuclear state, dismantling nuclear warheads and also signing the Nuclear Non-Proliferation Treaty in 1994. He has used presidential powers to rule by decree to overcome obstacles in the legislature, particularly over the transformation of the economy to a free-enterprise model, in which area Nazarbayev is strongly influenced by the advice of the Korean-American economist Chan Young Bang. Opposition and human rights groups have accused him of harassing those who express political dissent.

Nursultan Nazarbayev is married to Sarah Alplisovna Kounakaeva. There are three daughters by this marriage.

Daniel arap **Moi**

Daniel arap Moi has been president of Kenya since the death in 1978 of Jomo Kenyatta, the first president and founder of modern Kenya. Moi has been returned for further five-year terms in successive elections, including the first multiparty elections in December 1982 and the most recent poll, in highly disputed circumstances, in December 1997. As president he is both head of state and head of government, and appoints the members of the cabinet. Moi also leads the ruling Kenya African National Union (KANU) as party president. A teacher before he became involved in nationalist politics and the campaign for Kenyan independence, Moi then became a leader of the Kenyan African Democratic Union (KADU), whose post-independence merger into Kenyatta's ruling KANU party was the basis for the single-party regime of the next 27 years. Moi was Kenyatta's vice-president for 11 years before succeeding to the presidency and characterised his policies thereafter as following in Kenyatta's footsteps. Unlike many of the ruling élite of the 1960s and 1970s, however, Moi is not from the largest ethnic group, the Kikuyu. He is a Tigen from the smaller Kalenjin group, and has been criticised for exploiting inter-ethnic rivalries for his own political advantage.

Daniel Toroitich arap Moi was born on 2 September 1924 in the Baringo district in the Rift Valley. Orphaned at the age of four, he was educated at mission school, then in Kabartonjo and finally at the African school in Kapsabet. From 1945 he worked as a teacher, interspersing two spells as head teacher at the African school in Kabarnet with a long period teaching at the Tambach teacher training school there. During his spare time he studied for and passed the London matriculation examinations.

In 1957 Moi became an African representative on the legislative council, and from 1960 onwards he was chairman of KADU (making him in effect the deputy to party leader Ronald Ngala). He entered the House of Representatives at the 1961 elections. When KANU (the leading nationalist formation) refused to form a pre-independence government until its leader Kenyatta was released from detention, the less radical KADU accepted the opportunity do so, with the backing of the New Kenya Party (representing white voters).

Moi joined this pre-independence government as parliamentary secretary and then minister for education, and in 1962 moved to the ministry for local government. Kenya became independent in December 1963 under a KANU government. A year later, as a new republican constitution came into effect, KADU gave up its opposition role to merge itself into KANU, and Moi was rewarded with the post of minister of home affairs. He held this post until 1967, and thereafter the vice-presidency until 1978.

After the sudden death of Kenyatta, Moi became president and commander-in-chief of the armed forces on October 1978. He has held the presidency ever since, and for much of the time the home affairs and defence portfolios as well. Some powerful KANU "barons" and other leading Kikuyu figures initially saw him as only a stop-gap, but he tightened his grip after an attempted air force coup in 1982, and won election on his own account in a single-candidate poll in September 1983. Pro-Western on most foreign policy issues and an advocate of private sector business rather than of state socialism, Moi cultivated his support particularly among the Kalenjin and other minority ethnic groups, and among traders of Asian origin who had been the targets of economic nationalism in the latter years of Kenyatta's presidency.

Moi was again re-elected in April 1988 amid accusations of systematic electoral fraud and intimidation. That year's single-party legislative elections purported to offer some element of choice, under a much-criticised system where voters had to line up publicly behind their chosen candidate to cast their vote.

By the end of 1991, continuing pressure, both internally and from foreign donor countries threatening a freeze on aid, compelled the autocratic Moi to concede the need for a multiparty system. He had hitherto opposed this ostensibly on the grounds that it would promote tribalism. The main opposition party to register in the 1992 elections was the Forum for the Restoration of Democracy (FORD). Moi won the poll on 29 December with only 36 per cent of the popular vote, benefiting from the division of the opposition into three main contending factions.

Moi's critics accuse him of self-enrichment and repression, and complicity in engineering the death of several prominent opponents; they portray him as one of the last corrupt and autocratic survivors from his generation of former dictators in Africa. Moi himself fends off such charges, denies having accumulated great personal wealth, and points to his electoral mandate. The December 1997 elections, chaotically administered rather than massively fraudulent, gave him a further term of office once again because his opponents could not unite. He was assisted by the electoral system, which required only a simple majority, plus at least 25 per cent in at least five of the eight provinces. He was sworn in for his new term in early January 1998.

Daniel arap Moi was married from 1951 until 1976, when he divorced his wife Lena. They had five sons and two daughters.

Askar **Akayev**

Askar Akayev has been president of Kirgizstan since 1990, shortly before the country became independent upon the break-up of the former Soviet Union in 1991. Re-elected in October 1991, he won a further five-year term in December 1995. The president has considerable executive powers, increased by constitutional changes approved in 1996, although formally the head of government is the prime minister (whom the president appoints, along with the council of ministers). Akayev is an applied scientist and had a distinguished academic career, as well as heading the science and academic departments of the Kirgiz communist party in the 1980s. He now endorses the social democratic party, and has identified himself with the objectives of creating a market economy (heavily backed by international lending organisations) and making his country a financial services centre for central Asia.

Born into a farming family on 10 November 1944, in the village of Kyzyl-Bairak in the Kemin district of Kirgizstan, Akayev was academically gifted, becoming a doctor of technical science after he graduated from the Leningrad Precision Mechanics and Optics Institute in 1967. After a promising early career, he rose to be chairman of the Bishkek Technical University. He was elected vice-president of the Kirgiz Academy of Sciences in 1987, and president in 1989. Akayev is author of numerous scientific and political works, most notably a mathematical study of the problems of heating computers. He is a member of the New York Academy of Sciences, and is an honorary professor of the Moscow State University.

Akayev, a member of the Communist Party of the Soviet Union from 1981 to 1991, was head of the department of science and higher academic institutions of the Kirgiz communist party in 1986/87. In October 1990, parliament elected him president of the Kirgiz Soviet Socialist Republic. He was confirmed in a poll in 1991 as the first president of independent Kirgizstan, and commander-in-chief of the armed forces.

Having dismissed members of his government's economic team in early 1993 for obstructing the privatisation programme, Akayev backed the founding that year of a new social democratic party, and the following January he won overwhelming support for his economic reform programme. Resistance within the legislature persisted, however. In response, Akayev has pushed through, by referendum, changes to both the legislative structure and the distribution of power between president and parliament. In late 1995 he succeeded in getting presidential elections brought forward, to allow him to seek a fresh mandate. This he obtained in the poll on 24 December 1995, claiming over 70 per cent.

Askar Akayev is married to Mairam Akayev and they have two sons and two daughters.

Teburoro **Tito**

Teburoro Tito was elected to the presidency of Kiribati in September 1994, and on 1 October was sworn in for a four-year term as the third beretitenti *(president) since Kiribati gained independence in 1979. As president he has executive powers, as head of government as well as head of state, but is dependent on majority support in the legislature. A former education officer, Tito had been a member of parliament for seven years before becoming president, leading the Christian Democrat opposition to the Gilbertese National Progressive Party governments of Ieremia Tabai and Teatao Teannaki.*

Tito was born on 25 August 1953 at Tabiteuea North, and in 1971 was offered a government scholarship to study at the University of the South Pacific, Suva, Fiji. He studied there for seven years, leaving in 1977 with a science degree and a graduate certificate of education. In 1976 he became president of the USP students' association, and from 1977 to 1979 was the student coordinator. After returning to Kiribati in 1980 he entered the ministry of education as a scholarship officer, and in 1982 was offered a 30-day study tour of the USA intended for future leaders. In 1983 he became senior education officer in Kiribati, a post which he held until 1987. A keen soccer player, he also chaired the Kiribati Football Association from 1980 to 1994.

In 1987 Teburoro Tito was elected as a member of the *Maneaba ni Maungatabu* (parliament) for the constituency of South Tarawa. He was leader of the opposition until 1990 and its deputy leader until 1994. He was also a member of the parliamentary public accounts committee from 1987 to 1990, and sat on the Commonwealth Parliamentary Association executive committee for the Australia-Pacific region in 1988/89, attending numerous conferences and meetings abroad. In 1994, having been nominated for the presidency alongside three other candidates, he won a landslide victory in the national presidential elections, in the wake of a constitutional crisis and claims of misconduct by the outgoing government.

Teburoro Tito is married to Nei Keina Tito, and they have one child.

Kim Jong Il

Kim Jong Il's presumed leadership role in North Korea, following the death of his father Kim Il Sung in July 1994, was not reflected in his formal assumption of top posts until October 1997. In that month he became general secretary of the ruling communist party, the Korean Workers' Party (KWP). As of the end of 1997, however, the state presidency remained vacant. According to the 1972 constitution the president is elected normally for a four-year term by a plenary session of the Supreme People's Assembly, but no plenary has been held since Kim Il Sung's death. The head of government is, formally, a premier who is also elected by the Assembly, and this role is currently being filled on an acting basis by Kim Yong Nam.

Kim Jong Il, the eldest son of Kim Il Sung, was born on 15 February 1942. There are two versions of where this took place. The North Korean official version is that he was born in an anti-Japanese guerrilla camp at Mt Paektu in North Korea (the site of which is now visited as part of his cult of personality), and grew up lonely because of his father's frequent absences owing to the duties of political leadership. Others say he was born at a Soviet army camp in Vyatsk in the vicinity of Khabarovsk, the far eastern region of the ex-Soviet Union, where his father was being groomed by the Soviet military to set up and lead a communist party in Korea.

Kim Jong Il is said to have attended several different schools, including two in China where he was taken for safety during the Korean war. He graduated from Namsan Senior High School in 1960. He learned to fly in East Germany, graduated from Kim Il Sung University in Pyongyang in 1964 after studying political and economic sciences, and entered politics after spending some time as a guidance worker.

His rise was predictably rapid as he was groomed for the succession by his father, who was venerated in the North Korean state and party system as the Great Leader. Starting as his father's personal secretary, he moved on to the propaganda and agitation department and the party headquarters, was made deputy director of culture and art, and secretary for organisation and propaganda in 1973. He was officially designated heir to Kim Il Sung in 1974 when he was put in charge of party operations against South Korea.

In 1975 Kim Jong Il acquired the title "Dear Leader". This remains the best known of his epithets abroad (where he also has a reputation as a playboy), although North Koreans have been encouraged successively to regard him as Guiding Leader (1983), Great Guiding Leader (1986), Unprecedented Great Man (1994) and latterly Outstanding Leader.

In October 1980, after the conclusion of what was believed to have been a power struggle over the succession, Kim Jong Il's position was confirmed by his election to a new presidium of the KWP politburo, the innermost leadership circle. He also joined the party secretariat (headed by his father as general secretary) and the military commission, although it was generally believed that he could not rely on the strength of his support within the armed forces. It was announced for the first time in 1984 that he was to succeed his father as president. In confusingly vague terminology, he was named in 1991 as leader of the party (and supreme commander of the armed forces, with the rank of marshal).

During the 1980s in particular, Kim Jong Il was linked directly with a number of acts of state-sponsored terrorism, notably the bombing in 1983 which killed 17 members of a top-level South Korean government delegation in Burma, and the November 1987 bombing of a Korean Airlines plane. There was speculation at this time about his health and stability, and suggestions that Kim Il Sung was displeased by unpredictable actions which he had not himself approved.

When Kim Il Sung died in July 1994, the expectation of a dynastic succession was apparently confirmed by the announcement that Kim Jong Il was taking over all his functions. However, there were no formal appointments (until he became party general secretary in October 1997) and his public appearances were unexpectedly infrequent. This encouraged the suggestion that he was ill and that a power struggle was under way, masked by the official explanation that posts were not being filled formally out of respect and mourning for Kim Il Sung.

Kim Jong Il has latterly begun encouraging the notion of "Red Flag ideology", a so far unspecified development of the "juche ideology" first formulated in the 1950s, which emphasises national self-reliance and the special role of the leadership, and which is defined in the constitution as the guiding principle of all party actions.

Kim Jong Il married Kim Yong Suk in 1973, and they have one son and two daughters. He is also believed to have one daughter by a previous marriage and a son by a former mistress, Sung Hye Rim; her reported presence in Europe in 1996 contributed to press speculation in 1996 about the impact of defections on the North Korean ruling élite.

Kim Dae Jung

Kim Dae Jung was elected president of South Korea on 18 December 1997, to take office formally in February 1998 for a five-year non-renewable term. It was the fourth time that veteran opposition leader Kim had contested the presidential elections in a 40-year political career, much of which he had spent in prison, in exile or under house arrest. The executive president is head of state and forms and leads the government, appointing the members of the state council, although formally the prime minister is designated head of government.

Kim Dae Jung was born in southwest Korea at Mokpo, near Kwangju in the Cholla region, on 3 December 1925 (or by some accounts one or even two years earlier). Raised as a strict Catholic, he excelled at school, winning entry to the local school of commerce, but his education was interrupted by the Second World War. The ending of 40 years of Japanese rule in 1945 brought *de facto* partition, Soviet forces having liberated the north and US troops the south. When the Republic of Korea was declared in 1948, Kim was running the local newspaper in Mokpo.

He fought in the Korean war (1950–53), was captured by the forces of the communist north, and upon his release began a political career, managing on his fifth attempt in 1960 to win election to the National Assembly. The legislature was abolished after Gen. Park's military coup in 1961, but elections held in 1963 and 1967 saw Kim again elected and, as a gifted orator, becoming spokesman for the opposition to Park's authoritarian regime. During this period he was also attending Kyung-Hee University Business School from 1964 and reading economics at the graduate school there in 1970.

For the 1971 presidential elections Kim was chosen as the candidate of the left-of-centre opposition New Democratic Party (NDP), with a support base among blue-collar workers and students augmented by Kim's personal popularity in his native Cholla region. Despite the Park government's attempts to discredit him as a communist, and a car accident often seen as the first of several assassination attempts against him, he sustained an unexpectedly strong challenge, obtaining 45 per cent of the vote. Refusing an ultimatum to join Park's party, he fled instead to Japan, but in 1973 was abducted from Tokyo (allegedly in a CIA-backed secret service operation) and returned to Seoul. He was imprisoned from 1976 to 1978 for his criticisms of the Park regime.

The May 1980 Kwangju rising, brutally crushed by the army, led to Kim's arrest on charges of plotting to overthrow the government. A death sentence passed on him in September was commuted to life imprisonment as a result of international pressure, and later reduced to 20 years, but in December 1982, due to his ill health, Kim was released in a general amnesty and allowed to travel to the USA for medical treatment.

While abroad, Kim Dae Jung issued a joint declaration with the other main opposition leader Kim Young Sam committing themselves to work together to end the military regime, now led by President Chun Doo Hwan. He was placed under house arrest when he returned to Seoul in 1985 ahead of legislative elections, in which his supporters performed strongly. A merger with Kim Young Sam's party in April 1987 was reversed, however, just one month before the presidential elections which the regime had unexpectedly agreed to hold by direct ballot that December. This debilitating division in the opposition let Chun's successor Roh Tae Woo retain power; Kim Dae Jung, as leader of his new Party for Peace and Democracy (PPD), polled almost 27 per cent of the vote and finished third, just behind Kim Young Sam.

In 1989, in the latest of many attempts to portray him as "soft" towards the communist north, Kim was indicted over talks between a PPD representative and the North Korean government. The following year the ruling party achieved a dramatic political coup by absorbing two former opposition groups, co-opting Kim Young Sam on the understanding that he would succeed Roh as the first government-backed civilian candidate for the presidency in 1992. In that election Kim Dae Jung, having helped create a new Democratic Party in 1991 in an effort to rally the remaining opposition, came second behind Kim Young Sam with 34 per cent of the vote.

Although Kim Dae Jung retired from the political arena in 1993, the growing disillusionment with Kim Young Sam's government encouraged him back in mid-1995. His National Congress for New Politics (NCNP), despite attracting defectors from the Democratic Party, performed unexpectedly poorly in legislative elections in April 1996, when Kim himself failed to win a seat.

In the run-up to the 1997 presidential elections, the NCNP formed an alliance with the United Liberal Democrats, who had split off from the ruling party in 1995. Kim became their joint candidate, and in a closely contested campaign he emerged as the ultimate winner. His 40.3 per cent of the vote in the 18 December poll put him just ahead of the ruling New Korea Party's candidate, Lee Hoi Chang, who was damaged by a third candidate splitting the ruling party vote. Kim's victory, the first ever by an opposition candidate, was greeted with particular jubilation in Seoul and in Kwangju in his native Cholla, as tributes poured in to his character and political rectitude. His promises on the release of political prisoners were followed up with a wide-ranging amnesty which included ex-presidents Chun and Roh, who had both persecuted Kim while in power, and were serving long prison terms for corruption and in Chun's case for instigating the 1980 Kwangju massacre.

The election had been fought in the context of a major crisis in the South Korean economy, and it was agreed that Kim Dae Jung should work closely with incumbent president Kim Young Sam to direct policy even before his official inauguration on 25 February 1998. Kim Dae Jung thereupon confirmed that he would respect the terms being demanded by the International Monetary Fund for a massive infusion of vital credits, and continue the current Korean peninsula peace talks, while maintaining a strong "non-political" army and security co-operation with the USA.

Kim Dae Jung is married to Lee Hee Ho.

Shaikh **Jabir** al-Sabah

Shaikh Jabir became amir of Kuwait on 31 December 1977, succeeding his uncle Shaikh Sabah. He is the 13th amir chosen from within the al-Sabah family, the Sunni Muslim ruling dynasty since 1756. The amir rules through an appointed cabinet, or council of ministers, which is headed by the prime minister. Since 1992 Shaikh Jabir has agreed to include some opposition National Assembly members in his cabinet, previously made up entirely of members of the royal family.

Shaikh Jabir al-Ahmad al-Jabir al-Sabah was born in 1928, educated at the Mubarkiah, Ahmadiah, and Shaquiah schools, and tutored privately in English, religion and the sciences. He started his public life in 1949 as chief of public security in the oilfields area, a post he held until 1959, when he was made head of the finance department. After Kuwait gained its independence in 1961, the finance department became the ministry of finance and economy, and Shaikh Jabir was appointed its first minister. In 1965 he was appointed prime minister, and on 31 May 1966 he was elected crown prince by the National Assembly. Proclaimed amir of Kuwait on 31 December 1977, he was unanimously given the pledge of allegiance on 1 January 1978.

Since 1986 he has been a member of the board of directors of the Kuwait Investment Authority, and since 1987 a member of the higher planning council. Since 1989 he has been chairman of the committee for measures to activate the economy.

When Kuwait was invaded by Iraq in August 1990 the al-Sabah family went into exile, returning on 14 March 1991 after the country had been liberated and Iraqi forces defeated by a US-led alliance. On 20 April the first cabinet since the liberation of Kuwait was announced by amiri decree, and on 9 July the amir opened the second session of the National Council, relaying his thanks to those countries which had come to Kuwait's aid. In response to pressure for a measure of democratisation, elections were held (on a non-party basis) in October 1992 to the National Assembly, which had been in abeyance since Shaikh Jabir dissolved the previous assembly in 1986. Some opposition assembly members were then brought in to the council of ministers.

Nouhak Phoumsavanh

Nouhak Phoumsavanh has been president of Laos and chairman of the People's Supreme Council since November 1992. He is now serving a second five-year term, having been re-elected by the Supreme People's Assembly in December 1997. A long-standing member of the politburo of the Lao People's Revolutionary Party (LPRP), he is one of the few remaining influential members of the older generation of pro-Vietnam Marxists, particularly since the death in 1995 of "Red Prince" Souphanouvong. The nominal powers of the state presidency under the 1991 single-party constitution are extensive and include the appointment of the council of ministers and the prime minister. However, the separation of the party and state presidency since 1992, the appointment of the prime minister as party president at that time, and the omission of Nouhak Phoumsavanh from the party politburo since 1996, have diminished his real political significance.

Born on 9 April 1914 in Phalouka, in the Moukdahane district of Savannakhet province, Nouhak Phoumsavanh left school to work as a bus and truck driver, establishing his own business in 1941. He became involved in politics in the 1940s during growing resistance to French colonial rule. Liaising with members of the Vietminh – the Vietnamese communist independence movement – he joined their cause, going on to help form with Prince Souphanouvong in 1950 the "Pathet Lao" (Lao state), the military arm of the communist, anti-French and anti-monarchist Lao Patriotic Front. Following Lao independence in 1953, he attended the 1954 Geneva Conference on Indochina as a Pathet Lao representative with the Vietminh delegation, and then helped direct the LPRP's forerunner, the People's Party of Laos.

A deputy in the National Assembly from 1957, he was arrested in 1959 for his Patriotic Front activities, but escaped the following year. He was a member of the LPRP from the time of its formation in 1972, working for the establishment of a single-party state in 1975 after the Front's victory in the protracted civil war and the abolition of the monarchy.

Nouhak Phoumsavanh was vice-chair of the council of ministers of the Lao People's Democratic Republic from its inception until 1990, and also finance minister from 1975 to 1980. In 1989 he became president of the Supreme People's Assembly, and in the same year chaired the drafting committee on the new constitution, which took effect in 1991 and enshrined the LPRP's leading role as sole party.

On the death in 1992 of the long-term LPRP leader and incumbent state president Kaysone Phomvihane, Nouhak Phoumsavanh as the most senior LPRP politburo member was elected to succeed him as state president by a special session of the Supreme People's Assembly on 25 November. The party presidency, however, went to the prime minister Gen. Khamtay Siphandone.

Nouhak Phoumsavanh's presidency was affirmed by the newly elected National Assembly in February 1993, and he was re-elected for a further term in December 1997, despite having been dropped from the LPRP politburo at the sixth party congress in March 1996 and relegated to an advisory board of old revolutionaries.

Guntis **Ulmanis**

Guntis Ulmanis has been president of Latvia since 1993 and was re-elected for a second three-year term in June 1996. The president is elected by the Saeima *(unicameral parliament) and the post is primarily a ceremonial one. Ulmanis is now honorary chairman of the conservative Latvian Peasants' Union (LZS), which he joined in 1992. During Soviet rule he had been a member of the communist party and worked as an administrator in Riga, the capital, as well as lecturing in economics.*

Guntis Ulmanis was born in Riga on 13 September 1939. His great uncle, Karlis Ulmanis, was Latvian president during the period of Latvian independence between the two world wars. When the Soviet Union annexed Latvia and the other Baltic states in 1940, the infant Guntis was taken with his family into exile in Siberia. Returning in 1946, they only narrowly avoided a second deportation in 1949.

Ulmanis received his secondary education at Pumpuri school in Jurmala, and graduated in 1963 with a degree in economics from the Latvian State University, spending the next two years doing military service in the Soviet army. He joined the communist party in 1965 but did not hold party office. He worked for the Riga Tramways and Trolleybus Board from 1965 until 1970. From 1970 to 1980 he lectured in economics at the Latvian State University and from 1971 was also employed as an economist for Riga District Communal Services, where he remained (as director) until 1992. He was appointed to the executive board of the Bank of Latvia in 1993.

Ulmanis left the communist party in 1989, two years before Latvia's renewed declaration of independence in August 1991, and joined the LZS in 1992. In the parliamentary elections of June 1993, the first free elections for 60 years, Ulmanis was elected as an LZS deputy to the *Saeima*. One month later, on 7 July, the *Saeima* elected him as state president, as a compromise candidate on a third round of voting.

On 18 June 1996 Ulmanis was elected for a second three-year term of office, the last to which he can be elected under the constitution. He polled 53 out of 100 votes in the *Saeima*, against 25 for his rival, parliamentary speaker Ilga Kreituse.

As president, Ulmanis has pledged to maintain internal stability, to improve relations between the different ethnic groups within Latvia, including in particular the Russian minority which makes up one-third of the population, and to improve the education system. He has also emphasised the importance of foreign policy, especially Latvia's full membership of international organisations such as the European Union and NATO and the importance of improving relations with neighbouring Russia.

Guntis Ulmanis is married to Aina Ulmanis, and they have a daughter and a son.

Elias **Hrawi**

Elias Hrawi has been president of Lebanon since 1989. A Maronite Christian businessman and Assembly deputy from 1972 onwards, he was first elected as president for a six-year term after the assassination of the just-elected René Mouawad. Hrawi had his term extended by three years in 1995. The Lebanese constitution and the 1943 national pact created a division of powers among the institutions of state, so that the president is traditionally drawn from the Maronite Christian community, while the prime minister is traditionally a Sunni Muslim, responsible to a National Assembly with a Shi'ite Muslim speaker. The Taïf accord of 1989 greatly reduced the president's executive powers, correspondingly strengthening the role of the prime minister as head of government.

Elias Hrawi was born in 1926 in Hawch al-Umara, Zahlé, into a land-owning family. He graduated in commerce from the Beirut Jesuit University, and by the 1960s he owned a successful food manufacturing factory in the Beqaa Valley. Hrawi founded the first agriculture co-operative in 1970, becoming president of the Confederation of Co-operatives the next year. In 1974 he headed the Beqaa sugar beet co-operatives and the Beqaa Federation of Agricultural Co-operatives. In the civil war Hrawi's plant was destroyed, but he successfully switched his business to the import of oil.

Hrawi was first elected to the National Assembly in 1972, following in the steps of his two brothers. A series of projects to build highways, roads and bridges linking the Lebanese regions was initiated by him as minister of public works between 1980 and 1982. Unlike some Maronite Christian leaders, he maintained good relations with Syria, and was involved in the negotiation of the Taïf agreement of 1989, the first step in a national reconciliation process to end the protracted civil war. At the National Assembly session when this agreement was ratified on 5 November, he stood for the presidency but was eliminated on the first round, receiving only five votes. The assassination of newly elected President Mouawad 17 days later made necessary a fresh vote on 24 November, in which Hrawi was chosen overwhelmingly. As president he concluded a treaty with Syria in 1991 giving formal expression to the significant Syrian influence, and military involvement, which has helped end some 15 years of inter-faction conflict.

An exceptional three-year extension of Hrawi's mandate was agreed, again overwhelmingly, by the Assembly on 17 October 1995. Prime minister Rafiq al-Hariri had been pressing for such an extension to provide the necessary institutional stability for the implementation of his ambitious economic reconstruction plans.

Hrawi's wife is a Palestinian from Jerusalem. They have three sons and two daughters.

King **Letsie III**

King Letsie David Mohato III replaced his father, King Moshoeshoe II, as head of state of Lesotho, after Moshoeshoe's death in a car crash in February 1996. Letsie had already ruled for four years in the early 1990s, but had then abdicated to allow the return of the throne to his father, who had been head of state from the time of Lesotho's full independence within the Commonwealth in 1966 until he was forced out in 1990.

Born in Morija on 17 July 1963, and named Prince Mohato David Seeiso, the future King Letsie went to Iketsetseng private primary school in Maseru in 1968 and then to primary and secondary school in the UK, returning to Lesotho for vacations and spending much time at his father's cattle posts in the mountains. He attended the National University of Lesotho, graduating in 1984 with a degree in law. He then continued his studies at the universities of Bristol, Cambridge and London, studying English law, development and agricultural economics.

He became principal chief of Matsieng in 1989, and was installed by the military government as King Letsie in November 1990 following the dethronement of his father. Moshoeshoe had been effectively ousted in March, since when he had been ostensibly on sabbatical leave in the UK. Two years later, when Moshoeshoe returned to Lesotho, Letsie offered to step down in his favour, but this was opposed by the ruling military council. In a compromise formula Moshoeshoe was accorded the status of head of the royal family, but with Letsie still designated as monarch.

A return to civilian rule, and the holding of elections in March 1993, brought a Basotho Congress Party government to power under Ntsu Mokhehle. Amid unrest and continuing coup rumours, Letsie attempted a decisive intervention, announcing on 17 August 1994 that he had removed the Mokhehle government and was calling fresh elections. He was immediately challenged by the mobilisation of a large protest demonstration, precipitating a crisis which was eventually resolved only with mediation by Botswana, Zimbabwe and South Africa. Letsie agreed in September to reinstate Mokhehle and to abdicate in favour of his father. The necessary legislation was approved and Moshoeshoe returned to the throne on 25 January 1995, with Letsie reverting to the status of crown prince. However, just under a year later Moshoeshoe was killed in a car crash. Letsie succeeded to the throne on 7 February 1996, and his coronation took place on 31 October 1997.

Charles **Taylor**

Charles Taylor, who first rose to prominence as the leader of a guerrilla insurgency against the regime of Samuel Doe in 1989, was elected president of Liberia in July 1997, having seized power in 1990 but then been embroiled in a protracted civil war. As president he is both head of state and head of government.

Charles Taylor (who subsequently adopted the middle name Ghankay) was born in 1948, a descendant of the freed American slaves who first established Liberia in 1847 and ruled the country as an unchallenged élite until 1980. He studied economics in the USA. In 1979 President Tolbert appointed him director of the state General Services Agency, but Taylor switched allegiance in April 1980 to support Samuel Kanyon Doe in the bloody coup by which the latter seized power. However, Taylor later fled to the USA, amid allegations that he had embezzled government funds, and was arrested there in May 1984. He later escaped from custody and returned to Africa.

In late December 1989 Taylor led an incursion of the National Patriotic Forces of Liberia (NPFL) from neighbouring Côte d'Ivoire into Nimba province with the aim of overthrowing Doe. Advancing south and west, he seized control of the capital Monrovia in July 1990, deposed and killed Doe in September and declared himself president. During the civil war which followed Taylor was seen as an ally of Libya by the USA and was opposed by the Nigerian government, which had supported the Doe regime. An ECOMOG peacekeeping force of the Economic Community of West African States (ECOWAS) was dispatched to Liberia and in 1992 ECOMOG drove Taylor out of the diamond-rich western part of Liberia, but failed in an attempt to gain control of Monrovia later that year.

Fighting between different factions continued while various parties sought unsuccessfully to secure a peace agreement that would hold. Eventually an ECOWAS summit, chaired by Nigerian president Gen. Sani Abacha, was convened in Nigeria in July 1996 and on 26 August Taylor was among those signing a renewed peace accord. This provided amongst other things for a new six-member transitional council of state of which Taylor was a member.

Legislative and presidential elections were eventually held on 19 July 1997. Taylor, who owns a radio station and three newspapers, successfully dominated the election campaign and his National Patriotic Party secured 49 out of the 64 seats in the House of Representatives. In the presidential election he won over 70 per cent of the vote, his closest rival being Ellen Johnson-Sirleaf who secured just over 9 per cent.

Taylor was sworn in as president on 3 August 1997, when he pledged to set up commissions to protect human rights and assist reconciliation, and declared his priorities to be agriculture, health and education.

Col. Moamer al **Kadhafi**

Col. Moamer al Kadhafi, "Leader of the Revolution'" in Libya, has been in power since September 1969 when he led a coup to overthrow the conservative regime of King Idris. Originally president of the Revolutionary Command Council, he now holds no formal post but is the dominant political figure of the regime. He mounted his coup as leader of a Free Officers' Movement among junior officers, and was a pan-Arabist influenced by President Nasser, who at that time was still in power in neighbouring Egypt. Kadhafi's regime has virulently opposed foreign influences in Libya and any manifestation of what he denounces as Western imperialism and Zionism. His support for a range of foreign liberation movements and anti-government and terrorist groups has attracted particularly strong condemnation from the USA and has encouraged many states to treat Libya as an international pariah. Domestically, Kadhafi is an Islamic reformist as opposed to a fundamentalist, and his regime has sought to develop a new kind of model for participative democracy, while retaining the apparatus for strict control of any dissident activity.

Moamer al Kadhafi was born in the Sirte region in 1942, one of three children in a bedouin family. He attended a Koranic elementary school and the high school at Sebha, where his early involvement in politics led to his expulsion. He used a false birth certificate to enroll in another school in Misrata, then studied history and politics at university in Benghazi. In 1963, although known as a political activist and pan-Arabist, he was nevertheless accepted into the Royal Libyan Military Academy in Benghazi. Graduating in 1965, he was commissioned as an officer in the signals corps in Benghazi. A four-month training course in Beaconsfield, England, increased his knowledge of military signalling and armoured vehicle gunnery and his dislike of the British.

Within the armed forces Kadhafi built up his clandestine Free Officers' Movement, the group that he would lead in a bloodless coup in 1969. The intended coup date, twice deferred, was finally set for the early morning of 1 September. Kadhafi was already known to Western intelligence agencies and there has been speculation that they must have known something of his plans. When the date came the preparations worked smoothly and efficiently, and military and governmental installations in Benghazi and Tripoli were taken over with little bloodshed. Kadhafi made his first broadcast as head of the new regime within a few hours, and King Idris went into exile. Kadhafi's takeover reportedly pre-empted plans by more senior officers for a coup of their own.

Kadhafi became commander-in-chief of the armed forces, set up a Revolutionary Command

Council with himself as president, and, from 1970 to 1972, also held the posts of prime minister and minister for defence. In January 1976 he took the higher military rank of major-general but continued to use the title of colonel. In 1979 he relinquished all official positions, styling himself thereafter "Leader of the Revolution".

Economic, social and political changes after the coup, based on Kadhafi's brand of "natural socialism", included attempts to redistribute the country's oil wealth more equitably, and nationalisation of foreign-owned banks, insurance companies, factories and oil companies. (Some liberalisation of the economy did begin in the late 1980s, as did the development of steel manufacturing to reduce the country's near-total dependence on oil revenue.) Wage labour was declared to be abolished and workers were instead deemed to be partners in industrial ventures.

Instead of building a single-party state through mass membership of the Arab Socialist Union, Kadhafi instead embarked on the more idiosyncratic project of creating a structure for popular participation through a system of basic people's congresses and committees, with the parliament or General People's Congress at the centre. This was embodied in the 1977 constitution of what was henceforth known officially as the Socialist People's Libyan Arab Jamahiriya. The *Green Book*, published in three volumes between 1976 and 1979, contains Kadhafi's thoughts on what he describes as his "third universal theory" spanning socialism, Islam, development and political systems.

Kadhafi's pan-Arabist aspirations, and his inclination to seek solidarity and involvement with regimes elsewhere which he identified as progressive, led him into several declarations of union between Libya and other Arab and African states. Pan-Arabism also underlay his initial enthusiasm for the Arab Maghreb Union, formed in 1989 with Algeria, Mauritania, Morocco and Tunisia. His relations with neighbouring Egypt in particular have been tense, while his commitment to the Palestinian cause, something of an article of faith, has involved supporting "rejectionist" factions and criticising the mainstream Palestine Liberation Organization's "sell-outs" to Israel.

Palestinian groups are only some among many causes to receive his backing, others including the British miners' union in its long strike in 1995, the Irish Republican Army, and leftist radicals in many African countries. Kadhafi has himself survived a number of assassination attempts and attempted coups, and has withstood (and bolstered his own defiant image as a result of) actions to "punish" his regime on more than one occasion. The UK broke off diplomatic relations in 1984 over the shooting of a woman police officer at the Libyan embassy in London, and in 1986 the USA launched an air strike on Tripoli and Benghazi after a bomb attack on a West Berlin night club frequented by US servicemen. The bomb explosion on a Pan Am airliner over Lockerbie in Scotland in December 1988 was also laid at Kadhafi's door, leading to a long dispute about the extradition of suspects from Libya and the imposition of UN sanctions. More recently Kadhafi has kept a lower profile, notably remaining relatively silent during the Gulf war in 1991.

Col. Moamer al Kadhafi is married to Safiya Kadhafi. They have seven children, and their family also includes a number of adopted children, one of whom was killed in the US air strike against Tripoli in April 1986. Kadhafi has a reclusive aspect in his character and has been prone to spending long periods in a tent out in the desert.

Prince **Hans Adam II**

Prince Hans Adam II has been Reigning Prince of Liechtenstein since November 1989, succeeding formally upon the death of his father Prince Franz Josef II. An economics graduate with a business management background, he had already exercised the official powers of head of state, but without the title, since August 1984. Liechtenstein is a constitutional monarchy, and as head of state the monarch is described as exercising legislative authority jointly with parliament; the head of government is the prime minister, whom the monarch must appoint from the majority party in parliament.

Hans Adam von und zu Liechtenstein II was born on 14 February 1945. He went to the Schottengymnasium in Vienna, Austria, and completed his education in Switzerland, obtaining a diploma in national economy from the University of St Gallen in 1969. He worked briefly for a bank in London, before moving on to act as manager of the Prince of Liechtenstein Foundation from 1970 to 1981, during which time he was entrusted with the management and administration of the Royal House's property.

On 26 August 1984 Hans Adam's elderly father appointed him hereditary prince and passed all his official duties over to him as the representative of the head of state. When Franz Josef died on 13 November 1989 Hans Adam became head of state in his own right.

Prince Hans Adam married Countess Marie Kinsky von Wchinitz und Tettau in 1967. They have three sons and one daughter, their eldest son and heir apparent being Prince Alois, born in 1968.

Valdus **Adamkus**

Valdus Adamkus was elected president of Lithuania in a two-round election in December 1997 and January 1998, to take office for a five-year term in March 1998. The president's duties are mainly ceremonial but he is empowered to nominate the prime minister, to send legislation back to parliament for amendment, and represent the country abroad. Adamkus is a member of the conservative Homeland Union of Lithuania, the third largest party in parliament, but had only just taken up residence in Lithuania at the time of the election, having spent most of his adult life in the USA where he worked in the Environmental Protection Agency (EPA).

Adamkus was born in 1926 in Lithuania. As a teenager he joined the nationalist resistance, opposing both his country's forcible absorption into the Soviet Union in 1940, and its subsequent wartime occupation by Nazi Germany. During the Nazi occupation he ran an underground newspaper, but as Soviet troops advanced once again from the east he joined an anti-Soviet detachment supplied by the Nazis which fought for Lithuanian independence. When the Red Army took control of the country in 1944, he left Lithuania and fled to Germany.

Five years later he emigrated to the USA, where he got a job teaching Lithuanian, German, Polish and Russian at a US army school in Kansas. He then moved to Chicago (where there is the largest Lithuanian community outside Lithuania), completing a degree in civil engineering at the Illinois Institute of Technology. He joined the Republican Party and campaigned to prevent US recognition of the Soviet annexation of Lithuania, but had to cease party political activity when he started working for the US Environmental Protection Agency (EPA) in 1971. The following year he was on an EPA delegation to Lithuania, his first of a number of such visits to eastern Europe. In 1981 he was promoted to EPA district administrator for the mid-west region.

During his time in the USA, Adamkus was a leading member of the Lithuanian–American literary group *Santara-Sviesa*. In 1991, after Lithuania had gained independence from the Soviet Union, he applied for Lithuanian citizenship, and in 1994 he registered as a resident of the town of Siauliai.

In October 1997 he gave up his job at the EPA and returned permanently to Lithuania, having been chosen in July as presidential candidate for the Homeland Union. During the three-month campaign Adamkus toured much of the country, seeking to demonstrate that he had sufficient experience of Lithuanian affairs. He received greatest support outside Vilnius, the capital, where academics disliked his anglicised language and he was criticised for being too pro-Western, giving rise to concerns that he would upset relations with neighbouring Russia.

The first round of voting, contested by seven candidates on 21 December 1997, saw Adamkus take second place with 29 per cent of the vote, against 45 per cent for Arturas Paulauskas, who was backed by the former communist party and by the outgoing president, Algirdas Brazauskas. In the run-off on 4 January 1998, Adamkus secured a narrow victory with just 50.6 per cent of the vote. Paulauskas claimed that irregularities had occurred but the electoral commission was satisfied. As required by Lithuanian law, Adamkus immediately began the procedure to give up his US citizenship.

Valdus Adamkus is married to Alma Adamkus and they do not have any children.

Grand Duke **Jean**

Grand Duke Jean of Luxembourg succeeded to the throne on 12 November 1964, after the abdication of his mother Grand Duchess Charlotte. He had been heir apparent since 1939, and served with the British army during the Second World War after completing his education in Canada. As head of state the grand duke is a constitutional monarch, and executive authority is exercised, nominally on his behalf, by the prime minister as head of government responsible to parliament.

Jean of Luxembourg was born at Colmar Berg, Luxembourg, on 5 January 1921. Having spent most of his childhood at the Chateau de Colmar Berg, he completed his secondary education in Luxembourg and at Ampleforth College in Yorkshire, England. In 1939, aged 18, he became heir apparent to the crown of the grand duchy of Luxembourg, and received the titles of hereditary Grand Duke of Luxembourg, hereditary Prince of Nassau, and Prince of Bourbon Parma.

In 1940, following the outbreak of the Second World War, the ducal family left Luxembourg for France and then Spain. Jean continued his studies at the University of Quebec, Canada, reading law and political science. In the USA in 1941 he made a series of appeals for support for the "oppressed peoples" of Europe, delivering lectures in the mid-west and in New York. After spells in Washington and Brazil, he enrolled with the British army in 1942, rising to the position of colonel of the Irish guards. He also acted as president of the "Luxembourg Relief Fund in Great Britain", until he returned to Luxembourg in 1944.

Jean was a member of the Luxembourg state council from 1951 to 1961, and in April 1961 was appointed *Lieutenant-Représentant* of the grand duchess. On ascending the throne in 1964 he was also made general of the Luxembourg army.

Jean of Luxembourg married Princess Josephine-Charlotte of Belgium in April 1953. Their son Prince Henri is heir apparent.

Kiro **Gligorov**

Kiro Gligorov has been president of Macedonia since its declaration of independence in January 1991. (The country is recognised by the UN as the Former Yugoslav Republic of Macedonia, or FYRM, although it is designated under its own November 1991 constitution as the Republic of Macedonia.) Gligorov was returned to power for a five-year term in the country's first direct presidential elections in October 1994. A veteran Titoist partisan and Yugoslav politician, and leader of the former communist party now renamed the Social Democratic Alliance of Macedonia (SDSM), he was seriously wounded in an assassination attempt in October 1995. Despite his age and injuries, he remains the country's pre-eminent political figure, although the head of government is the prime minister responsible to parliament.

Gligorov was born on 3 May 1917, in Stip, Macedonia, in a family with a history of activity in the nationalist movement against Ottoman rule. Educated at the Skopje gymnasium and at the faculty of law, Belgrade University, he participated in the students' movement in Belgrade and completed his studies in 1938.

During the Second World War, Gligorov joined Tito's partisans in 1941, and was a member of the Anti-Fascist Assembly of the National Liberation Movement of Macedonia (ASNOM) and its all-Yugoslav counterpart AVNOJ. In the government of the People's Federal Republic of Yugoslavia set up at the end of the war he was an assistant general secretary for two years (1945–47), then went on to be professor of economics at Belgrade University (1948–49). Returning to government work, he specialised in finance and economic planning, and rose to be federal minister of finance (1962–67), then a vice-president of the federal executive council (federal government). During this time he led the team which initiated market-based economic reforms in Yugoslavia, an experiment unique in the socialist world. This gave him experience which was later to prove valuable in reorienting the Macedonian economy in the 1990s, but the suspension of the Yugoslav reform programme in the 1970s led to a hiatus in Gligorov's political career. He was a member of the executive bureau of the League of Communists of Yugoslavia from 1969 to 1974, while also sitting on the Yugoslav collective presidency in 1971/72, and then became president of the Yugoslav parliament for four years, but after 1978 he took no further part in political life until the late 1980s.

Brought back to join a government team responsible for tackling Yugoslavia's financial crisis and opening up the economy to market-oriented reforms, Gligorov became increasing involved with developments in Macedonia from 1989 onwards. Nationalists, reform communists and Albanian groups produced a three-way split when multiparty legislative elections were held there in late 1980. The new assembly issued a declaration of Macedonian sovereignty on 25 January 1991 (asserting a right of secession from Yugoslavia which was endorsed by a subsequent referendum and began gaining international recognition from early 1992 onwards). The assembly then turned to the veteran Gligorov as a compromise presidential candidate, electing him to office on 27 January 1991.

Gligorov successfully negotiated the removal of the Yugoslav national army from Macedonian territory in 1992, and prevented the outbreak of open conflict between rival nationalist and ethnic Albanian groups. International recognition was held up by Greek hostility to the country using the term Macedonia, and to its choice of national symbols which Greece claimed as part of its own heritage. Under the clumsy compromise name Former Yugoslav Republic of Macedonia, the new state eventually joined the United Nations in 1993, and by 1995 Greece relented at least to the extent of lifting sanctions.

Gligorov was re-elected president in October 1994 for a five-year term, winning over 78 per cent of the vote in a poll marred by allegations of vote rigging. He survived an assassination attempt on 3 October 1995, in which two people died and six others were injured. Relations with neighbouring Bulgaria were soured after allegations from within the Macedonian government that Bulgarian agents might have been involved.

Kiro Gligorov is married to Nada Gligorov and they have one son and two daughters.

Didier **Ratsiraka**

Didier Ratsiraka, who had been head of state from 1975 to 1993, returned to office as president for a five-year term in early 1997 after a narrow victory in elections the previous December. Trained as a naval officer, Ratsiraka had headed a single-party regime which progressively abandoned its socialist orientation, was eventually pressured into accepting democratic reforms, and lost a presidential election in 1993. He returned after three years' self-imposed exile in France to contest fresh elections after the incumbent president Albert Zafy had been impeached. The president is head of state, whereas the head of government is the prime minister, who is chosen by the president from among candidates nominated by parties in the National Assembly, and whom the president also has power to dismiss.

Ratsiraka was born in Vatomandry on 4 November 4 1936, and educated at the Saint Michel College in Antananarivo and the Lycée Henri IV in Paris. He then embarked upon a long period of military training in France, notably at the Ecole Supérieure de Guerre Navale in Paris. He gained experience in several naval postings in the 1960s, and from 1970 to 1972 he was the Malagasy military attaché in Paris.

Ratsiraka returned to Madagascar in 1972 to become minister for foreign affairs, instituting pro-Soviet and pro-Arab policies which undermined the close ties maintained with France since independence. Gaining the ascendancy in a military regime which was instituted in early 1975, Ratsiraka proclaimed himself president of the Supreme Council of the Revolution in June, and also prime minister and minister of defence. Elected president in a nationwide poll in December of the same year, he espoused radical socialist policies under a *de facto* single-party system.

In March 1976 Ratsiraka set up the Vanguard of the Malagasy Revolution Party (AREMA), which became the dominant party in a broader national front structure. A new constitution effectively outlawed political opposition. Beginning by nationalising the energy utilities and large-scale industries under a regime of Christian Marxism, he subsequently modified these policies as the country became increasingly dependent on the approval of the International Monetary Fund to secure foreign aid and investment.

Re-elected unopposed for seven-year terms in 1982 and 1989, Ratsiraka relinquished some of his executive powers in August 1991, in the face of an opposition campaign for the introduction of a pluralist system, and agreed to a transitional period in which the constitution would be altered. When a presidential election was eventually held in two rounds on 25 November 1992 and 10 February 1993, Ratsiraka was defeated by Albert Zafy, a professor of medicine, who took office in March 1993.

Ratsiraka spent several years in self-imposed exile in France, reorganising ARENA (which was formally renamed the Vanguard for Economic and Social Recovery, or ARES, with himself as secretary-general), and seizing the opportunity to return to Madagascar when Zafy was impeached by parliament in mid-1996 for unconstitutional behaviour. Renewed presidential elections were held in November/December 1996. Fifteen candidates contested the first-round poll, with Ratsiraka and Zafy going into a 29 December run-off. The final result was not announced until 31 January 1997, when the high constitutional court declared Ratsiraka the winner with 50.7 per cent of the vote, against Zafy's 49.3 per cent.

Since taking office on 9 February 1997 Ratsiraka has outlined plans to implement a market economy in Madagascar, while also promising to reduce poverty, and has undertaken to stand by the 1992 pluralist constitution.

Bakili **Muluzi**

Bakili Muluzi was elected president of Malawi in the country's first multiparty presidential and legislative elections held in May 1994. His election to the country's highest executive post, which combines the roles of head of state and head of government, marked the end of three decades of restrictive and personalised rule by Dr Hastings Kamuzu Banda. A rich Muslim businessman, who had been a government minister under Banda but left the sole and ruling Malawi Congress Party (MCP) in 1983, Muluzi stood against Banda as the candidate of the United Democratic Front (UDF). On 21 May 1994 he was inaugurated for a five-year term at a ceremony held in the Kamuzu stadium in Blantyre, the commercial capital of the country.

Muluzi was born on 17 March 1943, in Machinga, southern Malawi. He was educated at Thisted Technical School in Denmark from 1972 to 1973 and at Bolton College of Further Education in the UK in 1973, where he graduated with a diploma in the administration of technical education. On his return to Malawi later that year, he was appointed principal of Nasawa Technical College in Chiradzulu district.

Muluzi was active in the MCP as a regional party secretary from 1959, becoming secretary-general and administrative secretary in 1975, when he was elected to parliament for Machinga. He was appointed parliamentary secretary at the ministry of youth and culture in 1976, was minister of education from 1976 to 1977, and minister without portfolio between 1977 and 1982. However, in 1982 he was demoted to the post of minister of transport and communications. Fearing persecution by President Banda for gaining too much influence in the party, Muluzi resigned from the MCP in 1983.

Thereafter he worked for several years in a number of commercial jobs, as deputy head of the National Chamber of Commerce, and in the Road Transport Association. In 1992, as international aid was suspended because of Banda's poor human rights record, Muluzi formed the United Democratic Front (UDF), the first opposition group set up amid the growing pressure for democratic reforms. Facing widespread protests and international pressure, Banda agreed to allow a referendum on single-party rule, which produced a 63 per cent "no" vote when it eventually took place in June 1993.

On 17 May 1994 the first multiparty legislative and presidential elections were held. Muluzi was one of five presidential candidates and won 47.3 per cent of the vote, against 33.6 per cent for Banda. Muluzi's UDF, which had its power base in the populous south of the country, also secured the largest number of seats in parliament, subsequently forming a coalition government with the Alliance for Democracy (Aford).

Muluzi has placed a high priority on improving the protection of human rights; upon his election as president he immediately freed political prisoners and shut down three prisons which had reportedly been used as torture centres. He has also worked to reconcile divisions within his own UDF, Aford and the MCP, which have threatened to paralyse the parliament, where no party has an outright majority. In April 1997, the MCP agreed to end a ten-month boycott of parliament, while Muluzi said that he would introduce an amendment to remove flaws in the 1995 constitution and prevent such problems arising again.

Muluzi is married and has one son and one daughter.

Ja'afar ibni Abdul Rahman

Ja'afar ibni Abdul Rahman was elected in February 1994 as the tenth Yang di-Pertuan Agong *(supreme head of state) by the Conference of Rulers from among their own number, and was formally installed the following September for a five-year term. A UK-educated former diplomat and since 1967 the ruler of Negri Sembilan, he has also served two terms as Malaysia's deputy head of state. The elective monarch is the ceremonial head of state, political power residing with the prime minister as head of government.*

Tuanku Ja'afar ibni al-Marhum Tuanku Abdul Rahman was born on 19 July 1922 in the royal town of Klang, Selangor. His father Tuanku Abdul Rahman was ruler (*Yang di-Pertuan Besar*) of Negri Sembilan and was later elected as Malaya's first head of state in 1955 (but should not be confused with the country's first prime minister Tengku Abdul Rahman). Ja'afar's elder brother Munawir in turn became ruler of Negri Sembilan, but died in 1967, when Ja'afar succeeded him.

Ja'afar was educated at the Seri Menanti Malay School and then at the Malay College in Kuala Kangsar, but his subsequent studies at the Raffles College in Singapore were disrupted by the Second World War. During the Japanese occupation of what was then Malaya, Ja'afar worked at the land office in Seremban, and he afterwards became assistant district officer of Rembau, before obtaining a scholarship to study in England. He graduated in law from Nottingham University, and also enrolled for an economics degree at Balliol College in Oxford, and a course in economics and French at the London School of Economics, finally doing a one-year diplomatic service course in London before embarking on a diplomatic career. He was posted first to Washington D.C. and New York, then to London, where he rose to assistant high commissioner, and then successively to head the Malaysian missions in the United Arab Emirates, Nigeria and Ghana. His posting as ambassador to Japan in 1967 was never taken up because of his succession, in April 1967, as ruler of Negri Sembilan. Between that time and his own 1994 election as *Yang di-Pertuan Agong*, he was deputy head of state from 1979 to 1984 and from 1989 to 1994, and stood in on three occasions, in 1979, 1982 and 1993, when the head of state went overseas.

Ja'afar is a keen sportsman, having played tennis, squash, badminton and cricket competitively as a student, and takes a keen interest in the development of golf courses in his state.

Ja'afar Abdul Rahman married Ampuan Najihah Burhanuddin in 1943, and they have three sons and three daughters.

Maumoon Abdul **Gayoom**

Maumoon Abdul Gayoom, a former lecturer in Islamic studies, became president of the Maldives in November 1978 and has been re-elected on three occasions (in 1983, 1988 and 1993) for further five-year terms. The president is both head of state and head of government, but Gayoom's dominance in the family-based non-party political system was challenged by a coup attempt in 1988 and a bid by his brother-in-law Ilyas Ibrahim for nomination for the presidency in 1993; an educated younger generation is now pressing for increased freedoms.

Gayoom was born in the capital, Male, on 29 December 1937. Following early schooling in Male he went to Al-Azhar University in Cairo, where he graduated with a degree in Islamic studies and a diploma in education, going on to gain a master's degree in Islamic studies in 1966. He then embarked on an academic career, eventually becoming a lecturer in Islamic studies and philosophy at Abdullahi Bayero College, Ahmadu Bello University, Nigeria. He then taught at Aminiya School from 1971 to 1972.

On his return to the Maldives he became successively manager of the government's shipping department, director of the telecommunication department, special under-secretary in the office of the prime minister, deputy ambassador to Sri Lanka and under-secretary at the ministry of external affairs. In June 1976 he was appointed permanent representative at the United Nations. He then took on a cabinet post as minister of transport, holding this job until the 1978 presidential elections when long-serving President Ibrahim Nasir stood down. Nominated by the citizens' *Majlis* (parliament), Gayoom was endorsed by a 92.9 per cent vote in the popular ballot, and sworn in on 11 November 1978. His nomination for successive terms has usually been uncontested, although in 1993 Ilyas Ibrahim's rival candidacy attracted some support in the *Majlis*.

Gayoom took over the defence and national security portfolios in 1982, and since November 1993 he has also been minister of finance and of the treasury. His dependence on good relations with India was underlined when he had to be rescued by Indian intervention after a coup attempt in 1988. In the 1990s he has become better known internationally, along with Nauru's Kinza Clodumar, for drawing attention to the threat posed by global warming to small island states.

Gayoom was made a Knight Grand Cross of the Order of St Michael and St George in October 1997.

Maumoon Abdul Gayoom is married to Nasreena Ibrahim. They have two sons and twin daughters.

Alpha Oumar **Konaré**

Alpha Oumar Konaré was elected president of Mali in April 1992 in the country's first multiparty elections, and took office in June. He was re-elected for another five-year term in May 1997. A writer and educationalist, he was a government minister in the late 1970s, but in the 1980s became a leading opponent of the regime of Moussa Traoré, founding the Alliance for Democracy in Mali (ADEMA) which became the governing party following the return to multipartyism in 1992.

Konaré was born on 2 February 1946 at Kayes, western Mali, where he began his education. He went on to study at Dakar and Katibougou, graduating from the Ecole Normale Supérieure in history and geography in 1969. He was first involved in politics at this time, being secretary-general of the local political youth movement and launching a national strike movement against the recent military coup. For the next few years he taught at schools in Bamako, Markala and Badalabougou, and studied for a higher degree in history and archaeology, obtaining a doctorate from the University of Warsaw in Poland in 1975. The previous year he had been appointed director of the Human Sciences Institute in Bamako and in 1975 became head of the historic and ethnographic division of the ministry of culture. He also served as president of the International Council of Museums until 1978, when he was appointed minister of youth, sport, arts and culture. However, he lost the youth portfolio the following June and resigned from the Traoré government in August 1980.

After leaving the government he was appointed as a research fellow at the Institut Supérieur de Formation et de Recherche Appliquée (ISFRA), where he remained for nine years. In 1981 he wrote *Le Concept du Pouvoir en Afrique*, which was published by UNESCO. In 1983 he co-founded Jamana, a cultural co-operative. Three years later he helped to create a democratic people's front which co-ordinated the actions of clandestine political parties, Mali being at this stage a single-party state.

In 1989 he founded the first independent daily newspaper in Mali, *Les Echos*, and a monthly youth magazine, *Grin-Grin*. He also started publishing opposition proclamations against the Traoré regime and a news service in local dialects on cassette for the rural population. That year he left ISFRA to set up a training centre for formal and informal education. He has also been president of the West African Archaeological Association, a consultant for UNESCO and on their Council for International Funding for the Promotion of Culture, and a member of the administrative council of the World Centre of Islamic Education.

In October 1990 Konaré helped to form ADEMA, which was legalised in April 1991. He was elected as its president the following month. When multiparty elections were held in 1992, ADEMA won the legislative elections in February/March (although turnout was low and accusations of fraud were made), and Konaré headed the first-round presidential poll on 12 April, going on to win by a large margin in the run-off two weeks later. His term of office was beset by military and popular unrest, ethnic protests and unstable coalition government. Konaré's re-election on 11 May 1997 was marred by a low turnout, of under 30 per cent. His 96 per cent share of the vote was achieved in the face of a boycott by almost all opposition groups, protesting at the annulment of the previous month's legislative elections, although the latter were eventually re-run (and boycotted by the major opposition parties) in July/August 1997.

Konaré is married to Adame Ba and they have four children. With his wife he wrote a book on the history of Mali, and he has also written works on Mali's archaeology, its constitution and, most recently, its political parties.

Ugo **Mifsud Bonnici**

Ugo Mifsud Bonnici, a lawyer and former Nationalist Party education and interior minister, was elected as president of Malta by the parliament on 4 April 1994 in place of Vincent Tabone. Mifsud Bonnici's five-year term may be renewed only once. The post of president is primarily ceremonial, the government being headed by a prime minister responsible to parliament.

Ugo Mifsud Bonnici was born in Cospicua, south of Valletta, on 8 November 1932. His father Carmelo Mifsud Bonnici was a government minister, while his cousin (also called Carmelo or Karmenu Mifsud Bonnici) was later to become a political adversary and prime minister in the Labour government (1984–87). Ugo attended the lyceum, a prestigious state secondary school for boys, and the Royal University of Malta, going on after his degree to complete a doctorate in law. He took an active role in student literary societies concerned with the Maltese language. Practising as a lawyer in Cospicua until 1987, he also held a seat in the House of Representatives from March 1966 onwards, as a member of the Nationalist Party and opposition spokesman on education, and contributed frequently to party newspapers. In 1977 he was president of the party's general council and administrative council, and represented the party in talks which led to constitutional amendments approved in 1974 and 1987.

The narrow Nationalist Party victory in the May 1987 general election was followed by the formation of a government under Edward Fenech Adami in which Ugo Mifsud Bonnici was education minister. This was an especially high-profile role in view of the bitter dispute over the attempt by the previous Labour government (led by his cousin) to abolish fee-paying Catholic schools. Responsible for the 1988 Education Act, which amongst other things settled the matter of subsidising church schools and teaching religion in state schools, Ugo Mifsud Bonnici held the education portfolio for seven years, and was in addition minister of the interior from 1990 to 1992 and minister of human resources from 1992 to 1994.

During his first two years as president, Mifsud Bonnici worked with a politically sympathetic government led by Fenech Adami, but the October 1996 general election brought to power a Labour government led by Alfred Sant.

Ugo Mifsud Bonnici is married to Gemma, *née* Bianco; they have two sons and one daughter, all now lawyers, and three grandsons.

Imata **Kabua**

Imata Kabua was elected by the House of Representatives and inaugurated as the second president of the Marshall Islands on 22 January 1997. He succeeded his cousin Amata Kabua, the first post-independence president, who died the previous month. As president, Kabua acts as both head of state and head of government, and appoints the members of the cabinet. His constitutional powers are limited in that authority is vested in the parliament, but in practice, in a political system which is highly personalised and where there are no political parties, the president is the dominant political figure. The president's normal term is four years, but Imata Kabua was elected to the presidency to fulfil the remainder of Amata Kabua's current four-year term, running until November 1999.

Imata Kabua is the head of the Kabua family with the title of *Iroijlaplap* or paramount chief. Before becoming president, he had served as minister without portfolio in the previous government and was a senator for Kwajalein. He was elected with the support of 20 members of the parliament, against six votes each for two other candidates. Upon taking office Kabua reshuffled the cabinet, while retaining many of the previous ministers in their posts.

Kabua was much involved with representing the Marshall Islands in various regional and global contexts during his first year as president. Having inherited from Amata Kabua the current chairmanship of the South Pacific Forum, he visited its secretariat in Fiji in March. He was also a speaker at the annual conference of the Pacific Resources for Education and Learning, held at Majuro in the Marshall Islands, and an observer at the seventh economic summit of smaller island states, hosted by the Cook Islands. In September he attended the Pacific summit in Tokyo, and in December he went to Kyoto in Japan for the international summit on global warming, the impact of which could mean the Marshall Islands being submerged by rising ocean levels.

Meanwhile, in June, controversy had flared up over the plans by a US firm to store nuclear waste on one of the atolls of the Marshall Islands, which the US government had used in the post-war period for its nuclear weapons testing programme. After much pressure from the USA and from other Pacific Island governments, Kabua froze the waste disposal plans, while emphasising his concern over the loss of revenue this could entail. Later that month he went to Washington D.C. to discuss the future of the Compact of Free Association, the arrangement covering relations with and US aid to its former Pacific trust territories, which in the case of the Marshall Islands is due to run out in 2001.

Col. (retd) **Taya**

Col. (retd) Taya first seized power in a military coup in 1984. Having introduced a multiparty system in 1991, he was elected for further six-year terms in January 1992 and again in December 1997. A northerner and career army officer, he had taken part in an earlier coup in 1978 and launched his 1984 coup after being demoted from the prime ministership. As president he is the principal political figure; his Democratic and Social Republican Party (PRDS) dominates the National Assembly, and he appoints the prime minister, although the latter is formally designated as head of government.

Moaouia ould Sidi Mohammed Taya was born in 1943 into a small northern tribal group in Atar, Adrar. From 1976 to 1978 he was chief of military operations, then deputy chief of staff under the country's first president, Moktar Ould Daddah. In 1978 he was involved in a successful coup, and was subsequently appointed commander of the garrison at Bir Mogkrein in the north and then minister of defence, at a time when the army was fighting the Polisario Front in neighbouring Western Sahara.

The new military regime installed a Military Committee for National Salvation (CMSN), of which Taya became a member in 1979; he was also appointed commander of the national gendarmerie and minister in charge of permanent security. The following year he became minister of mines and energy and then, on 26 April 1981, prime minister and minister of defence. However, by March 1984 the then president Lt.-Col. Mohammed Khouna Ould Haidalla, perceiving Taya as a dangerous political rival, demoted him to the post of chief of staff of the armed forces and assumed Taya's government posts himself. The president's fears were realised in December 1984 when Taya led a bloodless coup and declared himself president and prime minister as well as chair of the CMSN.

Shortly after seizing power Taya pulled Mauritania out of the conflict in Western Sahara and recognised the independence of the Polisario's Sahrawi Arab Democratic Republic. This initially raised tensions with Morocco, although diplomatic relations were restored and a ceasefire declared the following year. Domestically Taya's main problems stemmed from tensions between Maures like himself who form the ruling élite, and the majority black population who are ethnically akin to the Senegalese peoples. His regime was accused of political oppression, executing opponents on charges of coup plotting, and repression of discontent especially in the south; cross-border friction erupted in 1989 when Senegalese resentment flared up and forced an exodus of Maures from that country.

Having first promised elections back in 1986, Taya's regime eventually held a referendum in 1991 which approved a new multiparty constitution. By July six parties had been legalised, including Taya's PRDS, and on 24 January 1992 Taya was elected president with just over 62 per cent of the popular vote in a poll against three other candidates. Opposition parties, however, rejected the result and boycotted the subsequent legislative elections. On 18 April Taya was inaugurated as president but did not retain the post of prime minister. Two years later he dropped his military title to emphasise the country's return to civilian rule.

On 12 December 1997 Taya was re-elected as president, with 90.25 per cent of the vote against four other candidates, but with opposition groups complaining of widespread multiple voting by presidential supporters.

Cassam **Uteem**

Cassam Uteem has been president of Mauritius since July 1992, the year in which Mauritius became a republic (former governor-general Sir Veerasamy Ringadoo having been interim president since 12 March). Uteem was re-elected by the National Assembly on 28 June 1997 for a second five-year term in this primarily ceremonial post. Uteem, at one time chairman of the Muslim Youth Federation, had been a member of parliament since 1976, was a member of the trade union-based Mauritian Militant Movement (MMM), and was deputy prime minister in the early 1990s.

Born on 22 March 1941 in Plaine Verte, Uteem attended the Royal College in Port Louis, the Mauritian capital, before receiving a diploma in social work from the University of Mauritius. He then went to Paris to study social sciences, receiving a degree and continuing his studies to gain a master's degree in psychology, again from the University of Paris VII. He began a commercial career as a supervisor at Cable and Wireless Limited, after which he became personnel manager at Currimjee Jeewanjee and Company Limited in 1960. He was also a founding member of the Old Royals Dramatic Association. In 1964 be became chairman of the Port Louis Youth Federation, and then chairman of the Muslim Youth Federation in 1966.

Uteem was a municipal councillor in Port Louis in 1969 and became secretary-general of the Mauritius National Youth Council in 1971. From 1971 to 1973 he was the treasurer of the Mauritius Council of Civil Service. Between 1974 and 1976 he was the country's representative at the World Assembly of Youth organised by UNESCO. In 1976 he became a member of the MMM central committee and politburo and was elected as a member of the legislative assembly for Port Louis East, retaining his seat since then. He was re-elected and served as a municipal councillor from 1977 to 1979, and again from 1986 to 1988.

From 1982 to 1983 he was minister of employment, social security and national solidarity, before being appointed opposition whip, a post he held from 1983 to 1987. In 1986 he was lord mayor of Port Louis. In 1988 he left the MMM politburo. From 1988 to 1990 he was chairman of the public accounts committee, before becoming deputy prime minister and minister of industry and industrial technology (1990–92). He was first elected as president of the republic by the assembly on 30 June 1992, and re-elected five years later. In March 1993 he was elevated to the rank of Grand Commander of the Order of the Star and Key of the Indian Ocean.

Cassam Uteem is married with two sons and one daughter.

Ernesto **Zedillo**

Ernesto Zedillo has been president of Mexico since 1994, when he was elected for a six-year term as the candidate of the ruling Institutional Revolutionary Party (PRI). He was sworn in that December, and as executive president is both head of state and head of government. A Yale-educated economist and former government minister, Zedillo became PRI candidate for the presidency only after the assassination of the previous nominee, Luis Colosio, for whom he had been campaign manager. Since the 1997 elections he has found himself governing without a majority in the legislature, a situation unique in his party's unbroken period in power since 1929. He presents himself as part of a new generation of modernisers within the party, with liberal economic policies combined with fiscal discipline but also with a measure of concern over social welfare issues.

Ernesto Zedillo Ponce de Leon was born on 27 April 1951 in Mexico City. He completed an economics degree at the National Polytechnic Institute in 1972 and, already a PRI party member, joined the president's economic policy office before going to do further study in the USA, obtaining a master's degree and doctorate in economics at Yale. From 1978 to 1980 he was a teacher at the National Polytechnic Institute and a lecturer at Colegio de Mexico.

In 1980, while working at the Banco de Mexico, Zedillo created an exchange risk management fund (FICORCA) which assisted Mexican companies in restructuring their debts and strengthening their financial situation. Between 1985 and 1988 he was head of the FICORCA division and then deputy secretary of the Banco de Mexico. He became secretary of the bank in 1988.

Brought into government under the presidency of his friend Carlos Salinas, Zedillo built up his image as a moderniser, as planning and budget minister from 1989 and from 1992 as minister of public education. In the latter post he launched a reform of pre-school, primary and secondary education in Mexico, and introduced programmes to reach the less developed areas of the country. His decentralisation of the management of education helped to reduce the power of the teaching union.

Propelled unexpectedly into the 1994 presidential contest himself following the assassination of Colosio in March, he topped the poll on 21 August with just under 49 per cent of the vote (adjusted to fractionally over 50 per cent after discounting invalid and blank votes) against two other principal contenders and six minor candidates. His margin of victory was the lowest ever for the PRI, which was racked by allegations of corruption, and the outcome was denounced as fraudulent by the centre-left opposition.

As president, Zedillo has sought to overcome hostility to the continuation of PRI rule by stressing openness and commitment to democratic principles, even appointing a member of the opposition to his cabinet as attorney-general. His reforms have focused in particular on the judiciary, on improving the credibility of the electoral process in Mexico, and on decentralisation of the administration to increase the powers of the states. He has also pressed ahead with privatisation of much of the state-run economy, to some extent making up for the disastrous currency crisis at the beginning of his term of office by delivering high economic growth in the subsequent period. The investigation of the Colosio murder, other assassinations linked to drug trafficking, and a number of high-profile corruption cases, however, have dragged down even further the image of the PRI and of the previous Salinas regime, and Zedillo's political reform agenda has been challenged as insufficiently far-reaching by rebel groups especially in the southern state of Chiapas. The July 1997 elections to the Chamber of Deputies left the PRI in opposition to the combined strength of the right-wing and centre-left opposition, although Zedillo has shown signs of sufficient flexibility to manage this situation to his party's advantage; more serious may be its loss of control of the government of Mexico City in the first direct election to the mayorship, held at the same time.

Ernesto Zedillo Ponce de Leon is married to Nilda Patricia Velasco. They have four sons and one daughter.

Jacob **Nena**

Jacob Nena was confirmed as the fourth president of the Federated States of Micronesia (FSM) on 8 May 1997, having acted as president since November 1996 because of the ill-health of President Bailey Olter. Nena is a political science graduate and former teacher who was the first governor of the state of Kosrae, his native island in the far east of the archipelago. The executive president is both head of state and head of government.

Nena was born on 10 October 1941 in Lelu, Kosrae, and attended school locally and on Pohnpei before attending the College of Guam, where he graduated in political science in 1968. In 1972 he obtained a master's degree in public administration and business management from the University of Hawaii, having in the meantime already begun teaching and working in local administration. When the island of Kosrae became a state at the time of independence in 1979, Nena was elected as its first governor, and for the next three years he was a member of the Micronesian Political Status and Transition Commission. In 1982 he was a member of the presidential delegation to the South Pacific Forum.

Throughout the 1980s Nena was involved in government both at local and statewide level. He was chair of the Lelu municipal government constitutional convention in 1986 and a member of the corresponding convention for Kosrae state. During the term of the fifth congress he was on the committees for justice and governmental operations, for health, education and social affairs, and for external affairs. He chaired the latter two committees during the sixth congress as well as the resources and development committee.

In May 1991 Nena was elected vice-president of the FSM under President Olter; both were re-elected to their posts in May 1995. In July 1996 Olter suffered a stroke and in November the congress appointed Nena as acting president pending a review 180 days later on 8 May 1997, when Olter was officially relieved of his duties.

Nena is married to Lerina Jack and they have ten children.

Petru **Lucinschi**

Petru Lucinschi was elected president of Moldova in December 1996, and was formally inaugurated for a five-year term on 15 January 1997. He shares executive power with a council of ministers (cabinet). The president designates a prime minister, who is head of government and who normally chairs cabinet meetings unless the president elects to do so on matters of particular importance. Lucinschi was a high-ranking communist party official during the Soviet period, but now styles himself as a social democrat. He was president of the parliament for three years before his election to the state presidency.

Petru Lucinschi was born on 27 January 1940 in the village of Radulenii-Vechi, within the Floresti district of what was then Romania. He was educated at the State University of Moldavia, where he studied history and philology, and at the Communist Party of the Soviet Union (CPSU) party school in Moscow. In 1962/63 he did his military service in the Soviet army.

He spent the years until 1978 working in a variety of positions in the civil service and in the communist party, initially within the Komsomol (youth wing), from 1971 as secretary to the party central committee at republican level, and from 1976 to 1978 as first secretary to the Kishinev city committee. However, after 1978 he left Moldavia and did not return until 1989. During this time he worked in senior positions in both the CPSU central committee, where he headed the propaganda department, and in the communist party of Tajikistan. He was also a member of the Supreme Soviet from 1986 to 1989 and after that of the Congress of People's Deputies in the Soviet Union until 1991.

On his return to Moldavia in 1989, Lucinschi was appointed first secretary of the Moldavian communist party. As a supporter of Mikhail Gorbachev's reforms, he was recalled to Moscow in June 1990, and served on the central committee secretariat and the CPSU politburo until the attempted coup of August 1991 and Moldavia's declaration of independence on 27 August as the Republic of Moldova. At this time Lucinschi worked for a period as a lecturer at the Institute for Social and Political Research at the Academy of Sciences in Moscow.

He was Moldova's ambassador to Russia in 1992/93, and in 1993 became president of the *Parlamentul* (unicameral parliament), a post in which he was confirmed the following year. He was a leading member of the Agrarian Democratic Party of Moldova (PDAM) from 1993 but stood in the 1996 presidential election as an independent, the PDAM nomination having gone instead to the then prime minister Andrei Sangheli.

In that poll, Lucinschi's main opponent was the incumbent president, Mircea Snegur, who had himself split from the PDAM the previous year, accusing it of obstructing his economic reform programme, and had founded his own rival centrist party. Lucinschi trailed Snegur on the first round in November 1996 but won 54 per cent of the vote in the run-off on 1 December. His victory reflected his support among broadly leftist forces and his deft handling of Moldova's intricate racial and linguistic politics. Now presenting himself as a social democrat, Lucinschi criticised his predecessor's plans to press ahead with radical market reforms.

Prince **Rainier III**

Prince Rainier III succeeded his grandfather, Prince Louis II, as the sovereign ruler of the Principality of Monaco in 1949. He has thus been head of state for longer than any other current incumbent in the world save for King Bhumibol of Thailand. The prince nominates the head of government (entitled minister of state) from a list of three diplomats submitted by the French government; he gave up his absolute powers in 1962, but as sovereign retains significant authority and represents Monaco in its relations with foreign powers, signing and ratifying treaties.

Born on 31 May 1923, Rainier inherited the throne through the female line, being the son of Prince Louis's daughter Princess Charlotte and of Prince Pierre de Polignac. He fought in the French army as a volunteer during the Second World War and was awarded the War Cross, followed in 1947 by the Cross of the Legion of Honour.

In 1951, shortly after his accession to the throne, he signed the Franco-Monegasque convention of friendship and mutual administrative assistance, one of a series of conventions on which relations between the principality and France are now based. In 1962 he reformed the constitution, which had first been promulgated in 1911 by Albert I, and abrogated his absolute powers. In 1966 he led Monte Carlo's centenary celebrations and has since then presided over Monaco's successful development as a tax haven and exclusive tourist destination for the international jet set. On 28 May 1993 Monaco joined the United Nations.

Prince Rainier married on 18 April 1956 the American film star Grace Patricia Kelly, and they had three children, Princess Caroline, Prince Albert (the heir to the throne) and Princess Stephanie. Princess Grace died in a car crash in 1982 while driving in the hills above Monaco.

Natsagyn **Bagabandi**

Natsagyn Bagabandi, the candidate of the former communist Mongolian People's Revolutionary Party (MPRP), was elected as the second president of Mongolia in a nationwide ballot in May 1997, convincingly defeating outgoing President Ochirbat of the Democratic Union Coalition (DUC). Bagabandi, a Moscow-trained food technologist and a MPRP central committee member since 1980, was chair of the parliament, the Great Hural, between 1992 and 1996. As president he has promised to slow down the pace of Mongolia's market reforms, and to increase spending on social reform programmes. He took office on 20 June 1997 for a four-year term in a post which has significant political powers, although he must "cohabit" with a DUC government, headed by a prime minister responsible to parliament.

Born on 22 April 1950, in Zavkhan province, Bagabandi was educated in the Soviet Union, studying at the Food Technological Institute in Moscow. After completing his education he worked in a food factory from 1972. Three years later he returned to Mongolia, continuing to work in the food industry.

Becoming active in politics in the 1970s, he made steady progress in the MPRP, serving on the central committee from 1980 onwards and becoming its deputy president in 1992, at the time of the country's retreat from communism. Also in 1992, when the MPRP won an overwhelming victory in Mongolia's first multiparty elections, Bagabandi was elected to represent his native province in the Mongolian Great Hural. He was chairman of the Great Hural for the next four years, and during this time made official visits to Russia, China and Japan, broadening parliamentary links.

In the June 1996 legislative elections the MPRP suffered a serious defeat and the DUC won 50 of the 76 seats in the Hural. The new government brought in a radical programme of privatisation and free-market reforms, with the aim of moving Mongolia rapidly from a centralised to a market economy, but leading initially to sharp increases in the cost of living and in unemployment.

In January 1997, when the MPRP decided at its 22nd congress to drop its Marxist–Leninist ideology in favour of "democratic socialism", the moderate Bagabandi was an obvious choice as chair of the party. In the presidential elections on 18 May 1997 he won 60.8 per cent of the vote. The DUC government remained in office, in an uncertain form of "cohabitation" with new MPRP President Bagabandi, and lacking the required two-thirds majority to overturn any presidential veto.

King **Hassan II**

King Hassan II has ruled Morocco since the death of his father Mohammed V in 1961. Hassan is the 17th sovereign of the Alaouite dynasty in Morocco, who claim direct descent from the prophet Mohammed. He rules his relatively conservative Islamic monarchy as a constitutional head of state, exercising considerable power but with a prime minister (appointed by him) as head of government.

Moulay Hassan was born on 9 July 1929 in Rabat, and was educated in the royal palace (where there was considerable emphasis on study of the Koran), at Imperial College in Rabat, and at Bordeaux University in France, where he obtained a master's degree in public law in 1951.

While a student in Rabat he joined fellow students in a number of public demonstrations in support of nationalist aspirations for full independence, Morocco being governed at that time as a French protectorate. The authorities warned his father to stop Hassan's involvement with the nationalists, but in 1947 his father took him on a trip to Tangiers and delivered a landmark speech demanding the country's independence, with Hassan himself appealing to the nation's youth to mobilise for liberation.

Hassan followed his father into exile in 1953 in Corsica and then, in 1954, Madagascar. During this period he acted as political adviser to his father. In February 1956, the family having returned from exile, he joined his father in negotiations for independence.

Following independence in April 1956, Hassan was appointed chief of staff of the Moroccan Royal Armed Forces. Later, in June, Hassan was the Moroccan representative at Spanish negotiations to achieve independence for Moroccan territory under Spanish rule. The following year, on 9 July 1957, Hassan was formally invested as crown prince. On 26 February 1961, on the death of Mohammed V, he became king of Morocco with the title Hassan II, and was formally invested in Rabat on 3 March with the title Commander of the Faithful.

He held the post of prime minister himself for much of the 1960s, but has gradually allowed the development of political parties in the parliamentary system introduced under a new constitution in 1972. Hassan has shown himself skilled in bringing moderate parties into participation in coalition governments under his regime. Royal amnesties have lately reduced the number of opponents of the regime held in detention, although the banning of Islamic fundamentalist groups, and the treatment of their members in Moroccan prisons, continues to arouse concern over human rights, and there have been fresh crackdowns in the 1990s.

In 1961, shortly before he became king, Hassan attended the conference of independent African states, known as the Casablanca Group, and in the same year he was in Belgrade as a participant in the founding of the Non-aligned Movement. He has managed throughout his reign to combine a pro-Western stance, and the rewards this has brought in aid from France and the USA in particular, with support for Arab causes. In 1969, Hassan chaired the first summit of the Islamic Conference Organization held in Rabat; he was also chair of the Organization of African Unity (OAU) in 1972, and hosted the Arab summit in Rabat in 1974, at which the Palestine Liberation Organization was recognised for the first time as the sole legal representative of the Palestinian people. He hosted a subsequent Arab summit at Fez in 1982, and the fifth Islamic summit at Casablanca in 1984.

King Hassan's profile in international organisations suffered from the opposition of many African states to the incorporation of the former Spanish Saharan territories within Morocco, in pursuit of which he had organised the "Green March" of October 1975 and fought a long war against pro-independence guerrilla forces in what came to be known as Western Sahara. For a time during the 1980s Morocco was isolated from the OAU over this issue as a succession of countries recognised a guerrilla-proclaimed "Sahrawi Arab Democratic Republic" (SADR) as the legitimate government of Western Sahara. Hassan began to win back some of the diplomatic ground after announcing that Morocco intended to organise a referendum on the future status of the territory, although the implementation of this promise became bogged down in disputes about voter lists and remained unfulfilled as of the end of 1997.

King Hassan is married with three daughters and two sons, the crown prince being Prince Sidi Mohammed, who was born on 21 August 1963.

Joaquim **Chissano**

Joaquim Chissano has been president of Mozambique since 1986, and was re-elected to the post for a five-year term in the country's first free presidential election in October 1994. The executive president is both head of state and head of government, and appoints the council of ministers, including the prime minister. Chissano was a guerrilla leader in the struggle for independence from Portugal, and co-founder of FRELIMO (the Mozambique Liberation Front), taking over as leader on the death in 1986 of Samora Machel.

Joaquim Alberto Chissano was born on 22 October 1939 in Malehice, Chibuto district, Gaza province, into a wealthy and influential family. He was one of the first black pupils to attend the grammar school founded by the Portuguese in Lourenço Marques (now Maputo) and was president of the Mozambican African Secondary Students in 1959/60. He went to Portugal in 1960 to study medicine at university, but left secretly in 1961 to join the liberation forces. In 1962, Chissano co-founded FRELIMO, becoming secretary to the president and joining the war as a guerrilla in 1964. He was FRELIMO representative in Tanzania from 1968 to 1974.

Chissano participated in the 1974 Lusaka negotiations between FRELIMO and the Portuguese government which established a framework for a rapid transition to independence. Samora Machel, the FRELIMO leader who was to become the first post-independence president of Mozambique, appointed him as prime minister of the interim government during this period, and as minister of foreign affairs for the first decade after independence. He became a member of the People's Assembly in 1977, and a major-general in the Mozambican armed forces in 1980. When Machel died in a plane crash in 1986, the central committee of the party elected Chissano as president and commander-in-chief in his place.

As president, Chissano oversaw the signing in 1992 of the UN-brokered agreement which signalled the end of the civil war between (former Marxist) FRELIMO and the South African-backed Mozambique National Resistance Movement (RENAMO). As part of that agreement, multiparty presidential and general elections were held in 1994, Chissano winning the presidential poll with 53 per cent of the vote against 33 per cent for RENAMO leader Afonso Dhlakama.

Chissano's chief task has been to rebuild a country devastated by the civil war, which left 900,000 dead and 1 million refugees. He has successfully overseen the process of demobilisation, although the government has had problems reasserting its authority in central districts. In 1995 Mozambique joined the Commonwealth, the first state to do so which was neither anglophone nor a former British colony.

Joaquim Chissano is married with four children.

Sam **Nujoma**

Sam Nujoma has been president of Namibia since independence in 1990, and was returned for a further five-year term in a nationwide poll in 1994. The leading figure for over 30 years in his country's long struggle for independence and the ending of South African control, Nujoma is president of the South West Africa People's Organization of Namibia (SWAPO). As state president he is both head of state and head of government, appointing the prime minister and members of the cabinet.

Sam (Shafiishuna) Nujoma was born on 12 May 1929 in Etunda village, Ongandjera district in northern Namibia. He is from the Ovambo ethnic group and was one of ten children in a family of subsistence farmers. He attended school at the Okahao Finnish mission school (1937–45) before leaving for Windhoek, where he began working for the South African Railways. Whilst working, Nujoma attended night school at St Barnabas, studying for his junior certificate by correspondence with the Trans-Africa Correspondence College in South Africa.

Nujoma began political life when he sought to mobilise workers in Windhoek, for which he lost his job. In 1959 he became leader of the Ovamboland People's Organization, the nucleus of what became SWAPO. Arrested for organising resistance to apartheid-style forced township removals, he went into exile in 1960. In New York, as president of the newly founded SWAPO, he lobbied the UN General Assembly, demanding an end to South African rule (which derived from a mandate originally entrusted to South Africa by the League of Nations). He was the Namibian representative at the founding of the Non-aligned Movement in Belgrade in 1961 and at the founding of the Organization of African Unity (OAU) in Addis Ababa two years later.

Nujoma was arrested again in March 1966 when attempting to return to Namibia, and deported to Zambia, where SWAPO began to mobilise its forces and to obtain weapons to smuggle into Namibia. For over two decades Nujoma was to be preoccupied with the armed struggle on the one hand, and ceaseless international lobbying efforts on the other. He was awarded the Lenin Peace Prize in 1973, the Ho Chi Minh Peace Award in 1988, and the Indira Gandhi Peace Prize in 1990.

The first leader of an African nationalist movement to address the UN Security Council, in 1971, Nujoma also led the SWAPO team in negotiations in 1977/78 involving the UN, South Africa and the southern African frontline states. The resulting UN Security Council Resolution 435 envisaged Namibia's independence by 1978. Implementation of this resolution was delayed by over ten years, repeatedly stalled by South Africa as a protracted military struggle developed, extending from Namibia to encompass the continuing civil war in Angola.

When a ceasefire agreement was eventually signed, SWAPO won a majority in elections for a Constituent Assembly in 1989, and Nujoma was elected unanimously by the assembly on 16 February 1990 to be first president of the Republic of Namibia. He was sworn in by UN secretary-general Javier Pérez de Cuéllar on the day the country achieved independence, 21 March 1990. In December 1994 he was re-elected for a fresh term, winning 73 per cent of the vote in a direct nationwide ballot.

Sam Nujoma is married with three sons and one daughter.

Kinza **Clodumar**

Kinza Clodumar has been president of Nauru since February 1997, when he was elected by the parliament for a three-year term. Head of state and head of government as well as minister of finance, public service and external affairs, he is best known internationally as an eloquent spokesman for small island states threatened by global warming and the risk of rising sea levels. A prominent parliamentarian with a background in the development of civil aviation and in financial administration, Clodumar had been speaker of the parliament before becoming president.

Born on 8 February 1945 on Nauru, Kinza Godfrey Clodumar went to school in Nauru and then in New South Wales in Australia. He completed his education at the Australian National University in Canberra where he graduated in economics and politics in 1969.

Returning to Nauru, he became a project officer in the island's development and industry department in 1970, rising to become director of civil aviation by 1976. He was first elected in 1971 to the Nauru parliament (which with only 18 members is one of the smallest in the world), and was minister of finance in 1977/78. In 1979 Clodumar resigned from parliament to become head of the island's development and industry department, a post he held until 1983. He re-entered parliament in 1984, but lost his seat during the 1992–95 term. Re-elected in 1995, he was speaker and a member of the cabinet before being elected president by parliament on 12 February 1997, ending a period of instability which had seen three changes of government within two months.

Abroad, he has represented Nauru at a number of international gatherings, signing the UN Convention on the Law of the Sea (UNCLOS) in Jamaica in 1981, attending the Earth Summit at Rio de Janeiro, Brazil, in 1992, and participating in the UN Review of the Nuclear Non-Proliferation Treaty in 1995 and the Kyoto conference on climate change in December 1997. As president, Clodumar faces the task of redirecting Nauru's economy following the depletion of phosphate reserves.

Kinza Clodumar has been married since 1968 and has three daughters and two sons.

King **Birendra**

King Birendra Bir Bikram Shah Dev has been king of Nepal since January 1972, following the death of his father, King Mahendra. An Old Etonian who has also studied social sciences in Tokyo and Harvard, he is the world's only Hindu monarch. Birendra is credited with recognising the need to concede the current multiparty democratic constitution in response to sustained pressure for the abandonment of the previous non-party system. The changes implemented since 1990 have transformed the role of what was effectively almost an absolute monarchy into that of constitutional head of state, although the king is still revered by many of his subjects as a god-like figure. Executive power is vested jointly in the king and the council of ministers, headed by a prime minister who is appointed by the king but responsible to the legislature.

Birendra was born in Kathmandu on 28 December 1945, the eldest son of King Mahendra and Princess Indra Rajya Shah. He traces his ancestry in a direct line from Nepal's founding monarch Prithvi Narayan Shah in the 18th century. He was educated in Darjeeling, India, and at Eton College in England, and in the mid-1960s spent a year travelling round Nepal as well as going to Tokyo University and then to Harvard, where he studied administration, economics and sociology in 1967/68.

Having been designated heir apparent in 1955, he was often included on official visits, attending the 1961 non-aligned summit conference in Belgrade, leading the Nepalese delegation to the Cairo non-aligned conference in 1964 and to Indonesia in April 1965, and meeting the Chinese communist leader Mao Zedong during a visit to China in June 1966.

After his accession to the throne in 1972 Birendra set up a national development council in April of that year and reorganised the national planning commission, with the aim of redressing regional economic disparities. He promoted a national referendum in 1980, which resulted in a reformed *panchayat* system, rather than an all-out return to multiparty politics. After an intense period of political unrest, and the dissolution of the *panchayat* system in May 1990, a new constitution was promulgated the following November.

King Birendra married Aishwarya Rajya Laxmi Devi Shah in February 1970 and they have two sons and one daughter. Dipendra, the elder son and heir apparent, was born in 1971. His coming of age in 1988 was marked by a major Hindu religious ceremony, held in the same year that Nepal hosted the World Hindu Conference.

Queen **Beatrix**

Queen Beatrix of the Netherlands succeeded to the throne on 30 April 1980, following the abdication of her mother, Queen Juliana. That day she was invested as Queen of the Netherlands, Princess of Orange-Nassau and a list of other titles, at a special plenary session of both houses of the States General (parliament) in the New Church in Amsterdam. As queen she is also head of state of Aruba and of the Netherlands Antilles, represented by a governor. Her role is ceremonial, although views which she has expressed on environmental and social issues in particular have had some political impact.

Beatrix Wilhelmina Armgard was born at the Soestdijk palace in Baarn on 31 January 1938, the eldest of the three daughters of Juliana and Prince Bernhard. Following the German invasion in May 1940 she was taken to England and on to Ottawa, Canada, for the duration of the Second World War. On her return to the Netherlands she continued her primary education, and received her grammar school certificate in 1956. When she reached her 18th birthday earlier that year, she became a member of the council of state. In the same year she entered the University of Leiden, studying sociology, jurisprudence, economics, constitutional law and international affairs. She passed her final doctoral degree examination in July 1961.

Queen Beatrix's interests include sculpture, painting, dramatic art and ballet. She enjoys riding and sailing, is patron of the National Fund for the Prevention of Poliomyelitis and also supports, among others, charities assisting handicapped children.

Queen Beatrix married Claus von Amsberg, a former German diplomat, on 10 March 1966, the nationality of her husband causing adverse reactions in some circles at the time. They have three sons, the heir to the throne being Prince Willem-Alexander, born in 1967.

Jaime **Saleh**

Jaime Marcelino Saleh has since January 1990 been governor of the Netherlands Antilles, in which capacity he represents Queen Beatrix of the Netherlands as titular head of state. Trained in law, he is a former judge and was chief justice before taking up his appointment as governor.

Born on 20 April 1941 in Bonaire in the Netherlands Antilles, Saleh went to secondary school and university in the Netherlands, obtaining a doctorate in law at Utrecht State University in 1966. From 1967 to 1968 he was a deputy public prosecutor in the district court in Zutphen, Netherlands. He then returned to the Netherlands Antilles where he worked in the public prosecutor's office for six years, and was also an attorney at law in Curaçao from 1971 to 1974. In December of that year he became a deputy judge, and in 1976 a judge, in the high court. From 1978 to 1979 he was vice-president of the military tribunal of the Netherlands Antilles. In September 1979 he became chief justice of the high court of justice of the Netherlands Antilles and Aruba, and concurrently president of the military tribunal.

He stood down as chief justice, after over a decade, to take up his appointment as governor with effect from 15 January 1990.

Jaime Saleh is married with four children.

Sir Michael **Hardie Boys**

Sir Michael Hardie Boys, a former appeal court judge, took office as the 17th governor-general of New Zealand on 21 March 1996, succeeding Dame Catherine Tizard. He represents the monarch, Queen Elizabeth II, as titular head of state, whereas the head of government is the prime minister.

Born on 6 October 1931 in Wellington, the son of a judge, he was educated at Hataitai School, Wellington College and Victoria University, Wellington, graduating in 1954 as senior scholar in law. He trained as a barrister and solicitor, working in private practice in Wellington for over 25 years until 1980. In 1973 he was appointed to the council of the Wellington District Law Society, becoming its treasurer in 1980. Also at this time he was on the legal aid board, chairing it from 1978 to 1980.

First appointed as a judge of the high court in 1980, he was appointed in 1989 to the court of appeal, and in the same year he also became a privy councillor.

In his early years Hardie Boys was a youth leader in the Methodist Church and he has a long history of involvement with the Boys' Brigade, of which he has been Wellington president and New Zealand vice-president. He has also served on the public and social affairs committee of the Anglican Church, on independent school governors' boards, and on the council of the Automobile Association in Wellington. In 1986 he was a visiting Fellow of Wolfson College, Cambridge, and in 1994 he was elected an honorary bencher of Gray's Inn, London. He is a Knight Grand Cross of the Order of St Michael and St George and in 1997 was appointed a Knight Grand Companion of the New Zealand Order of Merit.

Michael Hardie Boys married Mary Zohrab in 1957 and they have two sons and two daughters.

Arnoldo **Alemán**

Arnoldo Alemán was elected president of Nicaragua in October 1996 and sworn in for a five-year term on 10 January 1997. A successful lawyer, coffee grower and former mayor of Managua, Alemán was the candidate of the broad-based Liberal Alliance coalition. He replaced Violeta Chamorro who had been president since April 1990 but who was barred under the constitution from seeking a second consecutive term of office. The executive president is both head of state and head of government.

Arnoldo Alemán Lacayo was born on 23 January 1946 in the Nicaraguan capital, Managua. He studied law at the Universidad Nacional Autónoma de Nicaragua and graduated in 1967. During this time he was also leader of a Liberal Student Youth Organisation supporting the right-wing Somoza regime, in which his father was education minister. He practised law in Managua as a notary public and a specialist in banking and commercial law and in central American economic integration, working with various Nicaraguan banking and commercial institutions between 1968 and 1979.

Alemán was arrested in 1980 and held for seven months by the new left-wing Sandinista regime, which had emerged victorious in its insurgency against the Somoza regime and which remained in power until 1990 in the face of sustained contra rebel attack. Alemán, devoting himself after his release to coffee farming, was at various times during the next decade president of the Coffee Growers' Union of Nicaragua, vice-president of the National Farmers' Union and head of the Higher Council for Private Enterprise.

Alemán's return to active anti-Sandinista politics was fuelled by personal tragedy, the death of his wife María in hospital in the USA in 1989 while he was being held under house arrest in Nicaragua. In 1990, standing as a Liberal affiliated to the National Opposition Union (UNO), he won election as mayor of Managua, while the UNO candidate Violeta Chamorro defeated the Sandinista leader and incumbent Daniel Ortega in the presidential poll.

As president of one of several liberal factions, Alemán helped form in 1996 a broad-based Liberal Alliance, which backed his candidacy for the presidency. In the election on 20 October 1996 Alemán defeated Ortega and 21 minor candidates. He won 51 per cent of the vote, well above the 45 per cent threshold needed to make a run-off unnecessary, although Ortega complained of electoral fraud.

A widower since 1989, Alemán has four children.

Ibrahim Barre **Maïnassara**

Brig.-Gen. Ibrahim Barre Maïnassara seized power in a coup in January 1996, was elected president of Niger in July and was sworn in for a five-year term on 7 August. As president he appoints and chairs meetings of the cabinet (which includes a prime minister), the function of the cabinet being to implement policies as instructed by the president. Immediately following the January 1996 coup, launched by him as armed forces chief of staff, Maïnassara had been named chair of a newly formed National Salvation Council (CSN), but he had subsequently agreed and directed the return to constitutional rule.

Maïnassara was born in Maradi, Niger, in 1949 and trained as a soldier in Madegas, Niger, and in France. Following Niger's independence in 1960 he joined the army, rising rapidly through the ranks to become aide-de-camp to President Seyni Kountché, who seized power in 1974. In 1976 Maïnassara was appointed commander of the presidential guard, and he later became commander of the Niamey paratroopers.

In 1986 he went to Paris as military attaché, but returned the following year to take up the post of minister of health and social affairs in September, shortly before the death of Kountché in November. In 1990 he went as ambassador to Algeria, returning two years later as defence counsellor in the office of the prime minister. From 1993 he was chief of staff of the armed forces until he seized power in 1996.

Kountché's death in 1987 had unleashed pressure for democratic reform, which eventually resulted in the approval by referendum of a new multiparty constitution in 1992. Presidential elections the following year were won by opposition leader Mahamane Ousmane, but without a majority in the legislature, precipitating a protracted government crisis which was compounded when the former ruling National Movement for a Development Society (MNSD) and its allies won fresh legislative elections in 1995. This political confusion persisted, against a background of economic unrest, frequent strikes over non-payment of official salaries, and efforts to push through privatisation and restructuring measures required to obtain backing from the International Monetary Fund.

The institutional deadlock was broken on 27 January 1996 when Maïnassara denounced the factionalism underlying the political disputes and took power himself in a military coup. He suspended the constitution, dismissed both president and prime minister, dissolved parliament, banned political parties and set up a National Salvation Council (CSN) of which he himself was chair. Comprised entirely of army officers, the CSN nevertheless promised a return to civilian rule within a few months.

In May 1996 a revised multiparty constitution was approved by 92 per cent of voters, although the turnout was only around 35 per cent. Presidential elections followed on 7/8 July 1996. On the second day of polling, however, the independent National Electoral Commission was replaced, "in an attempt to reduce corruption by the opposition". The new pro-Maïnassara commission announced that he had won 52 per cent of the vote, a disputed result which was accepted by the Supreme Court on 21 July. Maïnassara was sworn in on 7 August.

Legislative elections on 23 November 1996 were again boycotted by the main opposition groups with the result that a pro-Maïnassara coalition, the National Union of Independents for Democratic Renewal, won 59 of the 83 seats in the National Assembly.

Since coming to power Maïnassara (who was promoted from colonel to brigadier-general in mid-1996) has successfully restored the international financial community's confidence in the regime (aid having initially been withdrawn after the coup) and agreed a major rescheduling of the country's debt. His regime maintains tight control of political developments and has arrested a number of opposition leaders in a clampdown on public protests.

Sani **Abacha**

Gen. Sani Abacha has ruled Nigeria since November 1993, when he proclaimed himself chairman of a new Provisional Ruling Council (PRC). A northern Muslim and British-trained army officer, he had backed the 1985 military coup and was chief of staff and defence minister under Gen. Ibrahim Babangida until his own takeover. He is head of state, head of government and commander-in-chief of the armed forces, and appoints the members of the PRC and of the federal executive council or cabinet.

Sani Abacha was born on 20 September 1943 in Kano, where he went to school, obtaining a West African School Certificate from Rumfa College in 1962. In December 1962 he enrolled at the Nigerian Military Training School in Zaria for a six-month course. The following June he went to England to spend six months at the Officer Cadet College in Aldershot, returning to Nigeria to take up an army commission as second lieutenant. Receiving further British military training at the School of Infantry in Warminster in 1971, he rose to the rank of brigadier by 1980, holding a variety of posts as both a commander and trainer. In 1981 he attended the senior executive course at the National Institute for Policy and Strategic Studies in Kuru, near Jos. In 1984, on his promotion to major, he became a member of the supreme military council.

In 1985 he was a key figure in Gen. Babangida's military coup, becoming chief of army staff and a member of the new ruling body, the Armed Forces Ruling Council (AFRC). By 1989 he was chairman of the joint chiefs of staff and in 1990 he was promoted to the rank of general. In September he became chief of defence staff and minister of defence, and retained the defence portfolio within a national council of ministers set up as part of a lengthy programme for the proposed return to civilian rule. Babangida was forced to resign in August 1993 after the fiasco of the holding of presidential elections, the annulment of the result, and the announcement but then scrapping of fresh elections.

An interim government, which included Abacha as minister of defence, yielded full power to him on 17 November 1993, whereupon he dissolved all levels of legislature and banned all parties. A week later he formed a predominantly military Provisional Ruling Council which would control a cabinet-style civilian federal executive council (both of which he chaired).

Abacha has been unspecific, and inconsistent, about concrete proposals for returning the country to elected civilian rule. A National Constitutional Conference (NCC) was adjourned soon after it opened in May 1994, and with political parties remaining banned, the reconvening of the NCC that September was boycotted by pro-democracy groups. Meanwhile in June 1994 M.M.K. Abiola, the winner of the annulled 1993 presidential election, was arrested when he came out of hiding to reaffirm his claims, and the resulting wave of protests and strikes were put down by the military. Plans drawn up by the NCC for a return to civilian rule were revised to extend the transition beyond an initially envisaged two-year period, and then in April 1995 the timetable was scrapped altogether, leaving only a complex system for successive levels of election with no deadlines attached.

Within the West African regional context the Abacha regime, notwithstanding its own lack of democratic credentials, has supported moves to defend and promote democracy elsewhere. Most recently it has spearheaded the ECOMOG peacekeeping force of the Economic Community of West African States (ECOWAS) despatched against a military junta which seized power in Sierra Leone. Internationally, the regime has been damaged by isolation, although not by effective sanctions, because of its non-democratic nature and its human rights record. Nigeria has been suspended from Commonwealth membership since 1995 over the execution of the minority rights campaigner Ken Saro-Wiwa and other Ogoni leaders. The problems of Nigeria's heavily indebted economy were also compounded when Abacha reversed the economic reforms begun by Babangida, thereby reducing any prospect of major support from the International Monetary Fund.

Gen. Abacha is married with six sons and three daughters.

King **Harald V**

King Harald V has been Norway's head of state since January 1991, following the death of his father King Olaf V. As with other Scandinavian constitutional monarchies, the functions of the sovereign are almost entirely ceremonial. Harald, who is also noted as an Olympic sailor and for his popular marriage to a commoner in 1968, served a long apprenticeship as crown prince during his father's 33-year reign.

Harald was born on 21 February 1937, at Skaugum, the estate which is still the home of the royal family. He was baptised on 31 March 1937 in the palace chapel. When the Nazis invaded in 1940, the royal family fled into exile and he spent most of the war years living in the USA near Washington D.C. He returned to Norway after liberation in 1945, attending Smestad primary school until 1950 and the Oslo cathedral school until 1955, taking his upper secondary diploma in science. Between 1956 and 1957 he attended the cavalry officers' candidate school at Trandum, and then the military academy where he remained until graduation in 1959. He has the rank of general in the army and the air force and admiral in the navy.

On 21 September 1957 he took his place beside his father, King Olav V, in the council of state following the death of his grandfather, King Haakon VII. He was made crown prince, taking the oath to the constitution on 21 February 1958.

Harald studied political science at Balliol College, Oxford, between 1960 and 1962, and subsequently devoted much time to foreign visits and the promotion of Norwegian business interests abroad. He took over his father's official duties after King Olav suffered a stroke in June 1990. He came to the throne on his father's death on 17 January 1991, and was sworn in as king four days later.

King Harald married Sonja Haraldsen on 29 August 1968. They have two children, Princess Martha Louise and Crown Prince Haakon, who was born in 1973. Prince Haakon is the heir to the throne, since legislation passed in May 1990 which gave equal succession rights to both sexes only applies to those born after 1990.

Sultan **Qaboos** bin Said al-Said

Sultan Qaboos has ruled Oman since July 1970, when he deposed his father Said bin Timur. Qaboos took control with the support of the armed forces and several members of the royal family after the alleged deterioration in the former sultan's health. As sultan he is head of state and head of government in what is in effect an absolute monarchy, with no constitution or legislature. His rule is authoritarian but paternalistic, combining a conservative perspective with cautious modernisation.

Qaboos bin Said al-Said was born in Salalah, in the southern province of Dhofar, on 18 November 1940, and is the latest heir to the Bu Said dynasty, the Ibadi Muslim clan which has ruled Oman since the 18th century; the sultanate of Muscat and Oman formally gained independence from Britain in 1951. Qaboos was educated privately in England and trained as an officer at the Royal Military Academy, Sandhurst, from 1960, including a one-year tour of duty with a British infantry battalion stationed in West Germany. Before returning to Oman he studied local government with Bedfordshire County Council for almost 12 months. In Salalah, from 1966, he studied Islamic history and culture under the guidance of his father.

Qaboos justified the 1970 coup in Salalah with reference to a need to modernise and develop Oman's international relations, and has maintained a consistently pro-Western stance, while also developing contacts within the Arab world and among the other conservative Gulf shaikhdoms. He has also framed a series of five-year plans, designed to create a modern infrastructure in Oman, which nevertheless remains relatively little developed and dependent on oil for its prosperity. He established in 1981 a state consultative council, which in 1991 became an all-elected body, albeit with only advisory functions. Since coming to power he has been minister of foreign affairs and minister of defence, and in 1994 also took the title of prime minister.

Muhammad Rafiq **Tarar**

Muhammad Tarar was elected by the federal parliament on 31 December 1997 as president of Pakistan, to take office on 1 January 1998. Tarar, a former Supreme Court judge, was the candidate of the Pakistan Muslim League (PML) and is a close friend of prime minister and PML leader Nawaz Sharif, a fellow Punjabi. The president is head of state, but the National Assembly in April 1997 repealed a constitutional amendment dating from 1985 allowing the president to dismiss the prime minister (a controversial power used on two subsequent occasions), and the main functions of the office are now ceremonial. The previous incumbent, Farooq Leghari of the Pakistan People's Party (PPP), had been forced to resign on 2 December 1997 at the end of a bitter power struggle with Nawaz Sharif over judicial appointments, the presidency being filled on an interim basis during the rest of December by Senate chairman Wasim Sajjad.

Muhammad Rafiq Tarar was born on 2 November 1929 in a small village in the Punjab, where he entered the judiciary after completing his law degree at Punjab University in 1951. He rose to the post of Lahore high court judge in 1974, served on the election commission from 1980, and became provincial chief justice in 1989. Two years later he became a Supreme Court judge. He gave up this post in October 1994. As a member of the PML he was elected by the provincial assembly in March 1997 to a seat in the federal Senate. During his short political career he has chaired the Senate committee on culture, sports and tourism.

Although Tarar describes himself as a liberal Muslim, he has been outspoken in opposing laws to give women the right to divorce, and his nomination to the presidency in December 1997 caused considerable surprise, as well as concern that the number of Punjabis holding top posts was creating a serious regional imbalance. The acting chief election commissioner, Justice Junejo, an appointee of Leghari, attempted to rule that Tarar's candidacy should be disallowed, on the grounds that criticisms of the judiciary in an interview he gave in June amounted to defamation and thus made him constitutionally ineligible. However, when an appeal against this ruling was heard on 23 December, Justice Qayyum allowed the nomination to stand pending further investigation. The PML's large majority in both National Assembly and Senate ensured that he emerged an easy winner in the presidential election, held at a joint sitting of the federal legislature on 31 December.

Kuniwo **Nakamura**

Kuniwo Nakamura was first elected president of Palau in November 1992, led the former US trust territory to full independence and membership of the UN in 1994, and was re-elected for a four-year term in November 1996. An economics and business graduate and former teacher, he was for many years a representative of Koror state in the Palau congress, becoming the republic's vice-president in 1989 and chairing negotiations on relations with the USA. As president he is both head of state and head of government, and appoints the members of the cabinet.

Nakamura was born on 24 November 1943 in Peleliu state. He attended a local elementary school, Palau Intermediate School and then Tumon High School (now JFK High School) in Guam. In 1967 he graduated from the University of Hawaii with a degree in economics and business administration. He worked as a teacher at Palau High School and became economic adviser to the US trust territory administration.

In 1975 he entered politics, serving two terms in the House of Representatives of the former Congress of Micronesia and chairing the appropriations committee. In 1978 he became a member of the Palau legislature, chairing the ways and means committee and the Palau Maritime Authority. At this time he was one of the delegates for Koror state to the first Palau Constitutional Convention, acting as leader from the floor. A republican constitution for Palau was adopted by referendum in October 1979, and the following year Nakamura was elected to the national congress for Koror state, retaining this seat in successive elections.

In 1989 Nakamura was appointed vice-president; he also held ministerial portfolios for administration and later for justice. His main preoccupation, however, was with chairing (from 1989) the commission on the future of Palau and its relations with the USA. Successive governments had sought throughout the 1980s to remove the anti-nuclear clause in the 1979 constitution, so as to open the way for Palau to move from its US trust territory status to full independence with a Compact of Free Association guaranteeing substantial US aid. The eventual solution to the intractable problem of obtaining the necessary three-quarters majority in a referendum was to include, with the 1992 elections, an amendment to remove this high threshold.

A change in the voting system to include primary elections for presidential candidates led to the elimination of incumbent President Etpison before the final ballot in the 1992 election, fought mainly on the Compact issue. Nakamura, standing like his predecessors on a non-party basis, narrowly won the election on 3 November 1992, with 50.7 per cent of the vote. The provision to make the constitutional amendment less difficult was also approved; a 64 per cent "yes" vote was obtained in a referendum a year later, and, with the Compact thereby secured, Palau became independent on 1 October 1994, with Nakamura as head of state.

He was re-elected to the presidency with a large majority in 1996, his popularity boosted by the islands' increasing prosperity arising from US aid and from his strategy of encouraging tourism and investment from Japan, Taiwan and the Philippines.

Yassir **Arafat**

Yassir Arafat was elected as president of the Palestinian legislative council in January 1996 and is president of the Palestinian National Authority. Although he is widely regarded, and treated, as head of state, a formal declaration of Palestinian statehood is not generally anticipated until the conclusion of ultimate talks with Israel. Arafat also acts as head of government, appointing the cabinet which is responsible to the legislative council. His international profile has changed over the decades. Condemned by many as a terrorist leader in the 1970s, he was being applauded by the 1990s as a pragmatic moderate, and shared the Nobel Peace Prize in 1994 with Israeli prime minister Yitzhak Rabin for their contribution to the Israel–Palestine peace process. Conversely, the halting of progress in the transfer of territory to Palestinian control leaves him more vulnerable to the accusation from radical critics that his dealings with Israel have compromised the Palestinian cause.

Mohammed Abdel-Raouf Arafat al-Qudwa al-Hussein was born on 24 August 1929 in Cairo, Egypt. He was nicknamed Yassir, meaning "easy", and spent most of his childhood in Jerusalem, living with his uncle after the death of his mother when he was four. In 1944 he joined the League of Palestinian Students. Aged only 17, he began procuring weapons for an anticipated battle for Palestinian territory. During the Arab–Israeli conflict which surrounded the creation of the state of Israel, Arafat fought with forces backing the grand mufti of Jerusalem, and in 1948 he fled to Cairo, one of some three-quarters of a million Palestinian Arabs left stateless. He began studies in engineering at Cairo University.

In 1952 he joined the Muslim Brotherhood and Union of Palestinian Students, of which he became president. At the outbreak of the Suez crisis in 1956, he participated in the Egyptian army. Moving to Kuwait that year, he worked as an engineer before founding his own company.

In 1957 Arafat co-founded *Al Fatah*, the Palestine National Liberation Movement and underground organisation which mounted several attacks on Israel. In 1968, Arafat and *Fatah* received international publicity when they fought off Israeli troops who had entered Jordan. *Al Fatah* soon became linked with the umbrella Palestine Liberation Organization (PLO), becoming its dominant faction. Arafat was himself elected as PLO chairman in 1969 and has retained this post ever since. From this time the PLO moved from a stand of pan-Arabism to an increasing preoccupation with the cause of a specifically Palestinian nationhood. When the PLO was forced out of Jordan in 1970, it switched its main activities to bases in Lebanon, from where it continued to carry out raids against Israel until it was again driven out, this time to Tunisia, by the Israeli forces which invaded Lebanon in 1982.

Arafat and the PLO had meanwhile won wide international recognition as "the sole legitimate representative of the Palestinian people", the UN voting in 1974 (after Arafat addressed the General Assembly) to give the PLO observer status and to recognise the Palestinians' claim to self-determination.

On 15 November 1988, an independent state of Palestine was proclaimed, at a meeting of the PLO's "parliament", the Palestine National Council, in Algiers. The territory of Palestine was defined as comprising the West Bank and the Gaza Strip, at that time in the throes of a popular uprising or *intifada* against Israeli occupation. Arafat went on to declare before the UN that the PLO renounced terrorism, and that it supported the right of all parties to live in peace. This declaration, going much of the way to meeting the Israeli complaint that the PLO opposed its right to existence as a state, led to an expansion in the international recognition of the PLO, and was a diplomatic success for Arafat. The following year, he was elected president of Palestine by the central council of the Palestine National Council, although a period of diplomatic setbacks followed, with the PLO's standing in the West in particular suffering from Arafat's backing for the Iraqi side in the 1991 Gulf war.

US-led negotiations in Madrid later in 1991, aiming to set in motion a comprehensive Middle East peace process, bore little positive fruit in respect of the Palestinian issue. Matters did progress, however, after secret negotiations, when in 1993 the Oslo agreement laid down a "land for peace" formula. Arafat's own international standing increased significantly when, in recognition of the importance of the Oslo agreement, he and Rabin won the 1994 Nobel Peace Prize. Israeli forces withdrew from Jericho, and Arafat returned at last to Palestinian territory, as chairman of a Palestine National Authority (PNA) set up under the 1993 peace agreement. On 20 January 1996, he was overwhelmingly elected first president of the Palestinian authority's legislative body, the 88-seat Palestinian council, governing the West Bank and the Gaza Strip.

Yassir Arafat married Suha Tawil in 1991.

Ernesto **Pérez**

Ernesto Pérez was sworn in for a five-year term on 1 September 1994 as president of Panama, an executive post combining the functions of head of state and head of government. He is a millionaire businessman and former banker, with experience in government and as a negotiator of the Panama Canal Treaty, and a professed admirer of the former National Guard leader and "Supreme Leader of the Panamanian Revolution" in the 1970s, Gen. Torrijos. Pérez was elected as president as the candidate of the Democratic Revolutionary Party (PRD) which he helped found in 1979 as a torrijista *populist nationalist party and which later became identified with the regime of Gen. Noriega, who was ousted by US intervention in 1989. Upon taking office, Pérez promised national reconciliation and an amnesty against those "unjustly persecuted" since the US intervention.*

Ernesto Pérez Balladares was born in Panama City on 29 June 1946. He was educated at the University of Notre Dame du Lac, where he graduated in business administration and gained a master's degree in economics, going on to study business administration in the USA in 1970. He was the director and corporate credit official for Panama and central America for Citibank from 1971 to 1975, and is the president of several companies.

Pérez entered politics in 1975, when he became a member of the Panama legislative commission, and served as the international delegate representing Panama for a hydroelectric power plant scheme. In 1976 he became minister of finance and the treasury. Heavily involved in the trade and governance of the Panama Canal, he was a negotiator and witness of the Panama Canal Treaty in 1977. In 1981/82 he was minister of planning and economic policy, and in 1983 he became director-general of the Electric and Hydraulic Resources Institute.

In 1992 Pérez was reappointed general secretary of the PRD, a post he had previously held in 1982, having helped found the party in 1979. In 1993 he was nominated as the PRD candidate for the presidency, winning election in the ballot on 8 May 1994 ahead of six other candidates on the basis of 33.3 per cent of the votes cast. In simultaneous legislative elections his party won 31 of the 72 seats, making it the largest party in the legislative assembly.

Ernesto Pérez Balladares is married, with two sons and three daughters.

Sailas **Atopare**

Dr Sailas Atopare has been governor-general of Papua New Guinea since November 1997, representing the monarch, Queen Elizabeth II, as titular head of state, and serving a six-year term.

Atopare, born in 1951, had been a member of parliament for the Eastern Highlands province before his election as governor-general. He emerged as the victor from a lengthy process of parliamentary balloting, after his predecessor Sir Wiwa Korowi had failed to win the two-thirds majority which is required by the constitution if an incumbent governor-general is to be re-elected to serve a second term. In the final ballot, held on 14 November, Atopare won 54 votes against 44 for Lutheran church leader Sir Getake Gam.

Appointed formally by Queen Elizabeth II and sworn in on 20 November 1997, Atopare is the country's seventh governor-general.

Juan Carlos **Wasmosy**

Juan Carlos Wasmosy Monti has been president of Paraguay since August 1993, serving a non-renewable five-year term as head of state and government. His party, the Colorado party (or National Republican Association), is the largest party in congress but has no overall majority and is riven by factional disputes. Wasmosy is a civil engineer by training. He made his fortune in power station construction before entering government in 1992, when he was almost immediately designated by the then President Andrés Rodríguez as his intended successor.

Born on 15 December 1938 in the capital, Asunción, Wasmosy comes from a family of Hungarian immigrant origin. He went to the Colegio San José and then the National University of Asunción, graduating with a degree in civil engineering in 1962. Later he became an assistant professor at the university's school of architecture. Most of his private career, however, has been in the construction industry. He became immensely wealthy as a leading member of the construction consortium which built the Itaipú dam and hydroelectric power station and which is currently involved in the construction of the even larger Yacretá hydro power scheme. Wasmosy is also president of the international association for breeders of zebu cattle.

Wasmosy joined the Colorado party in 1973, during the long period of the Stroessner dictatorship, but he was not active in politics until several years after the ousting of Stroessner in 1989 by Gen. Rodríguez. He was briefly minister of integration under Rodríguez, who chose him as his preferred successor as the 1993 presidential elections approached. The Colorado party primaries, however, were marked by bitter infighting and an internal election in December 1992 in which the pro-Stroessner party president, Luis María Argaña, claimed victory. Wasmosy's supporters on the party's ruling board overturned this result, encouraged by an open declaration of support from the regime's military strongman Gen. Oviedo. Wasmosy went on to win the election proper, on 9 May 1993, when he took 40.9 per cent of the vote against two other major and ten minor candidates. He faced the need to rule without a supportive congress, however, since the Colorados had lost their majority there, and his position was further weakened by the continuing hostility of the Argaña faction, which later called for his impeachment.

Wasmosy took office as president on 15 August 1993, and pledged to continue the process of political and economic liberalisation, but he repaid Oviedo's support by the controversial – and as it transpired misguided – decision to make him army commander-in-chief. Oviedo's ambitions led him subsequently to fall out with Wasmosy, whose remaining supporters, the *wasmosista* faction within the Colorado party, now faced the prospect of an alliance between *argañistas* and *oviedistas.* In April 1996 Oviedo tried unsuccessfully to force Wasmosy to resign. After initially seeking a compromise, Wasmosy eventually responded more firmly to the threat by purging the pro-Oviedo officer corps. Oviedo was charged in June 1996 with attempted insurrection, but was subsequently acquitted. Although Argaña appeared meanwhile to have strengthened his hand by winning Colorado party leadership elections in April 1996, Oviedo outflanked both him and the *wasmosistas* in the course of 1997 to win the party's nomination as presidential candidate for 1998. Wasmosy, reduced to the role of "lame duck president", gave assurances apparently under US pressure in December 1997 that he had no intention of overturning the due political process in order to seek an extension of his period of office.

Wasmosy is married to Maria Teresa Carrasco Dos Santos; they have four sons and a daughter.

Alberto **Fujimori**

Alberto Fujimori has been president of Peru since July 1990 and was re-elected for a second five-year term (having opened the way for this by changing the constitution) in a landslide victory in April 1995. Fujimori ran the National Agrarian University and had a political talk show on television until he launched his own political movement, the vehicle for his 1990 presidential campaign. In office, he has taken an authoritarian line, ruling largely by decree, and has clamped down hard on terrorism. Despite his populist image he has proven to be a neo-liberal on economic issues, pursuing free-market policies after applying a heavy dose of austerity measures to conquer hyperinflation, and advocating continuing Latin American regional integration.

Alberto Keinya Fujimori was born on 28 July 1938 in La Victoria, Lima. The son of Japanese immigrants, he converted to Catholicism. After his schooling in Lima he went to the National Agrarian University in La Molina, graduating in 1961 with a degree in agronomic engineering and joining the teaching staff in the mathematics department. Returning after a period spent studying mathematics abroad (at the University of Strasbourg in 1964, and then at the University of Wisconsin where he got a master's degree in 1969), he rose to be dean of the school of sciences, and eventually rector of the university from 1984 to 1989. In 1987 he was elected chair of the National Assembly of University Presidents.

Fujimori gained experience and a reputation as a skilful political analyst during his time as rector, hosting a television talk show "Getting Together". In 1989 he launched a political career, co-founding the political movement *Cambio 90* (Change 90) and becoming its candidate for the 1990 presidential election.

His unexpectedly strong performance in the first-round ballot on 8 April 1990 gave him second place and forced a second-round run-off against the novelist Mario Vargas Llosa, who was standing as the candidate of the right-wing Democratic Front (*Fredemo*). In the second ballot on 10 June Fujimori won convincingly, with 56.5 per cent of the votes cast, to his opponent's 34 per cent. This result was seen as a protest vote, supporting the claim of *Cambio 90* to be a new alternative to the traditional parties, and reflecting suspicion of his opponent as a member of the élite. Fujimori successfully projected a populist image, attracting strong support from the rural and urban poor. Known as El Chinito (the "little Chinaman"), he was seen by Peruvian Indians and *mestizos* (those of mixed race) as not belonging to the dominant minority who were of European descent.

Fujimori was sworn in on 28 July 1990, confronting an economic crisis, a crippling debt burden and hyperinflation. Upon taking power, Fujimori instituted austerity measures whose nature and severity shocked many of his supporters. Despite his populist campaign, his policies once in office were calculated to strengthen the free-market economic system by a combination of deregulation and decentralisation, and to restore confidence among international lenders. This approach did succeed in slowing down the rate of inflation, bringing it gradually below three figures and eventually down to just over 10 per cent by 1995. Meanwhile, between 1991 and 1993, Fujimori paid a series of visits to Japan, other parts of east Asia, Europe, the USA and Latin America, in an attempt to gain support and financial backing for the Peruvian economy.

Equally controversial, but more popular, was his hard line against the Maoist guerrilla insurgency of the Shining Path (*Sendero Luminosa*), whom he has confronted without paying much heed to criticism from human rights organisations. Already given extensive emergency powers by the congress in 1991, he launched an *autogolpe* or "self-coup" on 5 April 1992 to give himself a free hand, dissolving congress, suspending the national constitution, and dismissing top-ranking government officials and 13 of the 23 Supreme Court justices. In September the Shining Path leader Abimael Guzman was captured, and a year later Fujimori announced that he had received a letter sent by Guzman from prison, requesting talks towards an eventual "peace treaty".

Fujimori pushed through in the course of 1993 a new constitution which increased his own powers as president and removed the bar on a second term (enabling him to stand for re-election on 9 April 1995, when he won almost two-thirds of the vote). In 1996, moreover, he got congressional acceptance to seek a further term in 2000, on the grounds that the 1993 constitution allowed two terms, and that his first term did not count because he began it under the previous constitution.

Fujimori's image as a man of action was promoted by his personal direction of operations in a border conflict with Ecuador in early 1995. The international spotlight fell on him once again when left-wing *Tupac Amaru* guerrillas seized control of the home of the Japanese ambassador during a reception on 17 December 1996, initiating a long siege. Eventually, adopting a characteristically high-risk strategy, Fujimori on 22 April 1997 ordered in a commando unit which successfully stormed the compound, freeing the hostages (one of whom was killed, along with two of the soldiers) and killing all 14 of the guerrillas.

Alberto Keinya Fujimori married Susana Higuchi, a civil engineer, on 25 July 1974, and the couple had four children. A public dispute between them in 1994, when he issued a decree to try to prevent her entering politics, led to a high-profile rupture in their marriage, which ended in divorce in November 1995.

Fidel **Ramos**

Fidel Valdez Ramos became president of the Philippines on 30 June 1992, for a six-year non-renewable term. A Protestant leader of an overwhelmingly Catholic country, he is the 12th post-independence president, but the first to win a multiparty contest for this top executive post (which under the 1987 constitution combines the roles of head of state and head of government). His predecessor Corazon Aquino had come to power in February 1986 only after an upsurge of "people power" which drove out the Marcos dictatorship and reversed the rigged result of a highly controversial poll. Ramos, a US-trained officer and second cousin to Ferdinand Marcos, had risen under his regime to become its leading counter-insurgency commander and acting chief of staff. However, he became a crucial figure in the triumph of "people power", switching his support to Aquino at a critical moment, and he subsequently helped her government to weather a series of coup attempts.

Fidel Ramos was born on 18 March 1928 in Lingayen in the province of Pangasinan. His father was a lawyer and legislator who held government office as secretary of foreign affairs. From 1946 to 1950 he attended the élite US military academy at West Point, on a government scholarship, and in 1951 he qualified in civil engineering at the University of Illinois. Beginning his military career alongside US forces in Korea as a second lieutenant in the Philippines expeditionary force, he was chair of the Unconventional Warfare Committee by 1960, distinguished himself in Vietnam from 1966 to 1968 as head of the Philippines Civil Action Group, took a master's degree in national security administration at the National Defence College of the Philippines in 1969, and in 1971 was made head of the Philippines army special forces. The following year he was appointed chief of the Philippines constabulary, a position he retained throughout the Marcos years as a trusted key adviser and specialist in the counter-insurgency campaign against communist guerrillas.

Ramos became acting chief of staff in 1984, when Gen. Fabian Ver was suspended over involvement in the assassination of opposition leader Benigno Aquino (the event which propelled Benigno's widow Corazon into the political limelight). In his new role, however, Ramos began to make a name for himself as a campaigner against corruption in the military, expressing approval of the efforts of a "reform the armed forces" movement to ensure military impartiality and fair elections. The reinstatement of Ver in December 1985, the blatant rigging of the presidential elections in Marcos's favour the following February, and the prospect of his own imminent arrest in a clampdown on the opposition, pushed him (along with defence minister Juan Ponce Enrile) to declare allegiance to Aquino on 22 February 1986. To prevent Ver's troops from implementing Marcos's threat to "wipe out" Ramos, Enrile and the officers loyal to them, protest demonstrators massed around the national police headquarters. It was this popular defiance which was dubbed "people power" and which proved crucial in destroying the fast-ebbing credibility of the Marcos regime, precipitating his flight three days later.

Aquino, inaugurated on 25 February, promoted Ramos from lieutenant-general to full general and appointed him as armed forces chief of staff. In January 1988 Ramos entered the cabinet as minister of national defence, and he was also vice-chair of the National Peace and Order Council. During the six years of Aquino's presidency he quelled a total of seven coup attempts, the most serious being those of August 1987 and December 1989.

In 1991 Ramos declared his candidacy for the presidential elections due the following May. He benefited from Aquino's personal endorsement but failed to win the nomination in November 1991 of the main pro-government *Laban* party (LDP) and instead launched his own *Lakas* or People Power Party, which he later merged with the National Union of Christian Democrats (NUCD). His victory in the nationwide election on 11 May 1992 was achieved with only 23.6 per cent of the vote, topping the poll against six other candidates; he was sworn in on 30 June. The mid-term legislative elections in 1995 significantly strengthened his position in that his *Lakas*-NUCD, temporarily in alliance with the main faction of *Laban*, achieved a large majority in the House of Representatives. A major political talking-point in 1997, as the end of Ramos's term approached, was speculation that he might seek an amendment of the constitution to enable him to run for a further term, or to create a prime ministerial system under which he could continue in power.

As president, Ramos is also head of the National Disaster Co-ordinating Council, and holds a cabinet post with special responsibility for regional development in the southwestern Philippines.

Fidel Ramos is married, and has five daughters.

Aleksander **Kwasniewski**

Aleksander Kwasniewski has been president of Poland since December 1995. Elected for a five-year term in a nationwide ballot, the president is head of state while the prime minister (who is responsible to parliament) is head of government. The president nevertheless has considerable political influence and retains some executive powers, notably including the right to reject nominations made by the parliament for the post of prime minister. Kwasniewski is an ex-communist whose election caused some alarm especially in the USA, but represents a younger generation of pragmatic reformers in the party, which is now called Social Democracy of the Polish Republic (SdRP). An economist by training and editor of party youth publications, he was a junior minister in the last communist governments of the late 1980s, was active in the 1989 round-table debates on introducing a multiparty system, and became SdRP leader early the following year.

Kwasniewski was born in Bialogard, in the province of Kozazalin, on 15 November 1954. After attending high school in Bialogard, he graduated from the University of Gdansk with a degree in transport economics. He was an energetic political activist in the student socialist youth union, joined the then ruling communist party, the Polish United Workers' Party (PZPR), in 1977, edited the official student weekly paper from 1981 to 1984, and was editor-in-chief of the youth daily *Sztandar Mlodych* in 1984/85.

In November 1985 Kwasniewski joined the council of ministers and had special responsibility for youth affairs. By 1987 he had become chairman of the committee for youth and physical education and in October 1988 he was appointed head of the government socio-political committee. The following year he took part in the round-table debates on the creation of a pluralist system, held between February and April. After these talks had opened the way for partially free elections, and the PZPR had entered a Solidarity-led coalition government, the party held an extraordinary congress in January 1990 and reconstituted itself as the social democratic SdRP, with the youthful Kwasniewski a forward-looking choice as its first chairman.

Kwasniewski was elected in 1991 to sit as a deputy in the *Sejm*, the lower chamber in what had become a bicameral parliament. For two years from November 1993 he chaired the parliamentary constitutional committee and gained a reputation for seeking consensus in the interests of political unity. This even extended to giving his initial support to the conclusion of a concordat between Poland and the Vatican, to which many in his party were openly hostile. Kwasniewski also sat as a member of the foreign affairs committee and the economic policy, budget and finance committee.

In the 1995 presidential election, Kwasniewski led in the first round on 5 November with just over 35 per cent of the vote, narrowly ahead of the incumbent Lech Walesa in a field of 13 candidates. The run-off two weeks later was again close, Kwasniewski winning with 51.7 per cent. He was sworn in on 22 December, after the constitutional tribunal had ruled against Walesa's attempt to have him disqualified for allegedly misleading the voters about his electoral qualifications by claiming a postgraduate degree.

As president, Kwasniewski committed himself to promoting national consensus – a promise sorely tested the following year by the issue of abortion. (He eventually signed into law a bill permitting terminations but only within the early period of a pregnancy.) He also expressed his support for continuing economic reforms and concluding the formulation of a democratic constitution (which finally took effect in October 1997), and backed Poland's applications for membership of the European Union and the North Atlantic Treaty Organization (NATO).

Kwasniewski is married to Jolanta *née* Konty and they have one daughter.

Jorge **Sampaio**

Jorge Sampaio, a lawyer and former mayor of Lisbon, was sworn in for a five-year term as president of Portugal in March 1996. Formerly mayor of Lisbon, he was the candidate of the Socialist Party (PS). As president, Sampaio does not have a major executive role but acts as mediator in disputes, and may dissolve parliament and call an early election in the event of a political impasse.

Jorge Fernando Branco de Sampaio was born on 18 September 1939 in Lisbon. The son of a doctor, he spent part of his schooldays in England, and went to Lisbon University in 1956 to study law. His political career began at this time and he led student protests against the dictatorship of António de Oliveira Salazar. He went on to defend other opponents of the regime as a young lawyer in Lisbon.

After the "carnation revolution" in 1974 he initially supported the small Movement of the Socialist Left (MES) but distanced himself from the movement when it began to adopt Marxist policies. In 1978 he joined the PS, led by Mário Soares, and was elected as a parliamentary deputy in the 1979 general election and in subsequent elections. Throughout Sampaio has maintained a strong commitment to the defence of human rights and from 1979 to 1984 served on the Council of Europe's Commission for Human Rights in Strasbourg. In 1987 he was elected president of the PS parliamentary party, and he was PS secretary-general in 1989, but was replaced in 1992 by António Guterres.

In December 1989 Sampaio was elected mayor of Lisbon, a post to which he was re-elected in 1994.

The election of a socialist government in October 1995, and Sampaio's election as president on 14 January 1996, when he won 53.8 per cent of the vote, brought to end a decade of Portuguese politics dominated by Soares as president and the social democrat leader Aníbal Cavaco Silva as prime minister.

Sampaio lives in Lisbon with his second wife, and has one son and one daughter.

Shaikh **Hamad** bin Khalifa al-Thani

Shaikh Hamad bin Khalifa al-Thani acceded to power on 27 June 1995, ousting his father, Shaikh Khalifa, in a bloodless coup to become amir of Qatar. A Sandhurst-trained officer and head of his country's armed forces since 1972, he had played a major role in modernising army units and in increasing armed forces personnel.

Born in 1950 in Doha, he attended primary and secondary schools there before joining the Royal Military College, Sandhurst, from which he passed out in 1971. He joined the Qatari armed forces and was appointed commander of the First Mobile Battalion with the rank of major, a rank he held until his promotion to major-general and appointment as commander-in-chief of the armed forces in February 1972.

On 31 May 1977 he was appointed heir apparent and minister of defence, while remaining as commander-in-chief of the armed forces. In May 1989 he became chairman of the Higher Council for Planning, a position considered to be vital in the building of a modern state. He also chaired the Higher Council for Youth Welfare from its establishment in 1979 until September 1991, when the General Authority for Youth and Sports was established and a full-time chairman appointed.

Shaikh Hamad's takeover of power on 27 June 1995, while his father was abroad, was overwhelmingly supported by the armed forces and cabinet, and welcomed by neighbouring states. It was apparently motivated by disagreements when Shaikh Khalifa sought to resume closer control of the government, having effectively passed over its management to Shaikh Hamad three years earlier.

On becoming amir, Shaikh Hamad also became prime minister, but held this post for only a year, subsequently issuing an amiri decree to amend the Basic Temporary Amended Statutes of the Rule of the State, in order to separate the post of prime minister from that of amir.

Emil **Constantinescu**

Emil Constantinescu was sworn in as president of Romania on 28 November 1996, for a four-year term. A respected former professor and chancellor of the University of Bucharest, he was the candidate of the Democratic Convention of Romania (DCR), as he had been, unsuccessfully, at the previous election in 1992. His victory marked the completion of the political transition from the communist era, removing from power the former communist Ion Iliescu who had held the presidency since the ousting of Ceausescu in 1989.

Emil Constantinescu was born on 19 November 1939 in Tighina (now in Moldova), the son of an agronomist. He attended high school in Pitesti and from 1956 attended the law faculty of the University of Bucharest, graduating in 1960. After spending a year as an assistant judge in Pitesti he returned to the University of Bucharest in 1961 and enrolled at the faculty of geography and geology, graduating in 1966. He gained his doctorate in geology in 1979, became a lecturer in 1980, and a professor in 1990. In 1992 he was elected chancellor of the university.

In late 1989 Constantinescu participated alongside his students in the demonstrations which helped to topple the Ceausescu regime. In 1990 he was one of the founders of Universitarian Solidarity, an organisation set up after the Bucharest street protests in June to contest the intimidatory tactics of the new Iliescu regime. He was also a founder member and vice-president of the Civic Alliance, established in 1990. As a representative of the alliance he became the acting chairman of the Romanian Anti-totalitarian Forum in 1991, which was later transformed into the DCR centre-right electoral alliance. Constantinescu was elected president of the DCR in November 1992, having been the DCR candidate for the presidency in elections at which he finished runner-up behind the incumbent, Iliescu, the previous month.

In March 1995 he was re-elected president of the DCR and was nominated as the party's candidate for the 1996 presidential election. In the first round held on 3 November he came second out of 16 candidates, winning 28 per cent of the vote as against 32 per cent for Iliescu. However, in the second-round run-off on 17 November he overtook Iliescu, having secured the backing of most of the eliminated candidates, and obtained 54.4 per cent of the vote.

Following his election as president Constantinescu resigned as leader of the DCR and was replaced by Ion Diaconescu. At the swearing-in ceremony on 28 November he pledged to work for Romania's prompt accession to both the European Union and the North Atlantic Treaty Organization (NATO).

Constantinescu is married to Nadia Ileana, a lawyer at the ministry of justice. They have two children.

Boris **Yeltsin**

Boris Yeltsin is to date the only person to have held the post of president of the Russian Federation since it became an independent state upon the break-up of the Soviet Union at the end of 1991. Yeltsin was formerly a top communist party official in Sverdlovsk and then Moscow, and a protégé of Mikhail Gorbachev. He renounced his party membership in 1990, the year in which he was first elected as chairman of the Supreme Soviet of the Russian republic. In June 1991 he won a popular mandate at a direct presidential election, thereby strengthening his credentials as the advocate of more rapid and extensive reforms than were being implemented by the Soviet leadership under Gorbachev. Having taken a courageous stand in opposing the hard-line coup attempt in Moscow that August, Yeltsin enjoyed great prestige as Russia's first post-communist president, but faced an enormous task in terms of reconstructing the economy and reconciling conflicting political pressures. He was criticised for lacking a firm direction in liberalising the economy, and for an authoritarian intolerance of opposition, particularly when he called in the army in a violent power struggle against the conservative-led parliament in 1993. Yeltsin's popularity slumped thereafter as a desperate economic situation was compounded by an apparently unwinnable war against Chechen nationalists. In the 1996 presidential elections he nevertheless attracted enough support as the best available pro-reform option to defeat the communist challenge. His health at that time, his sometimes erratic public behaviour, and his relapses into illness linked to his major heart surgery at the end of 1996, have kept the succession issue in the forefront of Russian politics ever since.

Boris Nikolayevich Yeltsin was born on 1 February 1931 in Butka in Sverdlovsk region. His family had a peasant farming background, but his father became a construction worker and his mother a seamstress. In his youth, Boris blew off two fingers on his left hand while playing with a live grenade. Nevertheless, whilst he was a college student he played professional volleyball for Sverdlovsk, one of the leading Soviet teams at the time. Expected to pursue a career in industry, he completed his degree in construction engineering at Kirov Polytechnic School in Sverdlovsk (now Yekaterinberg) in 1955, then worked as manager of a heavy tubing manufacturing plant. Between 1957 and 1967 he was manager, then executive engineer, then director of the Yusgorstroy Construction Trust.

Yeltsin began to be heavily involved in politics from 1961, when he first joined the Communist Party of the Soviet Union (CPSU). From the late 1960s until the mid-1980s he was secretary, then chairman of the party regional committee in

Sverdlovsk, and in 1980 he became a member of the CPSU central committee. The election of Gorbachev as party general secretary in 1985 marked a turning point in Yeltsin's career. Moving to Moscow, he was made first secretary of the CPSU in the city, joined the central committee's powerful secretariat and became a candidate member of the politburo. Quickly identified as a radical, he grew increasingly popular with the people of Moscow for his informal manner and his willingness to criticise the Soviet system over such failures as poor housing and empty shops. Apparently disillusioned with the pace of *perestroika* (restructuring), however, he became involved in open confrontation with leading conservatives in the party at the end of 1987, and was dropped from the politburo, criticised by Gorbachev, and shunted from the Moscow leadership to a position with much lower visibility, as minister of construction.

Election by a huge majority in March 1989 to represent a Moscow constituency in the Soviet Union's newly restyled Congress of People's Deputies gave Yeltsin a fresh chance to demonstrate both his popularity and his political flair. A founder member of the oppositional Inter-Regional Group in the Soviet parliament, he dared to discuss multipartyism and called passionately for the transfer of more power from the centre to the republics. The Russian Federation Congress of People's Deputies, elected in early 1990, chose him in May as its speaker and, deciding that this was incompatible with party membership, he threw his party card on the floor in front of Gorbachev at the party congress in July 1990, expressing disgust with the slow pace of reforms.

Going for more radical change within the Russian republic with a 500-day "dash to the market economy" package and a declaration of sovereignty, Yeltsin was temporarily reconciled with Gorbachev to ward off a conservative backlash, until he strengthened his hand by holding and winning direct elections for the post of Russian president in June 1991, with 57 per cent of the vote.

Two months later, the hardline August coup in Moscow threatened not only to depose Gorbachev from the Soviet leadership, but to reverse the growing autonomy of the republics and to halt the whole reform experiment. Yeltsin famously led the resistance from the Russian parliament (the White House), emulating a pose of Lenin when he addressed the crowds from the top of a tank, and retaining the political initiative when the coup collapsed. The rapid dissolution of the Soviet Union within the remaining four months of 1991 left him in an apparently very strong position. He was a powerful and popular executive president of the Russian Federation, while the new Commonwealth of Independent States (CIS) offered him the prospect of maintaining links among the former Soviet republics in a manner which would reflect the role of Russia at its core.

In the course of 1992, however, Yeltsin became locked in a struggle with the conservative forces in the Russian parliament over the sometimes ill-conceived attempts of his liberal ministers to implement economic reforms. The constitutional court also opposed what it regarded as his attempt to assert excessive powers, successively over the creation of ministries, the banning of the communist party, the appointment of the prime minister, and his decision in 1993 that he would rule by decree. In parliament the conservatives fell narrowly short in a vote to impeach him in March 1993. The following month he won a vote of confidence in a popular referendum, but in September, when he issued a decree disbanding the parliament, conservative communist and right-wing nationalist forces combined to resist him by force. Proclaiming Gen. Rutskoi as president in Yeltsin's place, they attacked strategic points in Moscow, and held out in the parliament building when Yeltsin called in loyal troops. The shelling of the White House on Yeltsin's orders sent out an image of authoritarianism, at the scene of his own stand for freedom three years previously, from which his liberal democratic credentials never recovered. Elections to a new parliament in December 1993 returned large numbers of communists and ultra-nationalists, although Yeltsin did get his way with the narrow endorsement of a new constitution which gave him strong presidential powers.

Yeltsin's popularity touched an all-time low in 1995 as Russian troops fought a long and bloody war in Chechenya, where he had despatched them the previous December in a high-risk effort to end a separatist rebellion. Many of his erstwhile liberal allies condemned the war, while the economy languished in serious recession, organised crime undermined the authority of the government, and the president himself suffered two mild heart attacks. The communist party topped the poll in fresh elections at the end of that year, and pro-reform factions remained divided in the run-up to the presidential elections scheduled for mid-1996. A populist campaign of unexpected vigour, however, saw Yeltsin top the first round poll on 16 June. His support held up, in spite of a spate of fresh rumours about his ill health and frailty, to allow him to defeat the communist leader Gennady Zyuganov in the run-off on 3 July, with almost 54 per cent of the vote.

Sworn in again on 9 August, Yeltsin suffered a collapse and needed quadruple coronary bypass surgery in November. Many believed that his career was over. To great surprise, he made a recovery, marking his comeback with a complete reshuffle of his cabinet in March 1997. His government has continued to be marked by oscillation between an apparent strengthening of commitment to economic reform, and changes of personnel and periods of retreat in the face of unpopularity. The issue of his health, once again in the forefront at the end of 1997, has become a dominant factor as factions jockey for position in a post-Yeltsin era.

Boris Yeltsin is married to former fellow engineering graduate Naina Iosifovna Girina and has two daughters and four grandchildren.

Pasteur **Bizimungu**

Pasteur Bizimungu was inaugurated as president of the Republic of Rwanda in July 1994, after the previous regime, a genocidal Hutu-dominated military government, had collapsed in the face of the advancing forces of the Tutsi-dominated Rwandan Patriotic Front (FPR). Bizimungu, a former banker and businessman who joined the rebel FPR and fled Rwanda in 1990, is himself a moderate Hutu. His appointment as president was sometimes dismissed as a cosmetic exercise to diminish the perception that the new government was Tutsi-controlled. The FPR commander Paul Kagame is vice-president and defence minister and is often described as the strongman of the current regime. According to a transitional constitution adopted in 1995, the president appoints the council of ministers, whose head is the prime minister.

Pasteur Bizimungu was born in 1950 in Bushiri, Rwanda. He was educated in Rwanda until 1973 when he went to study in France and gained a master's degree. He began his career in banking and then rose to become director-general of the Rwandan national energy concern, Electrogaz. Towards the end of the 1980s he began to distance himself from the government and in 1990 joined the FPR. The same year he fled to Belgium and he remained in exile until 1994. He was an FPR representative at peace negotiations with the Rwandan government in Tanzania in 1993.

Any prospect of a peace settlement vanished when extremist Hutus took power in Kigali, encouraging their militias to launch a genocidal massacre of the Tutsi minority, following the death of President Habyarimana of Rwanda and his Burundian counterpart in an unexplained plane crash in April 1994. The FPR responded by stepping up its offensive in the northeast, capturing Kigali and other major towns by 19 July and announcing the formation of a new government with Bizimungu as president.

As president, Bizimungu has backed calls for a UN tribunal to investigate the 1994 genocide, and to bring to trial Hutu officials who were responsible for the massacres. An International Criminal Tribunal for Rwanda was eventually set up in Arusha, Tanzania.

Pasteur Bizimungu is married with children.

Sir Cuthbert **Sebastian**

Sir Cuthbert Sebastian was appointed governor-general of St Kitts and Nevis on 1 January 1996, succeeding the first governor-general, Sir Clement Arrindell. He is a doctor and had been for many years the chief medical officer at the general hospital in St Kitts. The governor-general represents the monarch, Queen Elizabeth II, as titular head of state.

Cuthbert Montraville Sebastian was born on 22 October 1921 and was educated at Basseterre Boys' Elementary School, teaching the younger boys for the last few years he was there. In 1939 he joined the St Kitts–Nevis defence force and started work as a learner dispenser at the Cunningham Hospital. Four years later he finished his training as a chemist and druggist and was promoted to medical sergeant. In 1944 he qualified as a laboratory technician. He then joined the Royal Air Force, serving as a rear gunner until the end of the war.

In 1945 Sebastian was appointed senior dispenser and steward (hospital administrator) at the Cunningham Hospital, where he remained for the next five years. He then went to study medicine in Canada, graduating from Mount Allison University and going on to Dalhousie Medical School, where he gained his doctorate in 1958 as well as a master of surgery degree. Having obtained licences from the Nova Scotia Medical Board and the Canadian Medical Council, he returned to St Kitts, becoming captain-surgeon of the defence force and working as a general practitioner for four years in many parts of St Kitts, Nevis and Anguilla.

In 1962 he decided to specialise in obstetrics and gynaecology and he attended the Dundee Royal Infirmary in Scotland for the next four years. On his return to St Kitts in 1966 he was appointed medical superintendent and obstetrician gynaecologist at Cunningham Hospital and again took up the post of captain-surgeon of the defence force, which he held until 1980. In 1967 he moved to the new Joseph N. France General Hospital and was made chief medical officer three years later.

In 1975, during a visit by the Prince of Wales to St Kitts, Sebastian was appointed as his local physician. Two years later he accompanied the then prime minister, Robert L. Bradshaw, to London for Queen Elizabeth's Silver Jubilee, acting as his aide-de-camp and personal physician. He continued to practise medicine until he was appointed to the governor-generalship in 1996.

Pearlette **Louisy**

Pearlette Louisy became the first woman governor-general of St Lucia on 17 September 1997. A former teacher and principal of a tertiary education college in the capital, Castries, she replaced Sir George Mallet who had resigned from the post, after only a year, on 31 August. Her predecessor's appointment had been controversial in that he had been embroiled in politics until only shortly before taking up his post. The governor-general represents the monarch, Queen Elizabeth II, as titular head of state.

Calliopa Pearlette Louisy was born on 8 June 1946 in the small village of Laborie on the west coast of the island. She attended St Joseph's Convent School in Castries and went on to the University of the West Indies in Barbados, graduating in English and French in 1969. By 1975 she had obtained a master's degree in linguistics from the Université Laval in Quebec, Canada. Between periods of study she taught in Castries, where she was a college principal in the 1980s and also national correspondent to the Agence de Coopération Culturelle et Technique, a position she held for ten years.

In 1986 she moved to the Sir Arthur Louis Community College at The Morne, Castries, as dean of the division of arts, science and general studies, a position she held for six years before her promotion to vice-principal and (in 1996) principal of the college. By 1994 she had obtained a doctorate in higher education from the University of Bristol. From 1996 until her appointment as governor-general she was secretary and treasurer of the Association of Caribbean Tertiary Institutions in addition to her role as college principal.

During her career Pearlette Louisy has written a number of papers and spoken frequently on a range of issues in tertiary education; she has also written several publications on learning the Creole language.

Sir Charles **Antrobus**

Sir Charles Antrobus was appointed governor-general of St Vincent and the Grenadines on 1 June 1996, representing the monarch, Queen Elizabeth II, as titular head of state. He is a former telegraph operator and had retired in 1993 as the islands' general manager of Cable and Wireless (C&W).

Charles James Antrobus was born on 14 May 1933 in Kingstown and attended St Vincent Grammar School. In 1951 he attended the C&W College in Barbados to train in telecommunications operations, and first worked as a telegraph operator for C&W in St Vincent until 1957. He then spent two years working in London for the Foreign Office in the diplomatic wireless service, first as a telecommunications officer and then at the traffic centre. He then returned to the Caribbean with C&W, spending some time working in the British Virgin Islands, Montserrat, St Kitts and Dominica. As general manager of C&W on St Vincent he was responsible for the introduction and extension of the automatic telephone dial system. While pursuing his long career with C&W he also held various other positions, including that of director and vice-president of the St Vincent Co-operative Bank, member of the board of income tax appeal commissioners and director of the St Vincent national insurance scheme.

After his retirement from C&W in 1993 he became a member of the central supplies tenders board, the St Vincent and the Grenadines appellate authority, chairman of the air transport licensing board and chairman of the civil service salaries review committee. He has also been vice-president of the islands' Chamber of Commerce and of the Employers' Federation, as well as a member of the board of the Duke of Edinburgh award scheme. He retired from all of these boards on his appointment as governor-general in June 1996.

Sir Charles Antrobus is married to Gloria Janet Vena.

Malietoa **Tanumafili II**

Malietoa Tanumafili II has been in office as monarch (O le Ao O le Malo) *since the country's independence (as Western Samoa) on 1 January 1962, initially as joint head of state and since April 1963 as sole monarch. The role is mainly ceremonial, and the office is an elective one; thus the next head of state will be chosen by the legislative assembly for a five-year term, although Tanumafili (and Tupua Tamasese Mea'ole, the other joint monarch until his death on 5 April 1963) held their positions for life as representatives of two of the country's four traditional royal families.*

Tanumafili was born on 4 January 1913, educated in New Zealand at St Stephen's College, Auckland, and Wesley College, Pukekohe, and succeeded to the title of *Malietoa* (head of one of the royal families) on the death of his father in 1940. In the same year he was appointed *Fautua* (adviser) to the New Zealand governor of Western Samoa.

Tanumafili was one of the prominent Samoan leaders in the period leading up to independence in 1962. In 1958 he joined the New Zealand delegation to the United Nations, and was joint chairman of the working committee on independence and the constitutional convention in 1959. In the same year he was awarded the CBE. When the country achieved independence from the New Zealand administration in 1962, he was appointed joint head of state. The death of Tupua Tamasese Mea'ole the following year left him as sole head of state, a post he holds for life. Celebrations held in 1990 marked his 50 years of continuous service to the government and people of the country (the name of which was changed officially in 1997 from Western Samoa to simply Samoa).

Malietoa Tanumafili's wife died in 1966; he has four surviving children.

Luigi **Mazza** and Marino **Zanotti**

Luigi Mazza and Marino Zanotti took office as captains-regent of San Marino on 1 October 1997. The captains-regent serve a six-month term, and together they act as both head of government and head of state. They are elected by the 60-member Grand Council (parliament) from among its members, Mazza and Zanotti each representing one of the two parties in the governing coalition. At the end of their term there is a three-day hearing when any complaints against their time in office can be voiced. This unique form of government was created in 1243 and has remained the same ever since.

Mazza is a lawyer and, since becoming involved in politics, has also worked increasingly in the econ-omic field within the Christian Democratic Party of San Marino (PDCS). His current term in office is his first as captain-regent. Born on 12 October 1960 in New York, he graduated in law from Bologna University and became a lawyer and solicitor. In 1978 he joined the PDCS. From 1982 he served on the council of the castle of the city of San Marino for six years, including two years as captain of the castle. Between 1983 and 1984 he was the central delegate for the youth movement of the PDCS. He has been a member of the Grand Council since 1988. He has been involved with the ministries of finance, budget, planning and information, industry, handicrafts and economic co-operation, commerce, and labour and co-operation as well as the special advisory council for the reform institute. Mazza is married to Lorella Conti and they have one daughter.

Zanotti was born in 1954, joined the San Marino Socialist Party (PSS) in 1976 and is now a member of the leadership. His particular experience lies in the fields of internal affairs, foreign affairs and urban affairs. Between 1987 and 1991 he was deputy secretary of the PSS. From 1983 he spent five years as a state councillor on the council of the castle of Serravalle, holding the captaincy of the castle from 1986 to 1988. Like Mazza, he has been a member of the Grand Council since 1988, and in 1992/93 he served a six-month term as captain-regent. Outside politics Zanotti is a department head in the private company, Colorificio Sammarinese. He is married to Carla Brusa and they have one son.

Miguel **Trovoada**

Miguel Trovoada has been president of São Tomé and Príncipe since April 1991, when he won the first nationwide election for this post following the abolition of the single-party system. As president he is head of state and commander-in-chief of the armed forces, although the formal head of government is the prime minister (whom he appoints). Trovoada is currently serving his second five-year term, having been re-elected in July 1996. A political activist from the time of the campaign for independence from Portuguese rule, he was the country's first prime minister from 1975 to 1979, but fell out with the single-party regime and spent most of the 1980s in exile.

Miguel dos Anjos da Cunha Lisboa Trovoada was born on 27 December 1936 in the city of São Tomé. He attended school in Angola and then went to Portugal to study law. An important figure in the movement opposed to Portuguese colonial rule, he co-founded the Committee for the Liberation of São Tomé and Príncipe (CLSTP) in 1960 with his former classmate Manuel Pinto da Costa, and became its first president. In 1972 the CLSTP renamed itself the Movement for the Liberation of São Tomé and Príncipe (MLSTP) and secured recognition by the Organization of African Unity (OAU). At that time Trovoada ceded the leadership to Pinto da Costa and assumed responsibility for foreign relations.

When São Tomé and Príncipe achieved independence in July 1975 Pinto da Costa was appointed as its first president and Trovoada its first prime minister, and the MLSTP was declared the only legal party. Trovoada held various ministerial posts, until 1979, when a disagreement between him and Pinto da Costa resulted in the abolition of the post of prime minister and Trovoada's demotion. Later that year he was imprisoned without trial, on charges of involvement in an alleged coup, until 1981 when he went into exile in Paris and then Lisbon.

The MLSTP agreed in 1989 to give up its monopoly on power (and it was redesignated the MLSTP-PSD the following year with the addition of "Social Democratic Party" to its name). Trovoada, having returned to São Tomé and Príncipe in May 1990, stood as an independent in the country's first democratic presidential elections held on 3 March 1991. The withdrawal of three other candidates, including Pinto da Costa of the MLSTP-PSD, meant that Trovoada was elected unopposed, and he was sworn in on 3 April 1991.

Economic problems during his first term of office engendered much discontent against government corruption and austerity measures imposed via the International Monetary Fund. Trovoada's support in the legislature was severely reduced at elections in October 1994, when the MLSTP-PSD won almost half the seats. After a series of short-lived governments, Trovoada was temporarily deposed in a military coup on 15 August 1995, but then reinstated on 21 August as a result of pressure from donor countries and an amnesty offer. In January 1996 a government of national unity was appointed.

In 1996, presidential elections due in March were postponed until 30 June. No candidate secured an absolute majority, but in a second-round run-off Trovoada won 52.74 per cent as against 47.26 per cent for Pinto da Costa. Although Trovoada did not enjoy a parliamentary majority, he refused to call fresh elections. Surviving another brief coup by junior officers in August, he went ahead with the formation of a broad-based government of national consensus, which was eventually sworn in in November 1996.

Miguel Trovoada is married with three children.

King **Fahd**

King Fahd has ruled Saudi Arabia since June 1982, coming to the throne following the death of his half-brother King Khaled. He is the son of King Abdul Aziz ibn Saud, founder of the Saudi state in the modern period, and has maintained a conservative absolute monarchy in which he is head of government as well as head of state, ruling by decree. Governing according to Islamic law, his official title also denotes his religious role as Custodian of the Two Holy Mosques.

Prince Fahd ibn Abdul Aziz was born in 1923 in Riyadh, and graduated from the Scientific Institute in Makkah. In 1953 he was appointed (Saudi Arabia's first) minister of education, and introduced a series of five-year development plans in an attempt to improve his country's education system. In 1962 he became minister of the interior, and by 1967 was second deputy prime minister. In March 1975, on the accession to the throne of his half-brother Khaled, Fahd was appointed crown prince and deputy prime minister. As crown prince he oversaw the implementation of successive five-year development plans.

Since his accession to the throne on 13 June 1982, Fahd has been responsible for the country's subsequent development plans, emphasising the growth of the private sector. On 1 March 1992 he introduced a Basic Law for the System of Government, and later that year restructured the *Majlis ash-Shoura* (the consultative council). He has introduced new laws governing the administration of the Saudi provinces and the council of ministers.

King Fahd has long taken an active interest in Saudi's international position. In 1977, he met with US officials to discuss solutions to the Arab–Israeli conflict, and in 1981 he outlined his own "Eight-Point Peace Plan", which became the basis for the Fez Declaration. He called in 1985 for increased US intervention in the Middle East. Under Fahd's leadership, Saudi Arabia attended the 1991 Madrid peace conference and the 1992 Moscow peace talks. In the 1990/91 Iraqi invasion of Kuwait he permitted the US-led allied forces to operate from Saudi Arabia. In 1992 Fahd donated emergency relief funds to Bosnia and established a Supreme Committee for the Collection of Donations for the Muslims of Bosnia.

King Fahd has three wives and six sons. His brother, Prince Abdullah, has been crown prince since Fahd came to the throne and deputised in 1995/96 when Fahd was described officially as resting, having reportedly suffered a stroke.

Abdou **Diouf**

Abdou Diouf has been president since 1981 and was last re-elected, for a seven-year term, in 1993. As president he is head of state and also head of government, and appoints the prime minister. Diouf, a former civil servant, had been prime minister for 11 years under the country's first post-independence leader Léopold Senghor, succeeding to the presidency on the latter's resignation.

Abdou Diouf was born on 7 September 1935 at Louga, northeast of Dakar. He attended primary school in Saint-Louis, near the border with Mauritania. He gained his baccalaureate in 1955, then went to university in Dakar and Paris, where he graduated in public law and political science in 1959. In 1960, he gained a diploma from the French overseas civil service school.

Following Senegalese independence in 1960, Diouf was appointed director of international technical co-operation and minister of planning in the government of President Senghor. He was also assistant secretary-general to the government and then secretary-general at the ministry of defence. Between December 1961 and December 1962 he was governor of Sine-Saloum region, then became *chef de cabinet* first to the minister of foreign affairs and from March 1963 to the president. In 1964 he moved on to become secretary-general in the president's office.

In 1968 he was re-appointed minister of planning and industry and remained in this post until he became prime minister on 28 February 1970. He has been a member of the National Assembly since 1973.

Diouf first became president on 1 January 1981, in a rare instance in Africa at that time of the voluntary retirement of an incumbent and the transfer of authority to a constitutionally designated successor. An early move under his presidency was the removal of the previous limit of four on the number of political parties allowed to operate within the multiparty system. Diouf has been elected to successive terms in 1983, 1988 and 1993, repeatedly defeating the leader of the rival Senegalese Democratic Party, Abdoulayé Wade. On the most recent occasion, on 21 February 1993, Diouf won 58.4 per cent against 32 per cent for Wade. In the same year a ceasefire was concluded with armed separatists in Casamance in the south, although this conflict continues to flare up.

Diouf was president of the Economic Community of West African States (ECOWAS) in 1981/82, has also been president of the Organization of African Unity (OAU), and was a vice-president of the Socialist International from 1992 to 1996. He is also the leader of the Senegalese Socialist Party (PS), which has an overall majority in the unicameral National Assembly.

Abdou Diouf was married in 1963.

France-Albert **René**

France-Albert René first became president of the Seychelles in June 1977, a year after independence. He has ruled continuously since then, managing the transition from a one-party state and winning a five-year term in the islands' first multiparty presidential elections held in July 1993. The president is both head of state and head of government.

René was born in Mahe on 16 November 1935. Having completed his early education in the Seychelles he travelled to Switzerland, and then to the UK, in order to complete his education at St Mary's College, Southampton, and at King's College, London. He qualified in law at the Middle Temple in a record five months and was called to the Bar in 1957, subsequently returning to the Seychelles, where he practised in the capital, Victoria, and was also involved in the trade union movement.

In June 1964 René founded and led the Seychelles People's United Party (later known as the Seychelles People's Progressive Front or SPPF), and was elected to the Seychelles legislative assembly in a by-election in 1965. He directed the governmental committee for three years from 1967. In 1970 he was the leader of the opposition in the assembly, pushing for the return of several islands, for universal suffrage, and for national independence. In 1974 René was re-elected to the legislative assembly, becoming the minister of works and land development in 1975.

On 29 June 1976 the Seychelles gained independence. René became prime minister (1976–77) in a coalition government with the Seychelles Democratic Party, whose leader James Mancham became president. However, one year later René deposed Mancham in an almost bloodless coup on 4/5 June 1977, while the president was attending a Commonwealth summit in London. As president and commander-in-chief, René ran a single-party state in which the newly formed Seychelles People's Progressive Front, of which he was secretary-general, was defined as having the leading role. Besides being head of state, René retained several ministerial posts himself.

At an extraordinary SPPF congress in December 1991, in line with the trends sweeping Africa, René announced the introduction of a multiparty democracy and inaugurated a period of constitutional reform. At the same congress he was unanimously re-elected secretary-general of the party. In the first multiparty presidential election, held on 23 July 1993, René was returned to office with 59.5 per cent of the vote as against 36.7 per cent for his closest rival, Mancham. In the concurrent legislative elections the SPPF won an absolute majority of seats.

France-Albert René has been married three times: to Karen Handley in 1956, to Geva Adam in 1975, and to Sarah Zarquani in 1993.

Lt.-Col. Johnny **Koroma**

Lt.-Col. Johnny Paul Koroma seized power in May 1997 in a military coup, ousting Alhaji Ahmad Tejan Kabbah who had been elected president of Sierra Leone in February/March 1996. A largely unknown figure, even within the country, Koroma suspended the constitution and declared himself president. After intervention by the Economic Community of West African States (ECOWAS), Koroma agreed in October 1997 to the restoration of the elected president Kabbah within six months, but the apparent breakdown of this agreement at the end of the year exposed him to the likelihood of military intervention by an ECOMOG peacekeeping force.

Born in 1964, Koroma comes from the Limba ethnic group. He trained as a soldier in the UK, Nigeria and Ghana, and joined the Sierra Leone armed forces in 1987, commanding a battalion attached to Sierra Rutile's bauxite mine in Moyamba district. In September 1996, six months after the election of Kabbah as president, Koroma led an unsuccessful coup, was imprisoned and was due to come to trial the following May. However, one day before his scheduled appearance in court, soldiers freed him from prison on 25 May 1997 and seized power in the country's third successful coup in five years.

On 26 May Koroma was named head of state and declared that he had led the coup for the sake of peace; the country had been embroiled for the past six years in a civil war with the rebel Revolutionary United Front (RUF), which the Kabbah regime had shown no sign of bringing back under control since the breakdown of a November 1996 ceasefire.

Two days later Koroma abolished the constitution and banned political parties. Although he said there would be a return to "proper democracy", he gave no timetable. On 1 June he formed an Armed Forces Revolutionary Council (AFRC), composed entirely of young army officers, and with the rebel RUF leader Foday Sankoh as its vice-president. Sankoh had signed a peace accord with Kabbah in November 1996 but later came to oppose the ceasefire and was in March 1997 placed under house arrest in Nigeria on charges of illegal possession of armaments.

The new regime was denied international recognition. In June ECOWAS sent a Nigerian-led peacekeeping force, ECOMOG, to restore civilian rule. On 23 October, representatives of the AFRC eventually signed a peace accord with ECOMOG in Conakry, in neighbouring Guinea where Kabbah was exiled, under which Koroma agreed that Kabbah would be restored to power within six months.

Koroma is married with four children.

Ahmad **Kabbah**

Ahmad Kabbah was sworn in as president on 29 March 1996, having emerged as the second-round winner in elections held to restore civilian government after a four-year period of military rule. A British-trained barrister and former UN Development Programme (UNDP) official, Kabbah contested the elections as the candidate of the Sierra Leone People's Party (SLPP). After barely more than one year in office, however, and with the country having relapsed into civil war with the rebel Revolutionary United Front (RUF), Kabbah was forced into exile by a coup on 25 May 1997. The new regime was not recognised internationally, and in October 1997 the coup leader Lt.-Col. Koroma agreed to the restoration of Kabbah's government within six months, although the prospects of a peaceful transfer soon began to recede. Under the 1991 constitution the president, who is both head of state and government, should normally serve a four-year term.

Ahmad Tejan Kabbah was born on 16 February 1932 in Pendembu, Kailahun district. He attended St Edward's School in the capital, Freetown, and studied economics at University College, Aberystwyth, Wales, before joining the colonial administrative service in 1959. He was an assistant district commissioner in the Bombali, Moyamba, Kono and Kambia districts before transferring to Freetown as deputy permanent secretary in the ministry of social welfare. He was promoted to permanent secretary and served at the ministry of trade and industry and the ministry of education.

In 1968 he studied law at Gray's Inn in London. On completion of his barrister's examinations he moved to the UN in New York as deputy chief of its West African division. He headed the UNDP offices in several southern African states between 1973 and 1981, when he was promoted to deputy personnel director, then director of UNDP's division of administration and management.

In the 1996 elections he won 35.8 per cent of the vote in the first round on 26/27 February and 59.5 per cent in the run-off on 15 March. Polling was disrupted by the RUF and some 27 people were killed. Kabbah was sworn in on 29 March.

Kabbah was forced to flee to Guinea on 25 May 1997 following Koroma's successful coup. Kabbah, however, retained recognition internationally as the lawful president, representing Sierra Leone in this capacity at the Commonwealth heads of government meeting in Edinburgh in October 1997. Intervention by an ECOMOG peacekeeping force of the Economic Community of West African States (ECOWAS) eventually resulted in agreement in October 1997 that Kabbah should be restored to power within six months.

Kabbah is married to Patricia Tucker.

Ong Teng Cheong

Ong Teng Cheong has been president since August 1993, and is the first president to have been chosen by direct nationwide ballot. A former architect, Ong was for several years deputy prime minister. The president, elected for a six-year term, is head of state, and appoints the prime minister and cabinet. The responsibilities of the presidency were increased when it was made a directly elective post, but the office is still mainly ceremonial, with most political power being exercised from the prime minister's office.

Ong Teng Cheong was born in Singapore on 22 January 1936. Educated initially at the Chinese High School, he then entered the University of Adelaide, Australia, where he graduated in architecture in 1961, and he spent the next three years working as an architect in Adelaide and Singapore. In 1967 he obtained his master's degree in civic design from Liverpool University, England. In the same year he joined the Singapore civil service, and worked for several years as an architect and town planner in the public sector, and was involved in the Urban Renewal and Development Project. He set up his own practice with his wife in 1971.

First elected to parliament in 1972, until 1993 he represented the Kim Keat constituency. He was active in the People's Action Party, and was chairman of its executive committee from 1981 to 1990. In 1975 he entered the government as senior minister of state for communications, and served in a variety of ministries until 1985. These included the ministries of labour and culture, as well as a ministry without portfolio. In 1985 Ong became second deputy prime minister, becoming deputy prime minister in November 1990. He was also deeply involved in the trade union movement, and was the secretary-general of the National Trades Union Congress (NTUC) from 1983 to 1993.

In 1991 the constitution of Singapore was altered to allow for the direct election of the president by universal adult suffrage, and to enhance certain presidential powers. Ong resigned from his positions in the cabinet and the People's Action Party in August 1993 in order to stand for the presidency. He was elected with over 58 per cent of the vote in the poll on 28 August.

Ong Teng Chung is married to Ling Siew May, and they have two sons.

Michal **Kovac**

Michal Kovac was elected president of Slovakia for a five-year term in February 1993, following the dissolution of the Czech and Slovak Federative Republic and the creation of an independent Slovakia on 1 January of that year. Before becoming president, Kovac spent many years in banking and financial analysis, and after the "velvet revolution" which brought down the communist regime in Czechoslovakia in 1989 he held ministerial office in the Slovak government. In 1993 he was the official candidate of the ruling Movement for a Democratic Slovakia (HZDS), from which he subsequently distanced himself, however, because of disagreements with Prime Minister Vladimir Meciar. The president is head of state and has some influence as a check on the powers of the executive branch, although Kovac has been accused by his opponents of going beyond these powers. Fundamentally the Slovak system is a parliamentary one in which the prime minister is head of government.

Kovac was born in Lubisa, Humenne county, on 5 August 1930. He was educated at the commercial academy and school of economics in Bratislava and joined the communist party in 1953. He worked for a year as an assistant lecturer before starting work at the state bank of Czechoslovakia in 1956. He was a financial adviser at the National Bank of Cuba in 1965/66, and deputy director of the Czechoslovak trade bank in London from 1967. He continued to lecture at the school of economics until 1967.

After Warsaw Pact troops invaded Czechoslovakia in 1968 to quell the liberalisation introduced during the "Prague spring", Kovac was recalled from London, expelled from the communist party, and demoted to the position of bank clerk. In 1978 he returned to research and teaching, specialising in monetary policy and banking.

After the "velvet revolution" of 1989, Kovac was appointed minister of finance in the Slovak government, a post he held until his resignation in May 1991. In June 1990 he was also elected to the Czechoslovak federal parliament for the radical Public Against Violence (VPN) movement. After the collapse of the VPN he joined the HZDS, becoming vice-president of the party in June 1991. In June 1992 Kovac was re-elected as an HZDS candidate to the federal assembly, which then elected him speaker of the federal assembly in succession to Alexander Dubcek. With the approaching split of the Czech and Slovak republics, Kovac was nominated for the presidency by the HZDS. He was elected in February 1993 by 106 votes to 20 by the members of the National Council (unicameral parliament).

Since his election, Kovac has repeatedly come into confrontation with Vladimir Meciar, Slovak prime minister since 1992, even though Meciar had strongly supported his candidacy. In March 1994 Meciar accused him of incompetence and populism and in August 1995, after an incident in which Kovac's son was abducted, Kovac was expelled from the HZDS. An investigation into the affair failed to prove or disprove allegations that the Slovak Information Service, which was led by a close ally of Meciar, had been involved in the kidnapping. Kovac has several times vetoed restrictive legislation passed by Meciar's government. He has received awards from the Institute of East–West Studies in the USA and from the American Bar Association for his role in advancing the rule of law in Slovakia.

A referendum was held in May 1997 on whether Slovakia should join the North Atlantic Treaty Organization (NATO) and on the possibility of holding direct presidential elections. However, differences between the government and Kovac over the validity of the referendum and confusion surrounding a ruling by the constitutional court resulted in a turnout of only 9.6 per cent and the vote was declared invalid.

Michal Kovac is married to Emilia Kovac, who teaches at the Bratislava school of economics, and they have two sons.

Milan **Kucan**

Milan Kucan has been president of Slovenia since April 1990 and was most recently elected in November 1997 for a further five-year term. A reform communist in the late 1980s, Kucan was first elected president when Slovenia was still a constituent republic of former Yugoslavia. Following Slovenia's declaration of independence in June 1991, he stood successfully as a non-party candidate in the country's first direct presidential elections in December 1992. The president is head of state but the office is primarily ceremonial, the head of government being the prime minister.

Milan Kucan was born on 14 January 1941, in the Prekomurje village of Krizevci near the Slovene–Hungarian border. He grew up in a teacher's family. His father, an officer in the resistance, was killed by the Nazis when Kucan was only three years old. He graduated from Ljubljana University in 1963, qualifying afterwards as a lawyer.

Kucan became involved in politics in 1964, and led the youth wing of the League of Communists of Slovenia, before working as a member of the secretariat of the League of Communists of Slovenia from 1969 to 1973. He was elected to his first government post in 1978, as president of the Slovene assembly. Between 1982 and 1986, he was the Slovenian representative on the central committee of the Yugoslav League of Communists in Belgrade. He returned to Slovenia in 1986 to become leader of the then League of Communists of Slovenia (ZKS), working to turn the ZKS into a reformist, social democratic political organisation and to introduce a multiparty system. In 1989 the ZKS was renamed the ZKS Party of Democratic Reform. Five years after his election as leader of the reformist wing of ZKS, the first free political parties were founded and the first multiparty elections were held concurrently with presidential elections in April 1990. Kucan won the latter with 58.4 per cent of the vote. Presiding over a peaceful transition to pluralist democracy, he was instrumental in preparing Slovenia for the independence declaration of June 1991.

As president he deliberately stood aside from party politics, renouncing ZKS membership at the time of Slovenia's first presidential election after independence, held on 6 December 1992. Kucan was elected from among seven other candidates, winning 63.8 per cent of the vote.

On 23 November 1997 he was re-elected, again on the first round, with 55.6 per cent of the vote against eight candidates, and sworn in on 22 December. His popularity is attributed to a combination of his diplomatic skill, his image as a moderate, and the relative smoothness of Slovenia's adaptation to the free market in the post-communist period. He has also promoted Slovenia's integration into western Europe, its application for membership of the European Union, and participation in NATO's "partnership for peace" programme from March 1994.

Sir Moses **Pitakaka**

Sir Moses Pitakaka became governor-general of the Solomon Islands for a five-year term on 16 May 1994, succeeding Sir George Lepping. Sir Moses is a former teacher, magistrate and administrator, and chairman of the citizenship commission. The governor-general represents the monarch, Queen Elizabeth II, as titular head of state. His powers relating to the dismissal of a government which lacks a parliamentary majority were tested in a political crisis shortly after he took office.

Moses Puibangara Pitakaka was born on 24 January 1945 in Zaru village in Choiseul province. He attended school in Sasamunga in his home province and then Goldie College on Banga Island in the Western province. In the early 1960s he spent two years at the Solomon Islands Teachers' College before starting work in 1964.

Over the next 15 years he held a variety of posts, first as a teacher and education officer and subsequently as a district officer, district commissioner and lands officer. He became a magistrate and was Honiara town clerk. During this time he continued his studies in education, attending a course at Birmingham University in 1967/68. In 1973 he spent four months at the University of the South Pacific in Fiji studying administration. Three years later he attended the University of Manchester in the UK for a course on public administration and trade relations, and the following year he attended St John's College, Oxford, studying diplomacy and foreign relations.

On returning to the Solomon Islands he became head of the foreign affairs department. He was also appointed chairman of the country's citizenship commission, a post he held for a decade. Also involved since 1980 with running the family business, he was human resources development manager for the local office of the Unilever Company from 1983 to 1985. At this time he was appointed chairman of the National Education Board – a position he held for six years – and a member of the judicial and legal services commission. In 1987 he joined the leadership code commission, becoming chairman two years later.

He was appointed as governor-general in May 1994, at a time when the prime minister, Francis Billy Hilly, had a parliamentary majority of only one. During a recess in October two government ministers joined the opposition, and the governor-general then moved to dismiss the prime minister on the grounds that he no longer held a parliamentary majority. Billy Hilly claimed this was not constitutionally legal, and refused to step down, even when the court of appeal upheld his dismissal. The court's decision was reversed by a judicial ruling that a vote of no confidence was required to dismiss the prime minister, but also stated that the governor-general need not follow the advice of a minority government. The crisis ended on 31 October when Billy Hilly resigned.

Sir Moses Pitakaka is married and has three sons and four daughters.

Ali Mahdi Mohammed

Following the overthrow of the regime of President Siyad Barre in January 1991, Ali Mahdi Mohammed was appointed interim president of Somalia by the United Somali Congress (USC), which he leads. However a split in the USC in July of that year led to tribal fighting and since then it has not proved possible to establish a functioning national government.

Ali Mahdi Mohammed was born in 1940 in Mogadishu. He is from the Abgal tribe, part of the Hawiye clan. He attended local schools and began his working life as a primary school teacher, before training in community health in Egypt and Italy between 1963 and 1966. Returning to Somalia, he served in the government of Mohammed Egal (see Somaliland) as director of the malaria control programme in the ministry of health, and worked as a parliamentary deputy for Jowhar, Benadir region, in 1969. However, following the military coup led by Gen. Siyad Barre that year, he was arrested and imprisoned. After his release he left politics for a while, running and owning the Makkah al-Mukarram Hotel in Mogadishu. He was also director of the UN Children's Fund (Unicef) in the capital.

In January 1989, when the United Somali Congress was set up by Hawiye clan members in central Somalia, Ali Mahdi became an active member and, as a successful entrepreneur, its principal financial backer. The USC won considerable support in the south of the country and by January 1991 was approaching Mogadishu, obliging Siyad Barre to flee the country on 26 January. Three days later Ali Mahdi was appointed interim president by the USC. (Another warring faction from the north, the Somali National Movement, declared the independence of Somaliland from Somalia in May of that year.) By July six of the tribal factions agreed to readopt the independence constitution of 1961 which had been in abeyance since the 1969 coup and they endorsed Ali Mahdi as interim president. However, at the party congress, Gen. Mohammed Farah Aydid of the Habr Gedir subclan of the Hawiye was elected chair of the USC. This caused a split in the party between the two subclans and violent fighting ensued with thousands killed by the end of the year and many more fleeing from the city.

Throughout 1991 and 1992 fighting continued between rival clans, while UN efforts to secure a ceasefire foundered. In December 1992 a US-led and ultimately abortive United Task Force (UNITAF) was sent to Somalia. Shortly afterwards Ali Mahdi and Gen. Aydid signed a peace agreement to end fighting between the two USC factions which did not, however, hold. In November 1993 Ali Mahdi was reported to have been appointed leader of a new alliance of 12 factions opposed to Gen. Aydid.

Talks the following month achieved little, but in March 1994 the two sides signed an accord agreeing to restore peace, disarm fighters and hold a national reconciliation conference in May. Once again, however, this agreement did not hold, and fighting continued, while two UN operations in Somalia (UNOSOM I and UNOSOM II) were unable to maintain peace and withdrew by March 1995. Talks have continued intermittently between the two warring factions. An attempted peace accord in October 1996 came to nothing, but on 3 January 1997 Ali Mahdi helped establish a National Salvation Council (NSC) uniting 26 factions and co-chaired by him and four other tribal leaders. In December 1997 in Cairo he signed a peace agreement on behalf of the NSC with Gen. Aydid's son, Hussein Aydid (see next entry), under which it was believed that he was to become president and Hussein Aydid prime minister. Since both are from the Hawiye clan, resentment among clans may prove an obstacle.

Hussein **Aydid**

Hussein Aydid was chosen by a council of clan elders as the successor of his father Gen. Mohammed Farah Aydid, who died from gunshot wounds on 1 August 1996. Gen. Aydid had been chosen unanimously as "president" of Somalia in June 1995 by representatives of 15 of his supporting factions. At Hussein's "inauguration" on 4 August he vowed to avenge his father's death but no functioning government of Somalia has thus far been able to establish control or to secure international recognition.

Hussein Mohammed Farah Aydid was born in Somalia and is the second eldest son of Gen. Aydid. His birth year is given variously as either 1961 or 1965. Hussein Aydid was educated in the USA and trained as a marine. He still holds both US and Somali citizenship. He joined the US-led and ultimately abortive United Task Force (UNITAF) which was sent to Somalia in 1992, working as an interpreter.

Except for his participation in this operation, Hussein Aydid did not return to Somalia until 1995 when he became his father's chief of security and arms buyer for the southern Mogadishu-based faction. In June of that year divisions within Gen. Aydid's Somali National Alliance (SNA) became evident when a meeting voted to install financier Osman Ali Ato as SNA leader. In response Gen. Aydid called a meeting of 15 factions allied to him which elected him "president" of Somalia for a three-year term. Ali Mahdi Mohammed (see previous entry), who had been appointed interim president of Somalia by the United Somali Congress (USC) in 1991, and Osman Ato both refused to acknowledge the appointment.

Fighting continued after Gen. Aydid's death in August 1996 and Hussein's appointment to the interim "presidency". The looting of UN property in September gained Hussein a reputation as a hardliner, who was opposed to any intervention in his country even from aid agencies. However, in October Aydid, Ali Mahdi and Osman Ato were persuaded to agree a ceasefire and to assist with the distribution of aid to the war-ravaged country, although fighting resumed two weeks later.

After lengthy negotiations held in Mogadishu, Yemen and Cairo throughout 1997, a peace agreement known as the Cairo declaration was signed on 22 December between Ali Mahdi, on behalf of the National Salvation Council, and Hussein Aydid for the SNA. The agreement provided for a ceasefire, the creation of a 13-member presidential council and a 189-member constituent assembly to head a transitional government for three years, leading to the eventual adoption of a federal structure. A reconciliation conference involving 465 delegates was to be held on 15 February 1998 in Somalia, when discussions on the presidency would take place. The Cairo agreement reportedly set it up for Aydid to become prime minister and Ali Mahdi president, but both are from the Hawiye clan, causing resentment among rival clans.

Aydid was married in 1995 in Mogadishu.

Mohammed **Egal**

Mohammed Egal was appointed "president" of the self-proclaimed Republic of Somaliland in May 1993 and was re-elected for a second five-year term in February 1997. Somaliland's secession from Somalia was declared in May 1991 but has not been recognised internationally. Egal is the leader of the Somali National Movement (SNM). At the time of independence in 1960, he was briefly prime minister of what had been the British Somaliland Protectorate (whose erstwhile territory was broadly that over which the Republic of Somaliland now claimed jurisdiction). He then became a government minister in United Somalia and was prime minister for two years prior to the 1979 Siyad Barre coup.

Mohammed Ibrahim Egal was born in 1928 in Odweine Town, Berbera, on the coast of the Gulf of Aden. His family belonged to the Habr Awal sub-clan of the Issaq tribe and was fairly wealthy. Egal was educated at the Koranic school and the nearby Shaikh school before travelling to the UK to study international relations in London. In 1956 he became secretary of the Berbera branch of the Somali National League Party, which was fighting for the independence of the territory from the UK.

Egal was appointed secretary-general of the party from 1958 until the independence of the British Somaliland Protectorate in 1960, when for a few months he was the country's prime minister. Somaliland then joined with neighbouring Somalia, a former Italian colony administered since the Second World War as a UN trust territory. This formed the United Republic of Somalia, with Egal as minister of defence until 1962, when he moved to education. In 1963 he resigned from the cabinet and founded the Somali National Congress (SNC), which became the main opposition party under his leadership. Egal was re-elected to parliament in March 1964 but resigned from the SNC leadership in 1965 and rejoined the governing Somali Youth League party.

In 1967 Dr Abdirashid Shermarke, in whose administration Egal had served, was elected president and he appointed Egal as prime minister of Somalia, also holding the foreign affairs portfolio. Egal improved relations with the UK and the USA, which had suffered as a result of the republic's pro-Soviet communist leanings. However, two years later, Gen. Siyad Barre ousted Egal in a military coup and imprisoned him without trial for six years. Following his release he was made ambassador to India, but was recalled in October 1977 and imprisoned again as an enemy of the regime. After another six years he was again released and was appointed president of the chamber of commerce, industry and agriculture.

In 1981 the SNM was formed as a rebel group, comprising mainly Issaq clan members and seeking to overthrow the Barre regime. It joined with Ethiopian troops in cross-border attacks from 1988 and together with other factions, including the United Somali Congress and the Somali Patriotic Movement, ousted Barre in January 1991. Ali Mahdi Mohammed (see Somalia) was declared president in the capital, Mogadishu, by his faction of the USC. With peace talks between the factions failing, Somaliland seceded from Somalia on 18 May 1991 with the SNM leader, Abdel-Rahman Ahmed Ali, as "president". His power faded however, and a meeting of tribal chiefs, soldiers and politicians was held in February 1993 to plan the country's future. On 5 May the SNM central committee initiated these plans, blocked Ahmed Ali's request for re-election and replaced him with Egal.

Ahmed Ali left for Somalia and, after negotiations with Gen. Mohammed Farah Aydid, demanded Somaliland's return to Somalia in April 1994. Egal branded him a traitor and expressed his determination to preserve Somaliland's independence and to obtain its international recognition, creating a Somaliland currency and issuing new passports. Fighting broke out in October 1994 in Hargeisa. By the end of the year many of the inhabitants had fled and the rebel soldiers occupied most of the city. The violence continued through 1995 while members of the SNM central committee, who were drafting a constitution, differed as to whether a parliamentary democracy style or a US presidential style of government should be instituted, the latter being favoured by Egal.

In February 1997 Egal was re-elected by the SNM for a second five-year term. Later in the year he turned down an invitation to join peace talks with the warring factions in Somalia, claiming he should not interfere with the internal affairs of a neighbouring country. On 16 December Egal resigned due to ill health, claiming he was tired of ruling alone. Two days later parliament voted by 124 votes to three to reject the request, amid massive popular demonstrations in support of Egal.

Egal married Aasha Saeed Abby in 1946 and they have three sons and two daughters.

Nelson **Mandela**

Nelson Mandela was chosen unanimously as president of South Africa by the National Assembly in May 1994, after the victory of his African National Congress (ANC) in elections which marked the abolition of the apartheid regime. As executive president he is both head of state and head of government. Mandela, a political prisoner for more than 27 years, had been released in 1990 and formally became ANC leader the following year. He was a rallying symbol for the international anti-apartheid movement while in prison, and as ANC leader and then president he became the embodiment of hopes for reconciliation in post-apartheid South Africa. Mandela has recently reaffirmed his intention of standing down from the presidency to make way for a new generation of leaders, and by the end of 1997 he had already ceded the ANC leadership to his erstwhile deputy Thabo Mbeki.

Nelson Rolihlahla Mandela was born in the village of Qunu, near Umtata, on 18 July 1918. He attended Methodist schools, and was simultaneously groomed for tribal duties and leadership. He later studied at the University College of Fort Hare, where he was elected to the Students' Representative Council (SRC). He was expelled after his participation in a student strike, and went to Johannesburg to complete his degree and study law. In Johannesburg he met Walter Sisulu, Oliver Tambo and others with whom he was instrumental in radicalising the ANC. Mandela joined the ANC in 1942, and in 1944 helped found the ANC Youth League, which quickly became more radical and militant than the old guard of the ANC.

In 1949, the Youth League's Programme of Action, to which Mandela had contributed, was adopted by the ANC. Mandela was elected to the ANC national executive in 1950, and by 1952 was national volunteer-in-chief for the ANC's Campaign for the Defiance of Unjust Laws. He received a suspended sentence for his contributions to this (non-violent) campaign. He spent the next 12 years working against the system of racial segregation imposed by the National Party in 1948. In 1952 he opened a law firm in the centre of Johannesburg with Oliver Tambo, and by the end of that year was president of the ANC Youth League and of the ANC in the Transvaal region. He developed a series of organisational plans intended to mobilise resistance to apartheid, especially to the nascent Bantustan policy whereby blacks were assigned to rural "homelands" as a pretext for denying them rights elsewhere in the country. In 1956 he was charged with high treason under the Suppression of Communism Act, together with ANC leader Albert Luthuli, Tambo, Sisulu and others, but the trial on this charge fell through in 1961 due to lack of evidence.

The ANC was banned in 1960. The following year Mandela was released from detention. No longer maintaining his commitment to the use of only peaceful means to resist apartheid, he oversaw the founding and first operations of *Umkhonto we Sizwe* (MK), the military branch of the ANC. He left South Africa illegally in 1962, travelling to many African countries, including Algeria for training in guerrilla tactics. He returned before the end of 1962, was swiftly arrested for leaving the country illegally and for incitement to strike, and was jailed for five years from November. While he was in prison, police found the MK headquarters, and he was charged once again with treason. The so-called Rivonia Trial of 1963/64, named after the farm where the police had uncovered the evidence of MK, ended in June 1964 with life sentences for Mandela and seven others. Most of his subsequent imprisonment, until 1984, was spent at the maximum security prison of Robben Island, just off the coast of Cape Town.

While he was in prison, Mandela's situation attracted global attention. He received numerous awards and honours, and thousands of people petitioned for his release during a worldwide campaign launched in the early 1980s. He was offered his freedom several times by President Botha in exchange for a renunciation of violence and acceptance of the Bantustan policy, which he declined, maintaining his refusal to condemn violence despite further government overtures during secret discussions with the minister of justice in 1987 and 1988. In 1989 Botha was replaced as president by F.W. de Klerk, who began a process of repealing many of the laws on which the apartheid system rested. De Klerk lifted the ban on the ANC, and Nelson Mandela was released on 11 February 1990. He was greeted by scenes of mass jubilation, and, although he made it clear that he had accepted no conditions on his release, he did subsequently call for the cessation of violence. In 1991, the ANC held its first national conference for decades inside South Africa, and elected Mandela as its president. In 1993 he received (with de Klerk) the Nobel Peace Prize. Sensitive negotiations over the dismantling of the apartheid state, and the creation of conditions in which democratic elections could take place, occupied Mandela for the period up to 26/29 April 1994, when the elections finally took place. The ANC won a landslide victory, with 62.6 per cent of the nationwide vote, and also dominated the elections in seven of the nine provinces. The National Assembly, meeting on 9 May, elected Mandela unanimously as president, and he was sworn in the following day.

A complex power-sharing formula was implemented in the creation of Mandela's first coalition government. Despite the subsequent withdrawal of the (white-backed) National Party, Mandela achieved a large measure of success over the ensuing period in presenting himself and his government as representing the whole "rainbow nation", and in engendering a positive spirit in the face of the awesome task of nation-building. A new constitution was worked out, and finally signed by Mandela on 10 December 1996. Delivering on the popular expectation of rapid economic improvements proved, however, more difficult to achieve, and in March 1996 Mandela announced the closure of the reconstruction and development office, with much of its work left to be done by government ministries. A further major problem was the high and rising level of violent crime.

Nelson Mandela married his second wife Nomzano Madikizela (Winnie) Mandela in 1958, and they had two daughters, the second born while he was in prison. Having spent much of their lives apart because of his imprisonment (while she also suffered periods of imprisonment, banning and house arrest), they separated in 1992 and were divorced in 1996, increasingly estranged both personally and politically. She nevertheless retained a strong following, especially among younger ANC activists, notwithstanding the evidence of her involvement in the violent "punishing" and even killing of people deemed to have betrayed the movement.

King **Juan Carlos I**

Juan Carlos I was proclaimed king of Spain in November 1975, following the death of Gen. Franco, whose right-wing dictatorship dated from his military uprising in 1936 at the onset of the civil war. The country had become a republic in 1931, but Franco declared it in 1947 to be a monarchy (without a monarch), and designated Juan Carlos as heir to the throne in 1969. Spain is now a parliamentary monarchy, and the duties of the king are mainly ceremonial, although Juan Carlos has gained considerable moral authority by showing his commitment on occasions of crisis to upholding the constitution.

Juan Carlos De Borbón y Borbón was born on 5 January 1938 in Rome. Initially educated in Italy, Switzerland and Portugal, Juan Carlos first went to Spain at the age of ten, when Franco announced his wish to groom him as his successor. He completed his schooling at the San Isidro School in Madrid in 1954, then studied at the army, navy and air force academies, and finally in 1961 studied law and economics at Madrid's Comlutense University. In 1962 he went to live at the Palacio de la Zarzuela near Madrid.

He became provisional head of state on 30 October 1975, in the last weeks of Franco's terminal illness, and was formally declared king on 22 November, becoming also commander-in-chief of the armed forces and head of the Supreme Council of Defence. In his first message to the nation as king he expressed his intent to restore democracy and to become king of all Spaniards, without exception. He hastened reform in July 1976 by appointing a new prime minister, Adolfo Suárez, and supporting him at critical junctures thereafter. Multiparty elections in June 1997 were followed by a referendum in December 1978 to approve a new constitution. This constitution was ratified by the king, who also supported the progressive devolution of powers to the regions.

Meanwhile in May 1977 his father the count of Barcelona transferred his dynastic rights to Juan Carlos, together with his position as head of the royal household. (He had abdicated in 1931 and subsequently ruled out his own reinstatement by refusing to swear allegiance to the principles of the Franco period.)

In February 1981, when a group of civil guards stormed the parliament building, Juan Carlos acted swiftly to secure the loyalty of the armed forces and thus restore the democratic process. His actions earned him widespread respect. Since then he has assumed a more traditional role as constitutional monarch, touring every continent and addressing many international organisations, including the UN. He has had a particular impact in relations with Latin America, emphasising the common cultural community.

Juan Carlos married Princess Sophia of Greece on 14 May 1962. They have three children, Princess Elena, Princess Cristina and Prince Felipe.

Chandrika Bandaranaike **Kumaratunga**

Chandrika Bandaranaike Kumaratunga became president of Sri Lanka for a six-year term in November 1994. The daughter of two former prime ministers, she herself had been prime minister for three months when she stood successfully for election as president, the highest executive position under a 1978 constitutional amendment. Her mother thereupon took over her position as prime minister.

Born Chandrika Bandaranaike in Colombo on 29 June 1945, she was educated initially at St Bridget's Convent in Colombo. Her father Solomon Bandaranaike founded the Sri Lanka Freedom Party (SLFP), became prime minister, but was assassinated in 1959. Her mother Sirimavo Bandaranaike was in 1960 the first woman in the world to be elected as prime minister, and held that office from 1960 to 1965 and from 1970 to 1977. Chandrika trained in political journalism with *Le Monde* in Paris. While in France she also took degrees in law and political science, and a doctorate in development economics. This served as preparation for a subsequent career which encompassed teaching and lecturing, research, and work in land reform.

Between 1972 and 1976, while her mother was head of government, she helped run the Land Reforms Commission of Sri Lanka, and then worked as an expert consultant for the UN Food and Agriculture Organization (FAO) until 1979. During this period she published a book entitled *Janawasa Movement: Future Strategies for Development in Sri Lanka,* chaired the poverty alleviation organisation Jana Savya, and carried out research projects in the fields of food policy, political violence and agrarian reform.

In 1974 she became a member of the executive committee of the Sri Lanka Freedom Party's Women's League. She married the prominent opposition leader and film idol Vijaya Kumaratunga in 1978. She was the chairman and managing director of the *Dinakara Sinhala* daily newspaper from 1977 to 1985. By 1980 she was a member of both the SLFP executive and its working committee. She also became the vice-president of the socialist Sri Lanka Mahajana Party (SLMP), formed by her husband in 1984, and its president by 1986. On 16 February 1988 her husband was shot dead in Colombo, one of a number of high-profile political attacks at this time which were attributed not to Tamil separatists but to Sinhalese extremists.

After 1988, she attended the Institute of Commonwealth Studies at the University of London as a research fellow, returning to Sri Lanka in 1991. In May 1993 she was appointed chief minister of the Western Provincial Council, a position she held until becoming prime minister following the election victory in August 1994 of her People's Alliance. Chandrika campaigned as the Alliance leader, with her mother retaining the leadership of the SLFP itself.

Besides the post of prime minister, Chandrika also held the portfolios of finance, policy planning and implementation, and national integration and ethnic affairs, until her election to the presidency in November. She fought the presidential election campaign largely on her promise of restoring peace to Sri Lanka, and received a record 62 per cent of the vote.

Inaugurated as president on 12 November 1994, she launched several initiatives over the succeeding years in efforts to negotiate with the Tamil separatists, pursuing a devolution policy to assist in this. However, she has also shown herself prepared to use the armed forces in efforts to break the Tamil separatists' military resistance in the north.

Gen. Omar **Bashir**

Gen. Bashir has been president and head of government in Sudan since July 1989, following a military coup. He won a non-party presidential election in March 1996, defeating a large number of relatively unknown opponents, and was sworn in on 1 April 1996 for a fresh five-year term. The president is both head of state and head of government, and appoints the members of the cabinet. Bashir, a career soldier from the north whose regime is dominated by Islamic fundamentalists, had risen through the army to the rank of major-general by the time he launched his 1989 coup and ousted the civilian government.

Omar Hassan Ahmad al-Bashir was born in 1935, educated in Khartoum, the capital, and was a soldier in the Sudanese army from 1960, having trained in Egypt and Malaysia. He fought for the Egyptians in the Yom Kippur war against Israel in 1973, and was involved also in the Sudanese government's long conflict with southern rebels, who continue to resist attempts to make Sudan an Islamic state ruled by sharia law.

On 30 June 1989 Bashir staged a coup, ousting the government of Sadiq al-Mahdi and dissolving parliament. He appointed himself chair of the Revolutionary Command Council for National Salvation (RCC), prime minister (a position he still holds) and minister of defence. He also banned political parties and suspended the constitution, imprisoning many government members and releasing soldiers implicated in previous military coup attempts. Still at war with rebel groups in southern Sudan, his regime is increasingly committed to the introduction of sharia law throughout the country, an objective kept in the forefront by the political dominance of the National Islamic Front (NIF).

In 1993 the RCC announced a return to civilian rule, after appointing Bashir as president and consolidating the power of the National Islamic Front. Non-party elections for a president and a new National Assembly were held in March 1996 but were boycotted by the major opposition factions which had formed a National Democratic Alliance. Forty independent candidates stood and, amid outcries of irregularities, Bashir was elected president for a five-year term with 76 per cent of the vote. The NIF won the majority of seats in the assembly, with their leader being elected chair (speaker) of the assembly.

Under the Bashir regime, diplomatic links have been severed with neighbouring countries whom Sudan accuses of aiding the southern rebels. Conversely, the country has suffered increasing diplomatic isolation as it is accused, by the USA and others, of harbouring terrorists. In January 1996 the UN Security Council passed a resolution criticising Sudan for supporting terrorism and in particular for its role in the attempted assassination of the Egyptian president, Hosni Mubarak, in June 1995.

Jules **Wijdenbosch**

Jules Wijdenbosch was elected president of Surinam for a five-year term by the parliament in September 1996. The president is head of state and head of government, and appoints the council of ministers. Wijdenbosch, who had briefly been prime minister in 1987 and again in 1991, is deputy leader of the right-wing National Democratic Party (NDP). This party, formed in 1987 under his chairmanship, is in practice the political vehicle of the former military regime's strongman, Lt.-Col. Desi Bouterse.

Jules Albert Wijdenbosch was born on 2 May 1941 in Paramaribo. After completing his education in the Netherlands with a doctorate in political sciences and government at Amsterdam University, he worked as a customs officer from 1962 to 1966, and during this period also chaired the Union of Customs Officials. In 1962 he co-founded the General Youth Organisation. Moving to the Netherlands, he worked in administration for the city of Amsterdam and was also vice-chairman of the Dutch Tenasu Foundation, concerned with Surinamese immigration issues.

During the 1970s Wijdenbosch was foreign minister in Surinam under the premiership of Henck Arron, whose government was overthrown by Bouterse's coup in 1980. He held ministerial office again from 1985, in a government headed by Bouterse and formed with the stated intention of returning the country to democratic rule under a new constitution. As a specialist in constitutional law, he contributed to the framing of this constitution, and the law on political parties and on elections. He was also prime minister under these circumstances from February 1987 until the November 1987 election, which produced a severe rebuff for the recently formed NDP. He was, however, brought back as prime minister, and also vice-president, by a pro-Bouterse coup in late December 1990, holding office (and standing down from his party chairmanship) until elections the following May.

By the time of the May 1996 general elections Bouterse had openly taken over the NDP leadership, with Wijdenbosch now the party's vice-chairman. As one of 28 pro-NDP members in the new 51-member National Assembly, Wijdenbosch was part of the strongest bloc, but an impasse developed because the NDP lacked the necessary two-thirds majority to elect a new president by vote of the assembly. It was thus necessary under the 1987 constitution for a broader National People's Assembly (also including local council representatives) to convene. This body on 5 September 1996 elected Wijdenbosch as president, by a vote of 437 to 407, and he formed a government in coalition with four other parties, the condition for their participation being the exclusion of Bouterse and of the NDP from certain key posts.

Jules Wijdenbosch is a widower.

King **Mswati III**

Mswati III was crowned king of Swaziland on 25 April 1986, becoming the youngest reigning monarch in the world at the age of 18. His father, King Sobhuza II, had died four years previously and a power struggle had ensued during the regency, with the result that Mswati was invested as king earlier than planned. He has strengthened the royal powers and rules mainly by decree, despite pressure for more democratisation.

Prince Makhosetive (as he was known before his coronation) was born on 19 April 1968. He was educated in Swaziland and then in England, at Sherborne Public School and Sandhurst Military Academy. His father died when he was 14 and Queen Dzeliwe, one of the royal wives, was appointed regent with the task of governing together with the *Liqoqo*, the traditional advisory council.

The following year she was ousted by members of the *Liqoqo* and replaced by Queen Ntombi, Makhosetive's mother. On the same day, 10 August 1983, Makhosetive was declared heir to the throne which, according to custom, he could not ascend until he was 21. A month later the *Liqoqo* requested that he return from school in England in the hope that his presence would reduce the unrest in the country.

Over the next three years the power struggle continued with the result that the coronation was brought forward and held on 25 April 1986. The following month the newly enthroned King Mswati abolished the *Liqoqo*, and in May 1987 he charged 12 government officials with sedition for their alleged involvement in the dethronement of Queen Dzeliwe and the subsequent intrigue. In September of that year he dissolved parliament. Fresh elections were held in November under a system whereby the electorate could vote for candidates nominated by local councils.

On his 21st birthday Mswati assumed the full powers and responsibilities of the paramount chief but there were already demands for multiparty elections and the restriction of the monarchy to a ceremonial position. In October 1992 he again dissolved parliament, appointed a council of ministers (cabinet) and with their help agreed to rule by decree until multiparty elections could be held. However, political parties have still not been legalised. Elections were held in September/October 1993 to the House of Assembly, but the assembly does not have full legislative powers and can only debate government policy and advise the king.

Mswati is under growing pressure within the region to accept a greater degree of democratisation. After an eight-day protest in January 1996 he agreed to begin talks on the future of the monarchy but refused to consider giving up his powers. Delays on political reforms caused significant social unrest again in 1997.

King Mswati is married and has children.

King Carl XVI **Gustaf**

Carl XVI Gustaf became king in 1973. The 74th king of Sweden, he belongs to the Bernadotte dynasty, which has been on the throne since 1818, and on his accession at the age of 27 became the youngest ever Bernadotte monarch. His duties and functions are defined in the 1974 Constitution Act. In common with other Scandinavian monarchies, the king's role is purely ceremonial and representative.

Carl XVI Gustaf was born on 30 April 1946 at the Haga Palace, the fifth child and only son of Hereditary Prince Gustaf Adolf, who was killed in a plane crash the following year. Carl Gustaf was educated privately, initially at the royal palace in Stockholm, after which he went on to Broms school and Sigtuna boarding school, where he matriculated in 1966. He then did two-and-a-half years of military service, training in the army, navy and air force. He passed his naval officer examination in 1968. His military training was later supplemented by a management course at the national defence college and commissioned service on board ships of the Swedish navy. In 1968 and 1969 the crown prince studied history, sociology, political science, financial law and economics at Uppsala University. Later he also studied economics at Stockholm University.

Under a programme designed to give him experience of the local, national and international political scene, he was attached to Sweden's permanent mission to the UN in New York and then spent time in London at Hambros Bank and at the Swedish embassy and chamber of commerce. When his grandfather King Gustaf VI Adolf died on 15 September 1973, Carl Gustaf became king.

He has been active representing Sweden at international events, was made honorary president of the World Scout Foundation in 1977 and is president of the Swedish branch of the World Wide Fund for Nature. He has been given an award by the US Environmental Protection Agency for his commitment to environmental protection, a subject in which he takes a special interest.

King Carl XVI Gustaf is married to Queen Silvia, *née* Sommerlath, the daughter of a German businessman. They met at the 1972 Munich Olympic Games where she was working as an interpreter and hostess. They have two daughters and one son. Their eldest child, Crown Princess Victoria, born in 1977, is heir to the throne under the 1980 Act of Succession, which now stipulates that the title passes to the monarch's eldest child regardless of sex.

Flavio **Cotti**

Flavio Cotti was elected in December 1997 as president for 1998 under Switzerland's presidential system whereby a new president is elected each December from among the members of the federal council (cabinet). The president is head of state, while executive power is held by the federal council and the post of federal chancellor is held by a public servant rather than an elected politician. Cotti, whose mother tongue is Italian but who is fluent in German, French and English, was active in politics in his native Ticino canton before his election to parliament in 1983. He had held the presidency once before, in 1991. He is a member of the Christian Democratic People's Party (CVP), one of the four parties which have governed the country in coalition since 1959.

Flavio Cotti was born on 18 October 1939 at Muralto, near Locarno (Ticino canton) to a family of merchants from Val Maggia, and went to school at Ascona and Sarnen (Obwalden canton). He studied law at Freiburg University and was elected to the Locarno legislative council while in his mid-twenties. In 1965 he began working as a barrister and notary public in Locarno, entering the Ticino cantonal parliament in 1966.

He joined the Ticino cantonal government at the age of 36, working successively as head of the departments of economic affairs, justice, military affairs and home affairs. In 1977 and again in 1981 he was elected as president of the Ticino cantonal government. Under his leadership new laws were introduced for the promotion of industry, tourism, agriculture and mountain areas, and the legal regulations regarding Ticino's economic development were reformed. Between 1976 and 1984 Cotti was also chair of the tourist office. He left the Ticino cantonal government in 1983, after 16 years of service, and having led the Ticino branch of the CVP for two years.

In the October 1983 general election, Cotti was elected to the National Council (lower house of the federal parliament) and he was elected president of the CVP in February the following year, the first Ticinese to hold this post. In December 1986 the Federal Assembly (comprising both houses of the federal parliament) elected him to the federal council (cabinet) and he assumed responsibility for home affairs, making him only the seventh Ticinese to hold a federal government post. Cotti was elected as federal president for the first time in December 1990 and held this post throughout 1991. On 1 April 1993 he moved from home affairs to foreign affairs. In December 1996 the Federal Assembly elected him federal vice-president for 1997, and a year later he was elected to be federal president for 1998, as was usual practice in Swiss politics.

Cotti is married to Renata *née* Naretto and they have one daughter.

Hafez al-**Assad**

Lt.-Gen. Hafez al-Assad seized power in a bloodless coup on 15 October 1970 and was declared president in November. His position was confirmed in a referendum in March 1971 and he has been re-elected unopposed for successive seven-year terms, most recently in December 1991. He is head of state, head of government and head of the ruling party, and runs a regime with an internal security system which has dealt effectively and ruthlessly with opposition in the past. In the 1990s, however, Assad has come to be viewed with less hostility than before by the USA and other Western governments, principally because of his stance against Iraq at the time of the 1991 Gulf war.

Hafez al-Assad was born in 1930 in Qardaha, near the coastal town of Latakia in northwest Syria. The family was originally called al-Wahsh meaning "son of the boar" but Hafez later changed this to al-Assad or "son of the lion". He was one of nine children of a poor farming family of Alawite Muslims, a traditionally downtrodden religious minority in predominantly Sunni Muslim Syria, but closely associated with the Ba'ath party which came to power in 1963.

Attending local schools, Assad became involved in politics as head of the students' committee to organise demonstrations against French rule. He joined the Arab Socialist (Ba'ath) party when he was 16. From 1952 to 1955 he attended the air force college at the military academy in Homs, after which he entered the air force with the rank of lieutenant. In 1958 he went to the Soviet Union for further training. On his return in 1959 he was posted to lead a night-combat squadron in Cairo at the time of the union of Syria and Egypt as the United Arab Republic. While there he helped to form the Ba'athist military committee, which opposed the secession of Syria from the union in 1961, costing Assad his commission.

On 8 March 1963 the military committee seized power in Syria. Assad, promoted to general, became commander of the air force and minister of defence. He held these posts at the time of the Arab–Israeli six-day war in June 1967 in which Syria was heavily defeated and suffered the humiliating loss of the Golan Heights. Assad continued to develop his power base within the military, however, and to identify with a nationalistic faction in the Ba'ath party which grew increasingly disillusioned with the more doctrinaire Marxist policies of its civilian leadership.

In 1970, having refused to commit his air force in an abortive attempt to come to the aid of Palestinians in Jordan, Assad used this fiasco as a pretext for a military-based coup, seizing power on 13 November as leader of the "Rectification Movement". He became prime minister and secretary-general of the Ba'ath party, and his election as president was confirmed by a national referendum the following March.

In an initial process of apparent liberalisation, he allowed more scope in the economy for private enterprise and trade, relaxed laws on freedom of speech and travel, and re-established the People's Council. Elections held in 1973 under a new constitution (defining Syria as a democratic, socialist state) resulted in an overwhelming victory for the Ba'ath-dominated National Progressive Front.

Externally, Assad promoted an effectively still-born Federation of Arab Republics with Egypt and Libya, and in 1973 joined other Arab states in attacking Israel in an unsuccessful attempt to reclaim the territory lost in 1967. This conflict, together with Assad's strong backing at this time for the Palestine Liberation Organization (PLO) and for other Arab groups engaging in acts of violence, contributed to the condemnation of Assad's regime by Western governments as a supporter of terrorism.

Assad was meanwhile establishing a reputation for the ruthless suppression of opposition within Syria. The Muslim Brotherhood, a fundamentalist movement among the majority Sunni population, conducted a protracted insurgency against the Ba'athist regime until it was effectively crushed by the massacre at Hama in February 1982, in which thousands of people were killed. Assad's internal security structures have been designed to divide power between a handful of men in charge of well-separated segments, so that only he has overall control. His initial reliance on family members was reduced after 1983, when he suffered a heart attack as a result of his diabetes and suspected his brother Rifaat of using this to plot against him.

Assad maintains a strongly anti-Zionist line, and there has been little relaxation in the mutual hostility between Syria and Israel, particularly during Israel's period of heavy military involvement in Lebanon in the 1980s. However, there has been a significant change in the way Assad's regime is perceived in the USA in particular. One factor in this has been successful Syrian involvement in Lebanon to end the faction-based conflict there. Another is the ending of the cold war, during which Syria had been identified as a pro-Soviet state. Most importantly, Assad has long opposed the aspirations of Iraqi leader Saddam Hussein for regional dominance. He backed Iran in the Iran–Iraq war of the 1980s, and his anti-Iraqi stance in the 1991 Gulf war went so far as the hitherto unthinkable decision to commit Syrian forces on the side of the US-led coalition. US aid to Syria remained for the most part debarred, however, by the retention of Syria on the list of states supporting terrorism.

Assad is married and had four sons, one of them now dead, and one daughter.

Lee Teng-Hui

Lee Teng-hui has been president of Taiwan (which officially designates itself as the Republic of China) since 1988. In March 1996 he was the clear victor in the country's first direct presidential election, winning a further four-year term. The president is a head of state with considerable executive powers, although there is also a premier, responsible to the parliament, who is formally head of government. A US-trained economist, Lee is a native of Taiwan, marking a break with the previous generation of mainland Chinese leaders who transferred the Republic of China government to the island after the Chinese communist revolution of 1949.

Born on 15 January 1923 in Sanchih, a rural area near Taipei, Lee graduated from Taipei High School and, with the island still under Japanese occupation, was one of the few Chinese to be given higher education in Japan, at Kyoto Imperial University. Returning to Taiwan in 1946 after the end of the war, he completed his degree in agricultural economics at the National Taiwan University in 1948, subsequently obtaining a US master's degree from Iowa State University in 1953 and a doctorate from Cornell in 1968. Between 1948 and 1958 he was assistant professor and then associate professor at the National Taiwan University, and for the next 20 years (apart from his three years at Cornell) he was professor of economics at the National Chengchi University, as well as a specialist consultant on rural reconstruction.

He first held government office as a minister of state from 1972 to 1978, and then became mayor of Taipei (1978–81). From 1981 to 1984 he was governor of Taiwan province, where he introduced regional planning techniques and a balanced development of urban and rural areas. In 1984 he was unexpectedly chosen by President Chiang Ching-kuo to be his vice-president of Taiwan, succeeding to the presidency after Chiang's death on 13 January 1988. On 21 March 1990 he was elected by the National Assembly for a fresh six-year term as president. He pushed forward democratic reforms and built up a consensus on constitutional reform. He ceased to refer to the mainland communist government of the People's Republic of China (PRC) as "rebels" and has promoted the policy of winning international recognition for Taiwan's separate existence, while retaining the eventual goal of Chinese reunification. This approach has allowed the ruling Nationalist Kuomintang (KMT) party under his chairmanship to claim credit for modernising itself, although not without suffering a split in 1993 with the departure of a dissident reformist wing. Internationally it has led to the energetic pursuit of invitations to visit foreign countries and attend international conferences, in the face of hostile reaction from the PRC, as for example when Lee went to Cornell University in June 1995 to receive a distinguished alumni award.

In 1994 the National Assembly adopted the Additional Articles of the Constitution of the Republic of China, making way for direct presidential elections. Lee stood for re-election in the nationwide poll in March 1996, when his vice-presidential running-mate was the KMT vice-chairman Lien Chan, and won an overall majority in the first round ballot on 23 March with 54 per cent of the vote. He was sworn in for his new term of office on 20 May, and subsequently piloted through a constitutional reform which boosted his own presidential powers.

The KMT's 15th party congress in 1997 gave Lee its endorsement as party chairman, with 93 per cent of the delegates voting for him in an uncontested poll, although a dissident element in the party was evident in the ballot for the central committee, which was topped by Taiwan province governor James Soong Chu-yu despite his having boycotted the conference proceedings.

Lee Teng-hui has been married since 1949 to Tseng Wen-fui. They have had one son (who died in 1983) and two daughters.

Imomali **Rakhmanov**

Imomali Rakhmanov has been in power in Tajikistan, amid conditions of civil war, since late 1992, and was confirmed in office as president by elections held in November 1994. The constitution adopted by referendum at the same time accords the president the principal executive role as both head of state and head of government, and specifies a normal term of five years. Rakhmanov is an ex-communist who, when he came to power, was seen as pro-Russian and a former ally of ex-President Nabiyev. He has promoted close links with the Karimov regime in neighbouring Uzbekistan.

Imomali Rakhmanov was born on 5 October 1952 in Danghara in the Kulob district of southern Tajikistan. He graduated in economics from Tajik State University, then worked as an electrician, salesman, government secretary and chairman of a trade union committee. Rising up through the communist party system, from 1988 he was a director of collective farms in the Kulob region, and in 1992 became chair of the executive committee of the Kulob regional soviet (i.e. council).

Following Tajikistan's declaration of independence in 1991 and the disintegration of the Soviet Union, the new state faced a period of civil war in which the former communist authorities were ranged against an Islamic fundamentalist opposition. The Islamic forces briefly gained the upper hand in September 1992, but the ex-communists regained control of the capital, Dushanbe, in December. Rakhmanov, chosen the previous month as speaker of the Supreme Soviet, thereupon formed a new government. His authority was effectively preserved by the intervention of a Russian-led peacekeeping force intended to prevent the re-escalation of the conflict.

In the presidential elections of 6 November 1994, held amid conditions of continuing civil war, Rakhmanov won 58.3 per cent of the vote, according to the official results, against 35 per cent for the former prime minister Abdulmalik Abdullajanov, whose supporters complained of alleged vote-rigging.

Although he has kept the Islamists from power, Rakhmanov faces the continuing threat of violence, with insurgents continuing to operate by infiltration from neighbouring Afghanistan. His support base is principally in the south and in the capital Dushanbe, but his regime has alienated pro-reform groups which criticise him for authoritarian methods. Rakhmanov was wounded in April 1997 when a grenade was thrown at his feet, killing two other people and injuring 60.

Benjamin **Mkapa**

Benjamin Mkapa became president of Tanzania in November 1995 after the country's first multiparty presidential and legislative elections which were held the previous month. A former journalist and for many years foreign minister, he was the candidate of the Chama Cha Mapinduzi *(CCM), the former sole and ruling party. Executive power is vested in the president, who is both head of state and head of government, although he has no power to legislate without parliament. The president is elected in a nationwide ballot for a five-year term, and is eligible for re-election once only.*

Benjamin William Mkapa was born on 12 November 1938 in Ndanda in the Masasi district in the southeast of what was then Tanganyika. Mkapa was educated locally and then went to Uganda to complete his studies, obtaining a degree in English from Makerere University in 1962. He began his career as a civil servant, working briefly as an administrative officer in Dodoma and Dar es Salaam and then as a foreign service officer from 1963. He joined the Tanganyika African National Union (TANU), which was renamed as the CCM after the 1977 merger with the ruling party of Zanzibar.

Switching from the civil service to journalism, Mkapa was managing editor of the *Tanzania Nationalist* and *Uhuru* in 1966, managing director of the *Daily News* and *Sunday News* newspapers in 1972, and founding director of the Tanzania News Agency, Shihata, between 1966 and 1976.

In 1974 he was appointed press secretary to the president. In 1976 he was made high commissioner to Nigeria. The following year he joined the cabinet as minister of foreign affairs until 1980, when he was appointed minister of information and culture. Two years later he returned to the diplomatic service as high commissioner to Canada and the USA in 1982/83, before returning to Tanzania, once again to the post of minister of foreign affairs between 1984 and 1990. He was minister of information and broadcasting from 1990 to 1992 and minister for higher education, science and technology from 1992 to 1995.

Mkapa was a member of parliament for Nanyumbu for ten years between 1985 and 1995, until his election as president in November 1995. This poll, held concurrently with the legislative elections, was the first since the transition from a single-party state to a multiparty democracy in 1992. Organisation of the elections was chaotic at times and opposition parties alleged electoral fraud but the high court eventually declared Mkapa to have won with 61.8 per cent of the vote as against 27.8 per cent for his closest rival, Augustine Mrema.

Mkapa is married with two sons.

King **Bhumibol**

King Bhumibol has been King of Thailand for over 51 years and is the world's longest-reigning current monarch, his official royal title being King Rama IX. He is head of state and titular head of the armed forces, and is revered as semi-divine by some of his subjects, but he rules as a constitutional monarch, the government being headed by a prime minister responsible to parliament.

Bhumibol Adulyadej was born on 5 December 1927 in the USA, in Cambridge, Massachusetts. The youngest of the three children of Prince and Princess Mahidol of Songkla, at the time of his birth he was not expected ever to become king, and there was little mention of his birth in the newspapers in Bangkok at the time. His early education was in Bangkok, but in 1934 his widowed mother took her children to Switzerland to continue their education. He attended the Gymnase Classique Cantonal in Lausanne, Switzerland, and graduated in political science and law from Lausanne University.

Bhumibol acceded to the throne in June 1946, aged 18, succeeding his elder brother Ananda Mahidol who had been found shot dead. He was formally crowned on 5 May 1950 as King Rama IX, the ninth ruler of the Chakri dynasty. Much of his energy has latterly been devoted to the Chaipattana ("Victory in Development") Foundation, which he set up in 1987 and of which he is president. It enables funds to be made immediately available to the king for urgent projects without need for approval by the government, as was formerly necessary. One of the earliest and better-known projects funded by the foundation has been the Chaipattana aerator machine, and in 1993 a patent was granted to the king for the invention of the Chaipattana Aerator Model RX-2. Other projects include the lessening of traffic congestion and better flood control. Aside from his skill in engineering, the king has a keen interest in jazz music and cartography.

He married Mom Rajawongse Sirikit Kittiyakara, daughter of Prince Chandaburi Suranath, on 28 April 1950. He and Queen Sirikit have one son, Crown Prince Maha Vajiralongkorn, born in 1952, and three daughters.

Dalai Lama

The Buddhist followers of the Dalai Lama believe him to be the incarnation of the Bodhisattva of Compassion, and recognise him as the spiritual and temporal leader of Tibet. However, he has been in exile since 1959, when he fled after an unsuccessful uprising against Chinese rule.

Tenzin Gyatso, who was born in a small village in northeast Tibet on 6 July 1935, was first recognised in 1937 as Dalai Lama. He was enthroned as the 14th Dalai Lama in 1940. His authority was exercised by a regency until 1950, when he assumed political power. Chinese forces invaded Tibet that year, and the Dalai Lama fled briefly to southern Tibet after abortive resistance. He negotiated an agreement with China in 1951, and continued throughout the 1950s to attempt to reach an accommodation with China, participating as vice-chair of the standing committee of the Chinese People's Political Consultative Conference from 1951 to 1959, and from 1955 to 1959 chairing the preparatory committee for the Autonomous Region of Tibet. At the same time he pursued his studies in Buddhist philosophy, completing a doctorate in 1959 after working in Tibet's monastic universities.

A Tibetan national uprising in 1959 was crushed by the Chinese, and the Dalai Lama and his government fled to Dharamsala, India, which remains his base in exile. In 1964 the Chinese declared Tibet an autonomous region of China. The UN passed resolutions in 1959, 1961 and 1965 calling for China's withdrawal.

While in exile the Dalai Lama has sought to work by peaceful means towards the goal of a free and independent Tibet, with the interim objective of a more representative form of government in Tibet. He also works for the resettlement of Tibetan refugees. His books include *My Land and People* (1962) and *A Human Approach to World Peace* (1984). In 1989 the Dalai Lama was awarded the 1989 Nobel Peace Prize, and he has also received the Congressional Human Rights Award (1989) and the US Freedom Award (1991).

In the 1990s the Chinese authorities have taken fresh steps to suppress any displays of support for the Dalai Lama within Tibet, and intensified their criticisms of him, while identifying and enthroning in late 1995 their own candidate for the position of Panchen Lama, the second ranking figure in the Tibetan religious and political hierarchy. The candidate identified by the Dalai Lama himself to succeed the previous Panchen Lama (who died in 1989) had been named in May 1995.

Gen. Gnassingbe **Eyadéma**

Gen. Eyadéma has been president of Togo since April 1967, after he ousted Nicolas Grunitzky in a bloodless coup in January. He was confirmed in power by a national referendum in 1972 and again in 1979, 1980 and 1986. The adoption of a new constitution in 1992 allowed him to seek a further five-year term, which he won in August 1993 in a nationwide poll which was widely criticised and boycotted by most opposition supporters. In the face of a sustained campaign by opposition parties calling on him to relinquish power, Eyadéma justifies his regime for having maintained continuity of government and economic stability, although his use of repressive force has caused rifts with Western aid donors. As president he is both head of state and head of government, and appoints the prime minister.

Etienne Gnassingbe Eyadéma was born on 26 December 1937 in the village of Pya, in the region of Kabye in northern Togo. Entering the French colonial army as a teenager in 1953, he saw action in Benin (then known as Dahomey), Indochina, Algeria and Niger. However, following Togo's independence in 1960, he returned to his country. He was made adjutant in 1961, captain in 1963 and lieutenant-colonel in 1965, when he was also appointed army chief of staff.

In January 1967 he led a bloodless army coup against Grunitzky's provisional government. In April 1967 he dissolved the committee of national reconciliation which had been set up, and appointed his own government. Concurrently with the post of president, he took over the post of minister for national defence. Since 1969 he has also been president of the ruling Rally of the Togolese People (RPT). In 1972 his presidency was confirmed in a national referendum in which he ran unopposed. In 1979 he declared a third republic and a transition to more civilian rule with a mixed civilian and military cabinet. A new constitution in 1980 provided for a national assembly as a consultative body. He was re-elected for a third consecutive seven-year term in December 1986 with 99.5 per cent of the vote in another uncontested election.

Between 1989 and 1991, there were clashes between anti-government demonstrators and security forces in Togo. Eyadéma agreed, under pressure, to the holding of a national conference on multipartyism. An interim constitution was drafted which provided for a one-year transitional regime followed by free elections and the formation of a new government. During the transitional period Eyadéma continued as chief of state, supposedly with limited powers, but he increased his role once again when the transition period was extended to the end of 1992.

In a national referendum in 1992 voters overwhelmingly supported the new constitution, thus initiating Togo's fourth republic. In the presidential election on 25 August 1993 Eyadéma won

96.42 per cent of the votes cast. The election was boycotted by opposition parties and he was once again unopposed. Eyadéma has survived a number of assassination attempts during his 30 years as president. He faced an opposition majority in the legislature after elections in 1994, but the lack of opposition unity assisted the president in his determination to make his own government appointments. In mid-1996 the RPT regained a parliamentary majority by winning several seats in by-elections, while Eyadéma strengthened his grip by appointing a new prime minister and reshuffling the cabinet.

King **Taufa'ahau**

Taufa'ahau Tupou IV, the son of the late Queen Salote Tupou III, became the king of Tonga in 1965. The Australian-educated king, a keen mathematician and Wesleyan lay preacher, is a direct descendent of King George Tupou I, who is considered to be the founder of modern Tonga. As hereditary head of state, Taufa'ahau presides over the Privy Council and appoints its members, including the prime minister who is formally designated the head of government.

Taufa'ahau Tupou was born on 4 July 1918 in the royal palace in Tonga. He was the first monarch to receive a Western education, attending Newington College and Sydney University, graduating both in the arts and law. His mother appointed him minister of education in 1943, and soon afterwards he established a teachers' training college and revised the Tongan alphabet; in 1947 he founded the Tonga High School. In 1944 he was made minister of health, a post he held until he became premier in 1949. While premier he was also responsible for foreign affairs and for agriculture.

Taufa'ahau succeeded to the throne on 16 December 1965 on the death of his mother. His coronation was held on 4 July 1967. He is a member of the International Mathematics Association and a lay preacher of the Free Wesleyan Church, holding a special position which gives him the conditional right to appoint an acting president of the church. Between 1970 and 1973 he was chancellor of the South Pacific University.

King Taufa'ahau and his wife Queen Halaevalu Mata'aho, whom he married in 1947, have three sons, one daughter and eight grandchildren. Their eldest child Prince Tupouto'a is heir to the throne and also minister of foreign affairs and defence.

Arthur **Robinson**

Arthur Robinson, the dominant political figure in the island of Tobago and prime minister of Trinidad and Tobago from 1985 to 1991, was elected in February 1997 for a five-year term in the largely ceremonial role of president. A lawyer by training, he had been part of the country's first post-independence government in 1962 and was active in politics throughout the following 35 years.

Arthur Napoleon Raymond Robinson was born on 16 December 1926. Having taken an external law degree with London University, Robinson travelled to Britain in 1951, passed his Bar examinations and graduated in philosophy, politics and economics from St John's College, Oxford. Returning to Trinidad and Tobago in 1955, he practised as a lawyer from 1957 to 1961, and was first elected to the federal parliament of the West Indies in 1958.

Robinson was one of the founders of the People's National Movement (PNM) which led Trinidad and Tobago to independence in 1962. At various times between 1962 and 1970, when he resigned from the PNM, he served as minister of finance, of external affairs, and as deputy prime minister to Eric Williams. He chaired the Democratic Action Congress from 1971 until 1986, when he was instrumental in its merger with other opposition parties to form the National Alliance for Reconstruction (NAR).

As the NAR's leader he was sworn in as prime minister after its sweeping success in the 1986 legislative elections. In a dramatic incident in July 1990, he was briefly held hostage in the parliament building by militant Black Muslims as part of an attempted coup. Robinson's government was unpopular because of its reliance on severe austerity measures to address its economic problems, and in the December 1991 legislative elections he was one of only two NAR members to retain their seats. Taking responsibility for this crushing defeat, Robinson resigned the party leadership.

From November 1995 until his election as president in February 1997, he returned to government (in which the NAR was a junior coalition partner) as minister extraordinaire for Tobago, the UN and international organisations, and adviser to the prime minister.

In the course of his long political career, Robinson campaigned from the mid-1970s to the mid-1980s for the devolution of power to Tobago, and since the 1970s he has advocated an international criminal court and sought to access UN funds to reduce local poverty. In 1971 he was consultant to the Foundation for the Establishment of an International Criminal Court, and as prime minister he became involved in several initiatives to promote the Caribbean region.

Arthur Robinson married Patricia Jean Rawlins in 1961, and they have a son and a daughter.

Zine el-Abidine **Ben Ali**

Gen. Zine el-Abidine Ben Ali has been president of Tunisia since November 1987, when former President Habib Bourguiba was deposed on grounds of senility. The president, who is elected for a five-year term, appoints the council of ministers and is also head of government. Ben Ali was elected president in direct elections held in 1989 and again in 1994. On both occasions he was the sole candidate and his election was approved by over 99 per cent of voters. A former military and intelligence specialist, Ben Ali is only the second president of Tunisia since independence in 1956.

Zine el-Abidine Ben Ali was born in Hamman-Sousse on 3 September 1936. He was expelled from school for political activism. Initially trained in electronics in Saint-Cyr in France, he was later educated in military intelligence at the artillery school in Châlons-sur-Marne (France), and at the senior intelligence school in Maryland (USA).

He began his working career as a military officer, and was the director of Tunisia's military intelligence security department from 1964 to 1974. For the next three years he was attaché to Spain and Morocco with general responsibility for defence, military and naval matters. By 1977 he had risen to the position of director-general of national security and was responsible for curbing protests by striking workers in 1978 and bringing under control an uprising by Islamic fundamentalists in the mining town of Gafsa in January 1980. Later that year, however, he was removed from his post and sent as ambassador to Poland.

In 1984 he entered the cabinet as minister of national security, and in 1986 was appointed secretary-general of the ruling Destour Socialist Party (PSD) which had been the sole legal political party from 1963 until 1981. From 1986 until he commenced his presidency, Ben Ali was minister of the interior and from October 1987 he was also prime minister. His assumption of the presidency on 7 November 1987, in a move backed by the military, signalled the first change in executive power since Bourguiba had led Tunisia to independence in 1956.

In 1988, Ben Ali changed the name of the PSD to the Constitutional Democratic Rally (RCD). He was re-elected with a massive majority in April 1989, while the RCD won all 141 seats in the national assembly. In March 1994 Ben Ali was re-elected for another term. The unanimity of his endorsement was tainted by the arrest, before the poll, of two politicians who had announced that they intended to stand against him.

Ben Ali has been criticised for failing to introduce a genuinely pluralist form of politics. Mindful of the turmoil in neighbouring Algeria, he has maintained a hard line against Islamic fundamentalists, in an attempt to preserve stability and thus ensure continued income from tourism. Ben Ali is a Muslim, even though his training and policies are primarily Western in orientation.

Ben Ali is married with three daughters.

Süleyman **Demirel**

Süleyman Demirel was elected president of Turkey for a seven-year term by the Grand National Assembly (unicameral parliament) in May 1993. Demirel, a former engineer, was leader first of the Justice Party and then of the centre-right True Path Party (DYP), and prime minister of Turkey on seven occasions from 1965 until his election as president. Known for his political astuteness and staying power, Demirel and his immediate predecessor Turgut Özal are the only two presidents since the foundation of a republic in 1923 who are not former army generals. The post of president is a powerful one in the event of a state of emergency (which the president may declare, and then rule by decree, in specified circumstances), and the president may also dissolve the assembly and call elections if there is an extended government crisis, but under normal circumstances executive functions are carried out by the prime minister (whom the president appoints) as head of government.

Süleyman Demirel was born on 1 November 1924 in Islamkoy, a remote village in the province of Isparta, some 200 miles southwest of Ankara. He completed his elementary school education in his home village, went to high school in Afyon, north of Isparta, and graduated from the engineering faculty of Istanbul Technical University in 1949. He then worked as an engineer before undertaking postgraduate studies on irrigation, electrification and dam construction in the USA, first in 1949/50 and then in 1954/55. He became director-general of the state hydraulic works department in 1955, holding the post until 1960 when he entered military service. After completing his military service he worked as a freelance engineer and was involved in the construction of many dams, power plants and irrigation facilities.

Demirel was elected to the general executive board of the Justice Party (JP) in 1963 and then as party chairman at the party's second grand convention in November of the following year. He took his party into a coalition government which ruled between February and October 1965, and in which he was deputy prime minister. In the general election of October 1965 his party won an unprecedented 53 per cent of the vote, allowing him to form a majority government as Turkey's 13th prime minister.

Demirel's party won a second general election in 1969 with a reduced share of the vote but an increased number of seats, and he re-formed his government (although it resigned briefly in February 1970, re-forming again after disagreements over the budget had been resolved). However, he was forced to resign in March 1971 as a result of a military coup. Demirel served as prime minister three more times, from March 1975 to June 1977, from July 1977 to December

1977 and from November 1979 until 1980, when he was again obliged to resign after a military coup in September.

Demirel was debarred from active involvement in politics for ten years after the 1980 coup. However, a national referendum in September 1987 lifted this ban and he returned to active politics as a DYP candidate, since the Justice Party remained a prohibited organisation under the 1980 ban. After an inconclusive general election in October 1991 he formed a coalition government with the Social Democratic People's Party. As prime minister for the seventh time he invested heavily in projects to improve the country's infrastructure.

Demirel was elected president on 16 May 1993, following the death of the incumbent President Özal. He resigned as leader of the DYP and was replaced in that capacity by Tansu Çiller, who then became Turkey's first woman prime minister. Since the inconclusive general election of December 1995, however, Demirel has overseen a period of coalition government, featuring in particular an unprecedented pro-Islamist prime minister, Necmettin Erbakan of the Welfare Party (RP), between June 1996 and June 1997. Demirel had agreed to the controversial appointment of Erbakan on the basis that he led the largest party in parliament and could command a majority with the backing of Çiller. However, when Erbakan offered his resignation the following year under severe pressure from the military establishment, Demirel immediately accepted it and appointed the leader of the right-wing secular Motherland Party (ANAP) in Erbakan's place rather than calling fresh elections.

Demirel is married to Nazmiye Demirel.

Saparmurad **Niyazov**

Saparmurad Niyazov became the first elected president of the Turkmenistan republic within the Soviet Union on 27 October 1990, and remained in office as the republic moved to independence with the collapse of the Soviet system. The 1992 constitution, under which he was re-elected in June 1992, defines the executive president as both head of state and head of government; it also fixes the president's normal term of office as five years, but a referendum in 1994 confirmed Niyazov in power until 2002. Niyazov, an engineer by training, had been communist party first secretary in Turkmenistan from 1985 to 1990 and chairman of the republic's Supreme Soviet since 1990.

Saparmurad Niyazov was born on 18 February 1940 and grew up in the capital, Ashkhabad. His father died in the Second World War, and in 1948 he lost most of his remaining close family in the Ashkhabad earthquake. He studied physics and mathematics at the Leningrad Polytechnic School from 1962 to 1966, graduating as a power engineer. From 1959 to 1967 he was a member of the All-Union Central Trade Union Council, working as a mineral prospecting instructor in Turkmenistan. From 1967 to 1970 he worked at the Bezmeinskaya hydroelectric power station.

In 1962 Niyazov joined the Communist Party (CP) of Turkmenistan, and by 1970 he had risen to the position of instructor, then department head, within the central committee of the Turkmen CP. He was first secretary of the CP central committee for Ashkhabad from 1980 to 1984, and in 1985 was appointed first secretary for Turkmenistan, the highest state and party post in the republic. In this capacity, like the 14 other first secretaries of the republics making up the Soviet Union, Niyazov was brought into the politburo of the Communist Party of the Soviet Union (CPSU) in the major restructuring of that organ in July 1990.

Niyazov became chairman of the Turkmenistan Supreme Soviet, in effect the republic's head of state, in January 1990. He held the republic's new directly elective presidency as a result of elections in October 1990 when he won what was recorded as 98.3 per cent of the vote, and became commander-in-chief of the armed forces. In the elections held after full independence, in June 1992, he was confirmed in his post with 99.5 per cent of the vote.

Niyazov chairs the former communist party, renamed in 1991 as the Democratic Party of Turkmenistan (DPT), and at present he is both prime minister and president. In 1993 the parliament conferred upon him the title *Turkmenbashi* ("father of the Turkmen people"). The apparent emergence of a cult of personality continued with the referendum in January 1994 on a five-year extension of his term in office, which was recorded as giving him a 99.9 per cent endorsement.

Saparmurad Niyazov is married and has one son and one daughter.

Sir Tulaga **Manuella**

Sir Tulaga Manuella has been governor-general of Tuvalu since June 1994. His current term in office as governor-general, as representative of the titular head of state Queen Elizabeth II, runs until March 1998. The 1978 constitution, under which the country became independent as a member of the Commonwealth with special status (but not participating in Commonwealth heads of government summits), requires that the governor-general should be of Tuvaluan nationality; an upper age limit of 65 was removed in 1987. Also at this time the government announced that the constitution was to be amended to redefine the governor-general's role as a largely ceremonial one, removing discretionary powers relating to the dissolution of parliament, the designation of a prime minister and the appointment of other cabinet members. Proposals for the adoption of a republican model, rejected in a nationwide poll in 1986, have been revived in the 1990s.

Sir Tulaga Manuella, an accountant by training, is a former senior member of the financial civil service. At the time of his appointment he was secretary of the Tuvalu Christian Church, a Congregationalist church which is a central element in national life and to which some 97 per cent of the islanders belong. Sir Tulaga was in addition secretary of the Pacific Council of Churches.

His appointment as governor-general was made at the insistence of the then prime minister Kamuta Latasi, who considered that the governor-general appointed on the recommendation of the previous government was politically biased. Sir Tulaga Manuella was sworn in as governor-general on 26 June 1994.

Yoweri **Museveni**

Yoweri Museveni has been in power in Uganda since 1986, and was most recently re-elected as president in a nationwide ballot in May 1996, for a further five-year term. As president he is both head of state and head of government, appoints the members of the cabinet including the prime minister, and leads the dominant National Resistance Movement (political party activity being still officially banned under the 1995 constitution). Museveni, who first came to prominence in the Tanzanian-backed intervention in 1979 to oust the Amin regime, reverted to guerrilla struggle for five years before coming to power himself, initially against the dictatorial rule of Milton Obote, and then going on to topple the military regime which deposed Obote. He is credited not only with having restored peace in the strife-ridden country, but also with having done much to revive the economy, and to build national consensus to prepare for the eventual introduction of pluralist politics.

Yoweri Kaguta Museveni was born in 1944 in Ntungamo, near Rwampara, in the Mbarara district of western Uganda. He studied locally before reading political science, economics and education at Dar es Salaam University in Tanzania from 1967 to 1970. Closely linked during his student days with the Marxist guerrilla Front for the Liberation of Mozambique (FRELIMO), he also chaired the University Students' African Revolutionary Front (USARF), a pan-Africanist and anti-colonialist organisation.

After university he returned to Uganda, working briefly as a research assistant at the office of President Milton Obote, until Gen. Idi Amin overthrew the government in 1971. Museveni fled back to Tanzania and, while teaching at Moshi Co-operative College, set up an exile Front for National Salvation (FRONASA). This organisation grew to the point where it could claim a fighting strength of up to 9,000, and in 1979 it was part of the *ad hoc* coalition which launched a bid to overthrow Amin. Heavily backed by Tanzanian forces, the Uganda National Liberation Front (UNLF) succeeded in driving out Amin. Museveni served briefly as defence minister in an interim government and vice-chairman of a subsequent military commission pending the holding of a general election in 1980.

Museveni stood as a candidate of the Uganda Patriotic Movement in the 1980 election, but returned to guerrilla resistance when Obote's Uganda People's Congress (UPC) hijacked the poll with blatant ballot-rigging to ensure its own victory. Museveni spent the next five years waging a gradually growing insurgency, as founder and leader of the National Resistance Army (NRA), against the Obote regime. Effectively without external support, his guerrilla forces gained ground in the south and west. When the NRA was unable to reach an agreement with a military government that had toppled Obote in mid-1985, it began a rapid advance towards the capital, Kampala, where in January 1986 the government of Gen. Tito Okello collapsed. Museveni took power himself on 26 January, combining the post of president with that of minister of defence.

In power, Museveni continued to project himself as a "freedom fighter". While urging national reconciliation, he had also to contend with continuing violence in the north in particular for the first years of his rule. Although his NRM-based regime emphasised non-alignment internationally, Museveni established sufficient credibility with international aid donors to attract sustained backing from the World Bank for economic reconstruction work. He built up regional links particularly through the southern African Preferential Trade Area, and was chairman of the Organization of African Unity in 1990/91.

A new constitution, the product of lengthy consultation over two years, came into effect in 1995, providing for an elective presidency and a mainly elective parliament. Museveni won the presidential election on 9 May 1996, campaigning with the slogan "No Change" and taking almost 75 per cent of the vote against two other candidates. The legislative elections held on a non-party basis in late June of the same year produced an assembly in which the president's supporters held a clear majority.

Museveni is married to Janet Kataaha, and the couple have four children.

Leonid **Kuchma**

Leonid Kuchma has been president since 1994, when he was elected in a nationwide ballot for a five-year term. A former engineer and manager in the weapons industry and space research, and a communist party member in the Soviet era, he became a leading advocate, after Ukraine's independence in 1991, of a rapid transition to a free-market economy. He attempted to pursue this objective as prime minister in 1992/93 against strong opposition from parliament. Under Ukraine's 1996 constitution, the president is head of state and commander-in-chief of the armed forces. The president's extensive powers include the power of appointment of the council of ministers, top officials and the heads of local and regional government, and powers to issue decrees. The prime minister, however, is head of government and chairs the council of ministers.

Leonid Danylovych Kuchma was born on 9 August 1938 in the village of Chaikino, in the Chernihiv region. In 1960 he graduated as a mechanical engineer from the University of Dniepropetrovsk. He spent the next 32 years working at the Pivdenmash machine-building factory, the Soviet Union's largest weapons manufacturer, rising to become managing director in 1986. From 1966 to 1975 he was also the technical manager at Baikonur cosmodrome in Kazakhstan, the centre of the Soviet space programme.

Kuchma joined the Communist Party of the Soviet Union (CPSU) in 1960, and was secretary of the party at the Pivdenmash factory from 1975 until 1982.

In March 1990 Kuchma was elected to the Ukrainian Supreme Soviet and served as a member of the parliamentary committee on defence and state security. The abortive coup in Moscow in August 1991 prompted the banning of the Communist Party of Ukraine, from which Kuchma resigned, and a declaration of independence by the Ukrainian Supreme Soviet, which was endorsed in a referendum the following December. In 1992 Kuchma retired from his directorship of the Pivdenmash factory and, on 27 October, was appointed as Ukraine's second post-independence prime minister.

Initially granted special powers to rule by decree for six months so as to be able to tackle the country's economic crisis, he introduced rapid and radical reforms, involving privatisation, severe cuts in government spending, and anti-corruption measures. These were popular with centrist and right-wing parties but opposed by the former communists and in May parliament refused to renew Kuchma's powers. Over the ensuing weeks Kuchma repeatedly sought to resign as prime minister and this was eventually accepted on 21 September 1993. In December he was appointed president of the Ukrainian Association of Industrialists and Entrepreneurs, a post he held until July 1994.

In the first round of the presidential elections held on 26 June 1994 Kuchma came second, behind the incumbent President Kravchuk. He was supported by the Interregional Reform Bloc (MBR) which had been founded in January as a less nationalistic party than that of Kravchuk. In the run-off on 10 July Kuchma won 52.1 per cent of the vote. The swing was due to support from the revived communist party and among ethnic Russians, especially in industrial areas.

As president he began a programme based on market reform, review of the electoral system, and better relations with Russia. Again his radical approach was disliked by both the communists and within his own party, as he had promised a slower pace during his campaign. Tensions between Kuchma and parliament eventually resulted in June 1995 in a constitutional agreement under which Kuchma agreed not to hold a referendum on his powers, in exchange for the presidential right to appoint a wider range of officials without parliamentary approval and to issue decrees with legislative force.

These increased powers were eventually approved by parliament in June 1996. That December, amid widespread unrest over non-payment of wages, Kuchma issued two decrees increasing his powers still further and making the internal, foreign, defence and information ministers directly responsible to the president. Tensions between president and government have persisted, with Kuchma making repeated government changes in an effort to ensure implementation of economic reforms.

In his March 1997 state of the nation address Kuchma blamed the government for the country's "financial crisis" and accused it of inefficiency and corruption. In Crimea, which was part of Russia until 1954 and has a substantial Russian minority, Kuchma has repeatedly had to assert Ukrainian control, even imposing direct presidential rule in April 1995. In foreign policy Kuchma has sought to develop closer relations with Russia, which had often been tense since the disintegration of the Soviet Union in 1991. In May 1997 he and his Russian counterpart Boris Yeltsin signed a treaty of friendship, co-operation and partnership resolving differences over the Black Sea fleet and confirming Crimea as part of Ukraine.

Kuchma is married with one daughter. He has won the Lenin prize of the Soviet Union and the state prize of Ukraine.

Shaikh **Zayed** bin Sultan al-Nahyan

Shaikh Zayed bin Sultan al-Nahyan has been ruler of Abu Dhabi since 1966 and president of the United Arab Emirates (UAE) since its formation in 1971. The rulers of the seven emirates together form a Supreme Council, which rules by decree. They elect the president and vice-president from among their number, for a five-year term, most recently in 1996; in practice, the ruler of the largest shaikhdom, Abu Dhabi, is president, and the ruler of Dubai is vice-president. The president appoints the prime minister and the council of ministers.

Shaikh Zayed bin Sultan al-Nahyan was born in 1916 in the Jahili fortress at the Al-Ain oasis. From 1946 to 1966 he acted on behalf of his brother, Shaikh Shakhbut, as governor of Al-Ain and the surrounding eastern province. In 1966 he succeeded his brother as ruler of Abu Dhabi.

In the circumstances created by the British withdrawal from the Gulf (announced in 1968 and completed in 1971), and the separate independence of Bahrain and Qatar, Shaikh Zayed pressed successfully for a closer union between the emirates, and this was formalised with the creation on 2 December 1971 of the UAE, with himself as president. The shaikhs, like most UAE citizens, are Sunni Muslim, and under Shaikh Zayed the country has retained a conservative Islamic social code, but oil has brought wealth and rapid development, contact with a Western expatriate community, and an influx of construction workers. Shaikh Zayed, noted for his "hands on" leadership style, has responded to criticism about the lack of democratic representation by reviving an advisory federal national council.

Shaikh Zayed's foreign policy has been based around co-operation among the Gulf states (with whom he helped to set up the Gulf Co-operation Council in 1981), promoting Arab unity, membership of the Non-aligned Movement, and a broadly pro-Western orientation. Although in the 1991 Gulf war he made bases available for US-led allied forces, to help drive Iraqi troops out of Kuwait, Shaikh Zayed has opposed the maintenance of UN sanctions against Iraq. His main security concern has been relations with Iran, particularly since a dispute over offshore islands in the Gulf flared up in the early 1990s.

As a major shareholder in the Bank of Credit and Commerce International (BCCI), Shaikh Zayed was badly affected by the bank's spectacular collapse in 1991, both financially (he had provided a large amount of money in an unsuccessful effort to save the bank) and in terms of damage to his prestige as the long investigation and winding up of the bank continued to generate publicity through to the mid-1990s.

Shaikh Zayed has many wives and children. First Lady Shaikha Fatima bint Murabak has been president of the Abu Dhabi Women's Society since 1975.

Queen **Elizabeth II**

Elizabeth II succeeded to the throne on 6 February 1952 on the death of her father George VI. Her coronation took place on 2 June 1953. She had been named as heir presumptive in 1936 following the death of her grandfather George V and the abdication of her uncle Edward VIII. As head of state, she is also the head of the navy, air force and army, and head of the Church of England with the title Defender of the Faith. In 1953 she succeeded as colonel-in-chief of all the Guards Regiments and the Corps of the Royal Engineers, and as captain-general of the Royal Regiment of Artillery and the Honourable Artillery Company.

Elizabeth II is not only Queen of the United Kingdom (i.e. of Great Britain and Northern Ireland), and of her "other Realms and Territories", but also head of the Commonwealth, in which capacity she is titular head of state (represented by a governor-general) of those 15 Commonwealth countries which do not have their own monarchies and have not adopted republican constitutions. These are Antigua and Barbuda, Australia, Bahamas, Barbados, Belize, Canada, Grenada, Jamaica, New Zealand, Papua New Guinea, Solomon Islands, St Kitts and Nevis, St Lucia, St Vincent and the Grenadines, and Tuvalu.

Elizabeth Alexandra Mary of Windsor was born in London on 21 April 1926, the first child of George VI and Queen Elizabeth (who were then the Duke and Duchess of York). She spent most of her early childhood in the London area, and was educated mainly by private tutors in French, art, music, law and constitutional history. In October 1940 she gave her first public broadcast in a message to the children of Britain and the Commonwealth. In 1944 she was appointed a Counsellor of State and had her first formal experience as future monarch while the king was at the front in Italy. She had joined the war effort as a member of the Auxiliary Territorial Service (ATS). In 1947 she made her first formal visit abroad, to South Africa. Her special dedication to the Commonwealth was re-emphasised when she came to the throne in 1952; her father's death was announced while she was on a state visit to Kenya, and a year after her coronation she resumed her tour of the Commonwealth, at a time when many colonies and territories were pushing for independence from British rule.

Her long reign has been characterised by far-reaching changes in the public face of the British monarchy, and its relationship with the nation. As an institution, the monarchy has faced increasing scrutiny in terms of the cost to the public and whether it yields "value for money", accompanied by pressure to streamline the civil list. The Queen is present at numerous public occasions, maintains the traditional weekly audience with the prime minister, and sees all cabinet papers and a daily summary of events in parliament. Besides being head of the Church, she is the patron of many societies and institutions. Her coronation ceremony was the first to be televised, and broadcast worldwide by radio, and she marked her silver jubilee in 1977 (celebrated in popular events and parties around the country) by an extensive tour of the UK and the Commonwealth.

Elizabeth married Prince Philip in November 1947. The son of Prince and Princess Andrew of Greece and Denmark, he was naturalised a British subject and created Duke of Edinburgh. They have three sons, one daughter and six grandchildren. Their eldest child, the Prince of Wales and heir to the throne, is Prince Charles, born in 1948.

The life of the royal family has been conducted under intense, and ever growing, media attention. The wedding of Prince Charles and Lady Diana Spencer in 1981 was immensely popular with the public. Princess Diana's glamour did much to change public expectations of the monarchy away from the family-centred ideal and the concepts of impartial service to the nation with which Elizabeth herself had grown up. While she continued to personify this ideal, it was undermined by the failure of the marriages of three of her children. The separation of Prince Charles and Princess Diana in 1992, the separation of the Queen's second son from his wife in the same year, and the coincidence of a destructive fire at the Queen's Windsor Castle residence, led her to describe 1992 in a famous phrase as her "annus horribilis". In 1997 a wave of public emotion and grieving over the death of Princess Diana in a car crash in Paris fuelled further criticism that the Queen and the royal family held too much to tradition in such a moment and were too reserved and out of touch with the "mood of the nation".

Bill **Clinton**

Bill Clinton has been US president since January 1993, having won election the previous November. He was re-elected in November 1996 and accordingly sworn in on 20 January 1997 for a second consecutive four-year term, the maximum permitted under the constitution. The executive presidency combines the functions of head of state and head of government. Clinton is a former lawyer from Arkansas in southern central USA, and served a total of six two-year terms as state governor of Arkansas between January 1979 and the end of 1992.

Bill Clinton was born William Jefferson Blythe III on 19 August 1946 in Hope, Arkansas. His father was killed in a car accident three months before he was born, and his mother Virginia remarried, to Roger Clinton, in 1950. While his mother was in New Orleans training as a nurse, Bill's Baptist upbringing as a young child was primarily the responsibility of his grandparents, Eldridge and Edith Cassidy. When he was 15, and his half-brother (born in 1956) reached school age, Bill had his name changed legally to the family surname Clinton. He had an unhappy relationship with his stepfather, and as a teenager found himself assuming responsibility for holding the family together, protecting his mother from her husband's abuse.

Bill Clinton attended Hot Springs High School and went on to Georgetown University where he graduated in 1968 in international affairs. From 1968 to 1970 he was a Rhodes scholar at University College, Oxford. In 1973 he completed law school at Yale University and became a junior professor at the University of Arkansas School of Law.

Interested in politics from his childhood onwards, and inspired by meeting the then President Kennedy at a "Boys Nation" youth leadership conference in Washington D.C. in 1962, Clinton registered as a Democrat, and first sought electoral office himself in 1974. He was narrowly defeated in a bid to unseat the Republican incumbent for an Arkansas seat in the US House of Representatives. Retaining his law professorship, he was in addition chair of the local housing development corporation in 1975/76. In 1976 he took a leading role in the Carter presidential campaign in Arkansas, and also won public office himself, as state attorney-general, holding this post for two years until his election as state governor of Arkansas.

Clinton was thus only 32 when he was inaugurated for the first time in January 1979 as state governor, the youngest governor in the country. His relative political inexperience told against him when he failed to win re-election at the end of his first two-year term, being branded as a high spender because of increases in highway taxes intended to finance the reform of public services. After two years with the law firm of Wright, Lindsey and Jennings, he came back to win re-election as governor in November 1982, taking office the following January and winning successive terms until his successful bid for the US presidency ten years later. His main achievements as governor centred around the improvement of the education system, the introduction of systematic testing of attainment standards for school students, and the raising of teachers' salaries. Additional responsibilities which he held at national level during this period included the chair of the National Governors' Association and co-chair of the Education Commission of the States in 1987, and co-chair of the Task Force on Education and chair of the Democratic Leadership Council in 1990/91.

In 1991 Clinton declared his candidacy for the Democratic Party nomination for the US presidency. His early position as front runner was damaged by allegations about an extra-marital affair, and the suggestion that as a student he had managed to defer being drafted for military service at the time of the Vietnam war by making a promise which he did not fulfil about joining a reserve officers' training programme (the draft later being replaced by a lottery system in which his name did not come up). His ability to overcome such reverses in his campaign attracted the nickname "the comeback kid", but opponents continued to regard the "character issue" as the most vulnerable point on which to attack him.

Winning the nomination and choosing Tennessee senator Al Gore at the Democratic Party convention to be his vice-presidential running mate on a youthful and relatively liberal ticket, Clinton campaigned successfully for the presidency, his ability to strike the right note on a range of issues being contrasted with the more aloof personality of Republican incumbent George Bush. In the 3 November 1992 poll Clinton took 43 per cent of the popular vote and won 370 of the 538 electoral college votes, defeating Bush, the independent Ross Perot and several minor candidates. On 20 January 1993 he took office officially as the 42nd president of the United States.

Clinton's first term of office was marked by the launching of several ambitious reform initiatives, on health and education in particular, which foundered on determined conservative opposition. Right-wing critics attacked his apparent preference for an active government role in social issues, whereas the previous 12 years of Republican administration had emphasised the need to "roll back" the government's involvement to "get it off the backs of the American people". The mid-term elections in November 1994 produced a severe anti-Clinton backlash in which the Democrats lost control of Congress to a Republican party with a pronounced right-wing agenda, codified as a "contract with America". Clinton showed his political flexibility in conceding an immediate round of tax cuts, beginning to win back the political centre ground. He managed to turn to his advantage a lengthy stalemate with Congress over the federal budget, presenting his Republican opponents as doctrinaire and obstructive, and came back strongly enough to win a further presidential term in the November 1996 elections, much assisted by the recently recovered buoyancy of the economy. He was able in addition to point to a positive balance on his foreign policy record. Initially marked by the failure of US intervention in Somalia, this record now included the fostering of an Israeli–Palestinian agreement, the Dayton agreement on former Yugoslavia signed in November 1995, the US intervention to restore democratic government in Haiti, and the conclusion of the North American Free Trade Agreement with Canada and Mexico.

The poll on 5 November 1996 gave Clinton 49.2 per cent of the popular vote, and 379 of the 538 electoral college votes, against 40.8 per cent for Republican candidate Bob Dole, and 8.5 per cent for Perot. In the campaign Clinton had once again faced attack more on his character, than on his record in office. In particular, he was unable to free himself from the long-running Whitewater affair. A federal investigation into this scandal centred on his role and that of his wife Hillary in a failed property venture while he was governor of Arkansas, and questioned the veracity of their accounts of this and apparently related events. Renewed allegations of sexual impropriety, the claim that he had used Arkansas state troopers to procure numerous female sexual partners for him, and efforts by former Arkansas state employee Paula Jones to bring a law suit against him for sexual harassment, ensured that the "character issue" remained at the forefront of US politics in the year following his inauguration for a second term on 20 January 1997. Clinton's popularity, however, remained high throughout the first year of his second term, in spite of several setbacks in particular over the continuing Whitewater investigations.

William Jefferson Clinton is married to Hillary Rodham Clinton, whom he met while studying at Yale. She is a lawyer and has been involved in a number of political campaigns, most prominently as the leader of the unsuccessful attempt to reform the system of health provision and insurance during Clinton's first term as president. They have one daughter, Chelsea, born in 1980.

Julio María **Sanguinetti**

Julio Sanguinetti is currently serving a non-renewable five-year term, which began in March 1995, as president of Uruguay, in which capacity he is both head of state and head of government. A career politician for some 40 years, he has already been president once before, from 1985 to 1990, after a 12-year period of military rule. Sanguinetti leads the Colorado Party (PC), which is the largest party (but without a majority) in both the Chamber of Representatives and the Senate, which together form the General Assembly. His government is a coalition with the Blanco Party (PN) and the smaller Party for the Government of the People (PGP) and the Civic Union (UC).

Julio María Sanguinetti Cairolo was born on 6 January 1936 in the capital, Montevideo. In 1961 he graduated from the faculty of law and social sciences in Montevideo with a degree in law.

He was first elected to the congress for the Colorado Party in 1963 and was re-elected in 1966 and 1971, holding his seat until the 1973 military takeover. He also worked as political editor of *Acción*, an evening newspaper set up by former President Luis Batlle. From 1969 to 1971, he was minister for industry and commerce; his membership of this government, which was engaged in fierce counterinsurgency operations, led to accusations many years later that he was responsible for human rights violations. In 1972 he became minister for education and culture, but left the government in 1973 amid the disturbances leading up to that year's imposition of full military rule.

During the ensuing period, while Uruguay was under a military regime, Sanguinetti worked as political editor and columnist for the newspaper *El Día* from 1973 to 1981, and he was also president from 1975 to 1984 of UNESCO's Latin American regional book promotion centre. Between 1976 and mid-1981 his political rights were suspended, but he nevertheless wrote a forthright editorial for *El Día* in 1980 urging a "no" vote in the plebiscite by which the military authorities tried to legitimise their rule.

In 1983 he became secretary-general of the PC and leader of its main faction, *Unidad y Reforma*, as a result of the political ban imposed on former PC leader Jorge Batlle Ibáñez by the military regime. The military had also proscribed the leaders of the other two main parties, the Blancos and *Frente Amplio*. In the elections in November 1984 Sanguinetti won the presidency with 39 per cent of the vote, and the PC became the largest party in both houses of the assembly. Sanguinetti wished to remove the legacy of the military regime, so rather than accepting the presidential sash from Alvarez, the military ruler, he requested that Alvarez should resign a few days earlier, allowing an interim president to officiate at the handover on 1 March 1985. His government released political prisoners and encouraged the return of 20,000 exiles, but in 1986 passed a controversial law ending trials of members of the armed forces for human rights violations committed under military rule. The middle years of his presidency were dominated by an opposition campaign to reverse this "punto final" legislation, which was, however, eventually upheld in a referendum held in April 1989.

At the November 1989 elections the Blancos overtook the PC as the largest party. The PC became a junior member of the coalition government, until in 1991 Sanguinetti, as leader of the largest PC faction (i.e. *Unidad y Reforma*), forced the party's sole ministerial representative to resign in opposition to privatisation proposals. In 1992 *Unidad y Reforma* split into two sections, the *Batllista Unido* led by the now restored Jorge Batlle Ibáñez and the *Foro Batllista* led by Sanguinetti.

In the presidential elections held on 27 November 1994, Sanguinetti was the leading PC candidate and the PC narrowly topped the poll (with 32.5 per cent of the vote in what was effectively a three-way split). He was accordingly declared president-elect under the so-called *Ley de Lemas*, the system whereby a party's leading candidate was deemed to have received all the votes cast for that party's various candidates. (His government subsequently succeeded in getting these arrangements replaced, under constitutional amendments passed in 1996, by a less idiosyncratic system of party primaries and two-round elections.)

Sanguinetti was sworn in on 1 March 1995, after having announced a government based on a "governability pact" with the Blanco Party. The principal issues of the first part of his period in office, which began under the shadow of economic austerity measures, were constitutional reform and the controversial restructuring of pensions and other social welfare arrangements, carried through against vehement opposition from organised labour.

Sanguinetti is married to the historian and writer Marta Canessa; they have one son and one daughter, and four grandchildren.

Islam **Karimov**

Islam Karimov has been president of Uzbekistan since it was a republic of the former Soviet Union. First elected by the republican Supreme Soviet in March 1990, he had his position endorsed for a five-year term in a popular vote in December 1991, following the declaration of independence that August. A March 1995 referendum extended his term of office to the year 2000. He is the dominant political figure in the country, appoints the cabinet (including the prime minister) and presides over its meetings, and is also commander-in-chief of the armed forces. Karimov is a former engineer who rose through the Uzbek state planning committee (Gosplan) to senior government and party roles under the communist regime, becoming first secretary of the Uzbek communist party in 1989.

Islam Karimov was born on 30 January 1938 in Samarkand. After completing his schooling he attended the Central Asian Polytechnic and Tashkent Economics Institute, gaining diplomas in mechanical engineering and economics. He began his working career in 1960 in the Tashkent agricultural machinery plant. The following year he moved to Tashkent's aviation factory as senior design engineer where he worked for five years.

Having joined the Communist Party of the Soviet Union (CPSU) in 1964, he became a member of the state planning committee (Gosplan) of Uzbekistan in 1966, rising from senior specialist in the scientific department to be its vice-chairman. He was appointed finance minister in the Uzbek council of ministers in 1983, and by 1986 was its deputy chair. For the next three years he was first secretary of the Kashkadarinsk district committee. From 1989 to 1991 he was first secretary of the Uzbek communist party and also a member of the Congress of People's Deputies of the Soviet Union. In 1990 Karimov, together with the party first secretaries of the other republics, became a member of the CPSU politburo as part of the restructuring of that body.

On 24 March 1990 he was elected president of the Uzbek Soviet Socialist Republic, a newly created position, as the republics began moving towards independence. However, he supported moves by the then Soviet president, Mikhail Gorbachev, to prevent the complete disintegration of the union. When the break-up of the union became a *fait accompli* following the August 1991 attempted coup in Moscow, Karimov resigned from the CPSU politburo but was reluctant to see the party itself dissolved.

Uzbekistan followed its neighbouring states by declaring independence on 31 August, and joined the Commonwealth of Independent States (CIS) on 21 December, but it was not until 29 December that a referendum was held to give formal popular confirmation to its independence. On the same day, Karimov was confirmed as president of the new republic for a five-year term. He was credited with winning 86 per cent of the vote against one other candidate, while the main secular nationalist opposition grouping *Birlik* (Unity) was debarred from contesting the election on the grounds that it was not formally a political party.

On 26 March 1995 a referendum extended Karimov's term of office until 2000, reputedly with 99.6 per cent support from a turnout of 99.3 per cent. The former communists, renamed the People's Democratic Party (PDP), remain the dominant political organisation in Uzbekistan. The 1992 constitution gives formal backing to multipartyism, and Karimov resigned the chairmanship of the PDP in 1996 to present himself in a non-party light, but *Birlik* remains subject to a ban imposed in 1992, and human rights organisations have been critical of the restrictions placed on political freedoms by the Karimov regime.

Although Karimov is himself a Muslim, like the majority of the population, his regime has taken a firm stand against Islamic fundamentalists. He is an advocate of the unification of the former Soviet republics in central Asia, and has seen some progress achieved in this direction with Kazakhstan and Kirgizstan, but is less enthusiastic about participating in an "inner core" of the Russian-dominated CIS. In the economic sphere his regime has retained characteristics of the centrally planned command economies of the communist era rather than pursuing a rapid transition to a free-market system. The development of the oil and gas resources of the region, however, has resulted in the conclusion of a number of joint ventures with foreign companies.

Islam Karimov is married to Tatyana Karimova and they have two daughters.

Jean Marie **Leye**

Jean Marie Leye has been president of Vanuatu since March 1994, having been chosen by indirect election for a five-year term. He is a member of the Union of Moderate Parties (UMP), the main francophone grouping since independence and a leading element in successive coalition governments in the 1990s. The president, as head of state, has a mainly ceremonial role but retains some formal power, including in certain circumstances the discretionary power to dissolve parliament and call elections. The political system is a parliamentary one; the head of government is a prime minister elected by the unicameral legislature.

Jean Marie Leye Lenelgau Manatawai was born on 1 May 1933 on Aneityum Island in what was then the New Hebrides, and attended French schools in Port Vila and in Luganville on Santo Island. He worked in telecommunications administration and various private sector jobs, and in 1957 became president of his native island's local council. As leader of the Union of the New Hebrides Communities Party he became a member of the pre-independence consultative council. He served on the drafting committee for the new constitution, which was adopted in September 1979 in readiness for independence, under the name Vanuatu, in July 1980. In 1983 Leye was elected to parliament as a member of the UMP alliance, of which he was a vice-president.

In the business world Leye is a member of the Vanuatu chamber of commerce and of the New Hebrides civil aviation committee, and is on the board of directors of Air Vanuatu.

On 2 March 1994 Leye was elected president of Vanuatu, two months after the end of the previous president's term. The delay arose from the fact that the governing coalition had only a tiny majority in parliament. It thus had difficulty achieving the required two-thirds majority in the electoral college, consisting of the parliament together with the provincial council presidents. The stalemate was broken in the third vote, when the opposition *Vanua'aku Pati* (Party of our Land) agreed to support Leye. He was sworn in to office immediately.

His presidency became highly controversial in late 1997, when he dissolved parliament and called fresh elections in a bid to end a political deadlock, following two years of government instability and factional disputes. He made the announcement that he was dissolving parliament in a radio broadcast on 27 November, but was then challenged by MPs who claimed that this infringed their right to have a debate on a no-confidence motion against Prime Minister Serge Vohor.

Jean Marie Leye Lenelgau is married and has four daughters and four sons.

Pope **John Paul II**

Pope John Paul II (Karol Wojtyla) has been head of state of the Vatican City since 16 October 1978, by virtue of his election as pope by the Sacred College of Cardinals. The Vatican City state, created under the 1929 Lateran treaty, and the papacy or Holy See, are indissolubly united in the person of the pope. The administrative affairs of the Vatican City are overseen by a Pontifical Commission appointed by the pope. John Paul II is the first non-Italian pope since 1523 and the first Polish pope in history.

Karol Jozef Wojtyla was born in Wadowice, Poland, on 18 May 1920 and received his early education there. His mother died in 1929, followed by his brother three years later. He was confirmed in May 1938 and commenced his studies at the Jagellonian University in Krakow in October. During the Second World War he worked in a variety of manual jobs, earning the name "worker cardinal", and from 1942 studied secretly for the priesthood in Krakow. During these years he was reputedly active in UNIA, the Christian democratic underground organisation, while some authorities have testified that he helped some Jews find refuge from the Nazis. He was ordained to the priesthood on 1 November 1946. In 1948, after two years of study at Rome, he received doctorates in theology from the Angelicum, and from the Jagellonian in Krakow.

Wojtyla returned to Krakow in 1948, working as a parish priest first in Niefowic, near Gdowo, and then at Saint Florian, in the Krakow diocese. In 1953 he received a doctorate in philosophy from the University of Krakow, and taught there from 1952 to 1958, and at Lublin from 1954, before he was appointed auxiliary bishop in Krakow in 1958. In 1963 he was nominated as the archbishop of Krakow, and was formally installed on 13 January 1964. Pope Paul VI appointed him a cardinal in June 1967.

Upon his election as pope, Wojtyla took the name John Paul II. Although he was treated by many in his native Poland as a symbol of freedom against the power of the communist state, theologically he is a conservative, espousing an exclusively male priesthood, while opposing birth control and extra-marital sex. He has survived two assassination attempts, the first in May 1981 in St Peter's Square, Rome, and the second a year later in Fatima, Portugal. Since his election to the papacy, he has made numerous official visits abroad, travelling to almost every region of the world.

Rafael **Caldera**

Rafael Caldera became president of Venezuela for a five-year term in 1994, having been elected in a nationwide ballot the previous December. The executive presidency combines the functions of head of state and head of government. Caldera is a veteran politician who stood in 1993 as an independent, but had on five previous occasions contested the presidency as candidate of the centrist Social Christian Party (COPEI), of which he was a founder member in 1946. This is his second presidential term, the first having been from 1969 to 1974. Until 1968 he held chairs as a professor of sociology and labour law at the Central University and the Catholic University Andrés Bello in Caracas, and he is a member of the Venezuelan Academy of Political and Social Sciences.

Rafael Caldera Rodríguez was born in San Felipe in the state of Yaracuy on 24 January 1916, and went to school in Caracas. He graduated from the law school at the Central University of Venezuela, and later attended the Wharton School of Business at the University of Pennsylvania in the USA. As a student he was the secretary of the central council of the Society of Venezuelan Catholic Youth (1932–34), and helped found the National Union of Students. From 1941 to 1945 he was general secretary of the National Action Party, and in 1941 he was also a deputy to the congress for the state of Yaracuy. He was attorney-general in 1945/46 and representative for the federal district in the Constituent Assembly which met in 1946/47.

Caldera was a founder member of the Social Christian Party of Venezuela (COPEI) and from 1948 to 1969 was COPEI's secretary-general. In 1952 he was re-elected to the Constituent Assembly, but did not attend as a sign of his protest against dictatorship. He was president of the Chamber of Deputies from 1959 to 1962, when he was also co-chairman of the bicameral commission established to draw up the country's new constitution.

He stood three times unsuccessfully as the COPEI presidential candidate, in 1947, 1958 and 1963, before first winning election for a five-year term beginning in 1969. After his five years in office, he became a senator for life. He stood again unsuccessfully in 1983, and in late 1987 the COPEI general secretary Eduardo Fernández was chosen in preference to him as the (ultimately unsuccessful) candidate for the election the following December.

Caldera led the opposition in a successful campaign to force the suspension in 1993 of President Pérez, on the charge of embezzlement. However, Caldera was expelled from COPEI later that year for refusing to stand aside in favour of the party's official candidate in the forthcoming presidential elections. Standing as an independent on a populist and anti-corruption platform,

Caldera headed the 5 December poll with just over 30 per cent of the vote, in a four-way contest with the candidates of the traditionally dominant parties (the Democratic Alliance and COPEI) and the left-wing Radical Cause. Caldera was supported by a loose National Convergence alliance of smaller parties and the social democratic Movement Towards Socialism (MAS).

Sworn in on 2 February 1994, Caldera announced only a modest rise in the minimum wage and few price controls, while emphasising the need for stabilisation, an anti-inflationary programme, and more energetic pursuit of privatisation. Reconciling social spending with the continuing need for austerity policies, and containing angry demonstrations, became the major themes of his presidency, along with the extension of privatisation to include the state oil monopoly.

Rafael Caldera Rodríguez married Alicia *née* Pietri in 1941, and they have three sons and three daughters.

Tran Duc Luong

Tran Duc Luong was appointed president of Vietnam in September 1997 by the newly elected National Assembly. As president he is head of state, and part of a leadership triumvirate with the prime minister and the leader of the ruling Communist Party of Vietnam (CPV). Generally described as a technocrat and pragmatist, he is an engineer and geologist who came into government only in 1987 and first joined the CPV politburo in 1996.

Tran Duc Luong was born on 5 May 1937 in the central province of Quang Ngai. He studied engineering at Hanoi Mining and Geology University and in the Soviet Union and worked in the General Directorate for Geology, where he was general director from 1979 until 1987. He chaired the science and technology committee of the National Assembly, and in 1987 was appointed as a vice-chairman of the council of ministers, with responsibility for industry, external economic relations, capital construction, transport and communications. Tran headed Vietnam's delegation to the USA in 1994, which laid foundations for the normalisation of relations a year later. He joined the CPV politburo in 1996, when he ranked 12th of its 19 members.

With President Le Duc Anh, Prime Minister Vo Van Kiet and party secretary-general Do Muoi all due to stand down ahead of the 1997 party congress because of old age and poor health, the renewal of the leadership was a major issue for debate throughout the year. Tran was nominated for the presidency in September 1997 by the CPV central committee, and confirmed as president by the National Assembly the same month. In guiding Vietnam's transition from a centrally planned to a market economy, it was expected that he would take a more cautious approach than the new prime minister appointed at the same time, the prominent reformist Phan Van Khai.

Mohamed **Abdelaziz**

Mohamed Abdelaziz is the president of the Sahrawi Arab Democratic Republic (SADR), recognised by the majority of African countries and some other states as the legitimate government of Western Sahara following its proclamation in 1976 by the Polisario Front (Frente popular para la liberación de Saguía el Hamra y Río de Oro). *Endorsed at successive Polisario congresses from 1976 onwards as the movement's secretary-general, Abdelaziz was also elected to the newly created post of president of the Sahrawi Republic in October 1982. His leadership was endorsed by a newly formed SADR parliament in 1995. He has been involved for three decades in political and military resistance first to Spanish colonial power and then to the subsequent Moroccan occupation of Western Sahara.*

Abdelaziz was born in Smara, in what was then known as the Spanish Sahara, in 1948. He attended primary and secondary schools, but had to give up his medical degree before its completion, becoming involved from an early age in activities committed to ending Spanish colonial rule. In May 1973 he participated in the first congress of the Polisario Front, which undertook its first guerrilla action later that same month. From 1974 Abdelaziz was a member of the Polisario political bureau and also commander of a military region.

In February 1976 Spain withdrew from the territory. It was thereupon partitioned between Morocco and Mauritania; Mauritania later renounced its claim, whereas Morocco extended its occupation. The Polisario Front, however, declared the independence of the Sahrawi Arab Democratic Republic (SADR) on 27 February.

In August 1976 Abdelaziz was elected as a member of the Front's executive committee and was named secretary-general. He has been elected secretary-general of the Front at every congress since then. On 12/16 October 1982, he was also elected at the Front's fifth congress to the newly created post of president of the Sahrawi Republic, and thus became the first SADR head of state.

Between 1976 and 1991 Abdelaziz led a series of attempts to expel Mauritanian and Moroccan forces. During the 1980s and 1990s, he also attended summit meetings of the Organization of African Unity (OAU), achieving success in winning recognition for the SADR from the majority of OAU member states, including Mauritania (although some have recently reversed their stance) and from other countries including India. Abdelaziz has also negotiated with the UN's decolonisation committee. In 1991 Morocco eventually accepted a UN-brokered ceasefire to be monitored by the UN Mission for the Referendum in Western Sahara (MINURSO) and agreed to the holding of a referendum. Although disagreements have persisted over exactly who is entitled to vote, as of early 1998 the referendum was scheduled to take place later in that year, and the ceasefire was holding.

Mohamed Abdelaziz is married and is the father of six children.

Ali Abdullah **Saleh**

Ali Abdullah Saleh has been head of state of Yemen since unification in 1990. A soldier who began his army career as a non-commissioned officer (NCO), Saleh took part in the 1974 military coup in the Yemen Arab Republic (North Yemen) and in 1978 he succeeded to the North Yemeni presidency, in which capacity he was a leading advocate of unification with the People's Democratic Republic of Yemen (South Yemen). The approval of the new constitution in May 1991, and the defeat of a secessionist rebellion in the south in July 1994, enabled him to consolidate his position, and he was re-elected in October 1994 for a new five-year term, renewable once only.

Ali Abdullah Saleh was born around 1942 in Beit Al-Ahmar near Sana'a. His primary education took place locally in a Koranic school. He joined the armed forces in 1958, began attending the army's NCO school in 1960, and participated in preparations among fellow NCOs for the 1962 revolution, which ousted the ruling Zaidi Islamic theocracy and installed a republican military regime. A year later he entered the Armor school for further military training. He fought, and was wounded several times, in the civil war between Saudi-backed royalists and republicans, which ended in 1970 with a republican victory. He rose to become battalion commander and then company commander in Armor, and brigade commander in Taiz province.

In 1974 Saleh participated in an army coup in North Yemen. Between 1974 and 1978 he was part of the military government of Taiz province. In July 1978, following the assassination of President Ahmed Hussein al-Ghasmi, he was brought into a four-member presidential council and almost immediately elected by the parliament as president of North Yemen and commander-in-chief of the armed forces. Promoted in September 1978 to the rank of colonel, he was re-elected in 1983 and 1988 to further terms as president and commander-in-chief.

Upon unification in May 1990 Saleh was elected chairman of the presidential council (president) of the Republic of Yemen. His initial 30-month transitional term was extended pending delayed parliamentary elections, but in October 1993 the new House of Representatives confirmed his position. Under his leadership the government sought to modernise the country, building schools and hospitals and embarking on a literacy campaign to transform a society hitherto dominated by conservative clan allegiances. His failure to criticise Iraq's invasion of Kuwait in 1990 resulted in a temporary halt to foreign aid, and strained relations with neighbouring Saudi Arabia to the north.

Saleh has had to contend with continuing tensions between Islamist and secular groups, and between north and south Yemen. A brief but intense civil war erupted in 1994, ending with the defeat of southern secessionists. Saleh was re-elected as president by the House of Representatives in October 1994, the president's powers having been greatly enhanced by amendments to the constitution, and in April 1997 his General People's Congress (GPC) secured an absolute majority of seats in the republic's second general election, thus consolidating his hold on power. In December 1997 he was promoted to the rank of field marshal.

Saleh is married and has several children.

Slobodan **Milosevic**

Slobodan Milosevic was elected for a four-year term on 15 July 1997 as president of the Federal Republic of Yugoslavia (FRY), the rump state created in 1992 following the break-up of the former Yugoslavia. He was sworn in on 23 July. He thereupon gave up his position, due in any case to end in December, as president of the republic of Serbia, the main element (together with Montenegro) in the FRY. Under the 1992 constitution, the president is federal head of state but the federal government is headed by a prime minister responsible to parliament, while the governments of the two republics have control over most internal matters. However, Milosevic is widely recognised as the dominant political figure, and the powers of the presidency in practice are greatly strengthened by the fact that this is now his official position. Milosevic is a law graduate and was a business manager in the communist era, who rose to leadership of the communist party and became the leading voice of Serbian nationalism. As Serbian president he was identified in the early 1990s with the effort to preserve Serbian dominance and to prevent Yugoslavia being broken up by the secession of Croatia in particular. The onset of the subsequent war in Bosnia saw him cast as the main protagonist of a "Greater Serbia", and the controlling power behind the Bosnian Serbs, although in the latter part of that conflict he sought to deliver them to the negotiating table in order to hasten the lifting of international sanctions against his own FRY state. Within Serbia he took a strong line against domestic opposition, mobilising the military on several occasions against protest demonstrations.

Slobodan Milosevic was born in the town of Pozarevac in Serbia on 29 August 1941. His father, an orthodox priest and teacher of Montenegrin descent, left home when Milosevic was a child, and he was brought up by his mother. Both his parents later committed suicide, his father when he was 21 and his mother when he was 32.

In 1959 Milosevic joined the ruling League of Communists of Yugoslavia (LCY) and he was active in student politics before graduating in law from the University of Belgrade in 1964. He began a career in business, working for the national gas extraction company, Tehnogas, in Belgrade. He was also head of the Belgrade Information Service (1966–69), and an adviser on economic affairs to the mayor of Belgrade. By 1973 he had been promoted to director-general of Tehnogas, a position he held until 1978 when he moved to the presidency of Beogradska Bank. He left the bank in 1983, becoming a member of the presidium of the central committee of the LCY and, the following year, chair of the party's

Belgrade committee. In January 1986 he replaced his former mentor Ivan Stambolic as party leader in Serbia, with a reputation as a hardliner. He was also a member of the federal council's committee for a long-term stabilisation programme.

Milosevic's adoption as the leader of Serbian nationalism stems from a notorious occasion on 24 April 1987 when he addressed a crowd of demonstrators outside the town hall in Kosovo Polje. The gathering was a Serbian protest against the concessions being demanded by the majority Albanian population of Kosovo (an autonomous republic within Serbia). Reproving the riot police who had acted to restrain the crowd, Milosevic told the protestors: "No one has the right to beat you. No one will ever beat you again."

In 1989 Milosevic replaced Stambolic on the collective presidency of Serbia. In Serbia's first multi-party presidential elections in December 1990, Milosevic was the candidate for the Socialist Party of Serbia (SPS), the renamed communist party. He won a massive 65 per cent of the vote against 30 other candidates, while the SPS gained a large majority in the assembly, with 194 out of 250 seats. At his re-election in December 1992, under the FRY structure, he received some 57 per cent of the vote.

The break-up of former Yugoslavia in 1991/92, beginning with the secession of Slovenia and Croatia, represented a setback for Serbian nationalists, who had hoped to preserve a dominant position beyond the borders of Serbia itself. The subsequent bloody conflict in Bosnia, and the retention of Serb control over enclaves within Croatia until 1995/96, was played out against this background. The course of the fighting and "ethnic cleansing" in 1992/93 initially appeared to offer Milosevic the temptation of a "Greater Serbia". However, by the time Milosevic attended the late 1995 peace talks which marked the end of the conflict, and which thus opened the way for the gradual lifting of the international sanctions imposed on the FRY since 1992, he had been forced, at great cost, to settle for rather less. Signing the Dayton agreement, he accepted on behalf of the Bosnian Serbs the retention of a Bosnian state, but one within which there would be a Bosnian Serb republic as one of two distinct entities. Until the military defeat of the Bosnian Serb forces and the effective intervention of NATO forces earlier that year, Milosevic had not managed to impress upon the Bosnian Serb leadership that this was the best outcome achievable for them. His reduction in military support for them (which he always denied providing at all) had been forced upon him by the pressure of international sanctions. This was one of the elements which helped determine the eventual course of the Bosnian conflict, just as Milosevic's initial backing had given the Bosnian Serbs a military ascendancy with heavy costs in terms of killings and "ethnic cleansing".

Milosevic was elected unopposed as federal president in July 1997, and sworn in on 23 July. A joint sitting of both houses of the federal parliament had given him 88 out of 98 votes cast in the Chamber of Citizens and 29 out of 31 in the Chamber of the Republics in the 15 July ballot. The subsequent election of Milan Milutinovic (see Yugoslavia: Serbia) as president of Serbia in December 1997 ensured the continuing control of Milosevic's SPS over the key constituent element in the FRY.

Milosevic is married to Mirjana Markanovic, a professor at the University of Belgrade and a member of the Russian Academy of Social Sciences. Now a significant political figure in her own right, she comes from a leading Serbian communist family and attended the same high school as Milosevic. The couple have one son and one daughter.

Milo **Djukanovic**

Milo Djukanovic was elected in October 1997 to take office on 15 January 1998 as president of Montenegro, which together with Serbia forms the Federal Republic of Yugoslavia (FRY). He was previously prime minister of Montenegro. Both he and his closest rival, incumbent Montenegrin president Momir Bulatovic, belong to the former communist Democratic Party of Socialists (DPS), but Djukanovic is generally considered a pro-Western reformer, whereas Bulatovic is a staunch supporter of FRY president Slobodan Milosevic.

Milo Djukanovic is the son of a high court judge and was born on 15 February 1962 in the industrial town of Niksic where he went to school. He studied economics at Titograd University, where he first became involved in politics, joining the League of Communists of Yugoslavia (LCY) in 1979. By the age of 24 he had been appointed to the party's central committee. In 1989/90, when Milosevic secured first the presidency of the collective presidency of Serbia and then in 1990 the Serbian presidency itself, Djukanovic at first supported him, and was rewarded with the post of prime minister of Montenegro in January 1991. However, by 1996 Djukanovic had become an opponent of Milosevic, whom he accused of corruption and the destruction of Yugoslavia for his own ends. That year he gave his support to the Serbian protest movement and the DPS (the successor to the LCY in Montenegro) split into two factions, one led by him and the other by the Montenegrin president, Bulatovic. Djukanovic reportedly blamed Milosevic for the continuation of international sanctions against the FRY, and wanted to improve Montenegro's relations with Western countries to ensure that they were lifted.

In the first round of the October 1997 presidential election none of the eight candidates achieved an absolute majority, although both Djukanovic and Bulatovic secured well over 40 per cent. When Djukanovic won the 19 October run-off by a narrow margin, Bulatovic claimed that irregularities had occurred, demanded new elections, and threatened not to stand down as president, but international observers declared the elections valid. In the weeks leading up to Djukanovic's inauguration, there were widespread protests and fears were expressed by Djukanovic's opponents that as president he would want to break up the FRY.

Milo Djukanovic is married to Lidija Djukanovic and they have one son.

Milan **Milutinovic**

Milan Milutinovic emerged as the winner on 21 December 1997 from four rounds of voting held to elect a successor to Slobodan Milosevic as president of Serbia, Milosevic's second four-year term of office having ended in July. Milosevic had moved over to the presidency of the Federal Republic of Yugoslavia (FRY), of which Serbia is the main component together with Montenegro. Milutinovic is a staunch ally and aide of Milosevic and a long-standing member of the Socialist Party of Serbia (SPS), the successor to the League of Communists of Yugoslavia (LCY).

Milan Milutinovic was born on 12 December 1942 in Belgrade. He studied at Belgrade University, joining the youth movement of the LCY. He later joined the LCY itself, rising rapidly through its ranks. He was elected to the Yugoslav parliament in 1969 and was then appointed Serbian education minister. He became director of the Serbian national library, before joining the diplomatic service in the 1980s. In 1989 he was made Yugoslav ambassador to Greece, where he worked to strengthen relations after the disintegration of the former communist Yugoslavia and the imposition of international sanctions on the FRY. He won particular praise from his government for his handling of Yugoslav banking assets in Greece.

In August 1995 Milutinovic was appointed FRY minister of foreign affairs, and three months later he took part in the negotiations for the Dayton peace accord, where his tough negotiating stance brought him into the international spotlight. In July 1997, when Milosevic had to step down from the Serbian presidency because he had served his maximum term, Milutinovic became the SPS's candidate to replace him.

The turnout in elections held in September, October and November 1997 was below the required 50 per cent turnout and so those polls were declared invalid. In the last of them Milutinovic had trailed Vojislav Seselj, leader of the far-right Serbian Radical Party and an even less palatable prospect for Western countries than the pro-Milosevic candidate.

In the vote on 21 December Milutinovic won 59 per cent, against only 38 per cent for Seselj, while crucially the turnout reached 50.5 per cent. Prior to the vote international observers declared that the "overall process was fundamentally flawed" and requested more political debate and fairer media coverage, but no action was taken.

Milan Milutinovic is married to Olga Milutinovic and they have one child.

Frederick **Chiluba**

Frederick Chiluba was first elected president of Zambia, for a five-year term, on 13 October 1991 and was subsequently re-elected to the post on 18 November 1996. The executive president is both head of state and head of government, and appoints the cabinet. Highly experienced in trade union politics, Chiluba was the main opposition figure during the latter years of the single-party government of Kenneth Kaunda, but has lately been criticised himself for seeking to suppress effective opposition.

Frederick Chiluba was born in Kitwe in Wusakile township on 30 April 1943. The son of a miner, he won a scholarship to secondary school, from which he was expelled as a student agitator. After several years spent in odd jobs and intermittent education, Chiluba began work as an invoice clerk with the international engineering firm Atlas Copco in 1966. He remained with the company for the next 24 years, rising to the position of credit manager.

At the same time Chiluba also embarked on a career as a trade union leader. He was a shop steward within the National Union of Building, Engineering and General Workers (NUBEGW) from 1967 to 1970, and district chairman for the Zambia Congress of Trade Unions (ZCTU) in 1970/71. He went to Germany in 1971 to study trade unionism and industry. From 1974 until 1991 he was the most influential figure in the Zambian labour movement, as chairman-general of ZCTU.

By the early 1980s, Chiluba's prominence as union leader made him also the main focus of political opposition to Kaunda's single-party government. Chiluba was expelled in 1980 from the sole party, the United National Independence Party (UNIP), and in 1981 he was arrested and briefly imprisoned over an alleged plot against the government. Throughout the 1980s, however, Chiluba's international reputation was augmented by his work with the Geneva-based International Labour Organization (ILO), for which he chaired a number of committees.

In February 1991 Chiluba was elected leader of the new Movement for Multiparty Democracy (MMD), an ideologically disparate party which became the focus of opposition to Kaunda's government. In the October 1991 general election, the first at which opposition parties were permitted to compete, Chiluba's MMD won 125 out of the 150 seats in the unicameral National Assembly. Chiluba himself polled 75 per cent of votes cast in the concurrent presidential election. He thus became only Zambia's second president since independence in 1964.

The transfer of power from Kaunda to Chiluba was regarded as a model of democratic transition in Africa. However, Chiluba's commitment to genuine multiparty democracy came into question when his government took steps to prevent an effective opposition challenge in the run-up to the 1996 legislative and presidential elections. Constitutional amendments were approved which stipulated that anyone who had already served two or more presidential terms could not seek election (a provision affecting only Kaunda), and that only those with two Zambian-born parents could be candidates (whereas Kaunda's parents were born in what is now Malawi). The arrest of eight prominent UNIP leaders prompted donor countries to suspend foreign aid. The election on 18 November was boycotted by UNIP and other smaller parties. In the presidential poll Chiluba secured the support of 82 per cent of those voting, but the turnout was estimated at only around a quarter of the electorate. The arrest and detention of Kaunda in connection with an alleged coup attempt in late 1997 prompted further concern about the status of democratic freedoms in Zambia.

Frederick Chiluba is married to Vera Chiluba and they have five sons and four daughters.

Robert **Mugabe**

Robert Mugabe has been in power in Zimbabwe since independence in 1980, initially as prime minister and, from the end of 1987, as president. He was most recently re-elected, for a six-year term, in a nationwide ballot in March 1996. Under constitutional amendments introduced in 1987 the executive president is both head of state and head of government, appointing the members of the cabinet. He is also commander-in-chief of the defence forces. Mugabe was involved in the long struggle for independence and against white minority rule. He commanded the most effective of the guerrilla forces, and represented the more left-wing of the two main African nationalist movements at the 1979 Lancaster House conference, which established the framework for independence and majority rule. Accused of ruthlessness in eliminating opponents once in power, he has also recently caused controversy by his fierce condemnation of homosexuality, and by plans to redistribute white-owned farmland.

Robert Gabriel Mugabe was born on 21 February 1924 at Kutama Mission in Zvimba. A member of the country's majority Shona ethnic group, he had a Christian upbringing in mission schools, where he then became a teacher himself. He obtained a degree in history and English from the University of Fort Hare in South Africa in 1951. Returning to teaching, he worked in mission schools, in government schools in Salisbury (the capital, now Harare) and Gwelo, and at teacher training college from 1955. He did an external degree with the University of London at this time, graduating in economics in 1958. In that year he went to Ghana to lecture at St Mary's Teacher Training College in Takoradi, but returned in 1960 to chair the inaugural congress of the National Democratic Party (NDP). Chosen as NDP secretary for information and publicity, he began his long involvement in full-time African nationalist politics.

The proscription of the NDP in December 1961 prompted its leaders to reorganise as the Zimbabwe African People's Union (ZAPU). Joshua Nkomo, the erstwhile NDP president, headed the new party, of which Mugabe was a co-founder, acting secretary-general, publicity secretary, and editor of *The People's Voice*. ZAPU was soon banned in its turn, however, in September 1962. A split and realignment in the nationalist movement led to his becoming secretary-general in 1963 of a new Zimbabwe African National Union (ZANU), led by Rev. Ndabaningi Sithole.

Mugabe was detained from December 1963 until March 1964, and then imprisoned for over ten years, from August 1964 until December 1974, for his political activities. Imprisonment reinforced his political solidarity with fellow nationalist detainees, while he also completed three further academic degrees during this period. In 1975 he escaped to Mozambique, where he set about reinvigorating the armed liberation struggle as leader of ZANU's armed wing, the Zimbabwe African National Liberation Army (ZANLA).

Mugabe was at this point isolated in opposing a ceasefire with the white minority regime of Ian Smith, which had unilaterally declared independence, as Rhodesia, ten years previously. The better-known African nationalist leaders – Nkomo of ZAPU and Sithole of ZANU – favoured attending talks with Smith under the umbrella of the African National Council (ANC), formed in 1971 by Bishop Abel Muzorewa to co-ordinate internal opposition when the British government was considering an earlier constitutional proposal. Mugabe's stance split ZANU into internal and external wings, but was vindicated by the failure of the latest round of talks with the Smith regime. Nkomo and he set up a Patriotic Front alliance in 1976 between ZAPU and ZANU, pledging to fight on to achieve genuine black majority rule. Sithole began to be marginalised, leading a separate faction when Mugabe was elected president of ZANU at the party's congress-in-exile in Mozambique in 1977.

The Patriotic Front held together in rejecting a subsequent internal settlement, in which Smith and Muzorewa were the main participants, and in boycotting the 1978 elections held to legitimise their formula. The guerrilla struggle, backed by the African frontline states, was stepped up, until the internal regime agreed to attend a constitutional conference convened by the British government at Lancaster House in London in September 1979. Mugabe performed impressively as leader of ZANU in a joint Patriotic Front delegation, and the pre-independence general elections held in March 1980 proved a triumph for him and his party (renamed as ZANU-PF). He became prime minister, leading the country to independence as Zimbabwe on 18 April 1980, and announcing a policy of national reconstruction aimed at restoring peace and stability.

In power, Mugabe avoided alienating the international business community and the white minority, making only gradual moves towards the redistribution of wealth which he had propounded as a Marxist guerrilla leader, and keeping within the terms of the agreed constitutional settlement (although he launched in 1992, and relaunched in 1997, more far-reaching proposals for the compulsory acquisition of white-owned land). The main conflict in the 1980s was not with the white minority but with his former allies in ZAPU. Under a state of emergency which remained in force until 1990, Mugabe used troops with great ruthlessness in 1983/84 to crush resistance in Matabeleland, the main Ndebele-populated heartland of ZAPU support. The massacres at this time, and the detention and alleged torture of dissident opponents, were accompanied by the strengthening of ZANU-PF's political dominance. Elections in 1985 gave the party an increased majority, and by the end of the decade the abolition of the reserved white seats in parliament and the merger of ZAPU into the ruling party left it with little more than nominal opposition. Mugabe himself advocated the creation of a single-party state, but in 1991 he announced that he was abandoning plans to implement this.

Meanwhile Mugabe had moved over from the post of prime minister to the newly created executive presidency on 31 December 1987. Unopposed as first holder of the post, he was re-elected in March 1990 with just under 80 per cent of the vote against one other candidate, and again re-elected in 1996. Mugabe's mandate from this most recent poll, on 16/17 March, was marred by a turnout of only 31 per cent and no real opposition; both Muzorewa and Sithole, although named on the ballot papers, withdrew in protest over restrictive electoral laws and alleged intimidation.

In 1991 Mugabe hosted the Commonwealth heads of government meeting in Harare. This summit broadened his international profile,

Zimbabwe's main role having hitherto been as a frontline state in the anti-apartheid struggle and the confrontation with South African-backed forces in Namibia, Angola and Mozambique. In November 1995 Mugabe became the chairman of the Group of 15 developing countries. His ability to fulfil an "elder statesman" role on the international stage has been diminished, however, by the criticisms levelled at his regime over human rights and the restriction of political opposition, compounded by his intemperate denunciations of homosexuality on a number of occasions.

Robert Gabriel Mugabe married Sarah Francesca Hayfron in April 1961. She died in 1992. He married a second time in August 1996, to Grace Marufu. He has three children.

Index